I0739832

Richard Holt Hutton

Criticisms on contemporary thought and thinkers

Selected from the Spectator

Richard Holt Hutton

Criticisms on contemporary thought and thinkers
Selected from the Spectator

ISBN/EAN: 9783337278724

Printed in Europe, USA, Canada, Australia, Japan

Cover: Foto ©Thomas Meinert / pixelio.de

More available books at **www.hansebooks.com**

Richard Holt Hutton

Criticisms on contemporary thought and thinkers
Selected from the Spectator

ISBN/EAN: 9783337278724

Printed in Europe, USA, Canada, Australia, Japan

Cover: Foto ©Thomas Meinert / pixelio.de

More available books at **www.hansebooks.com**

CRITICISMS

ON

CONTEMPORARY THOUGHT

AND THINKERS

SELECTED FROM THE *SPECTATOR*

BY

RICHARD HOLT HUTTON, M.A. (LONDON)

FELLOW OF UNIVERSITY COLLEGE, LONDON

IN TWO VOLUMES—VOL. I

London

MACMILLAN AND CO., LIMITED

NEW YORK: THE MACMILLAN COMPANY

1900

All rights reserved

TO THE MEMORY OF MY NEPHEW

THE LATE

REV. WILLIAM RICHMOND HUTTON

SOMETIME CURATE OF KIRKSTALL, NEAR LEEDS

AND OF WEST HESLERTON, YORK

I DEDICATE THESE ESSAYS

WHICH BUT FOR HIS REQUEST AND VALUABLE HELP

IN SELECTING THEM

WOULD PROBABLY HAVE BEEN LEFT IN THE TEMPORARY

FORM FOR WHICH ALONE THEY WERE INTENDED

CONTENTS

CARLYLE'S FAITH

1874

MR. CARLYLE has mended his religious faith since he last described the damnable condition of the world in which he is compelled to live, and in his letter to Sir Joseph Whitworth on the relations of capital and labour, he speaks of Almighty God with a pious simplicity which is a surprise and a pleasure after those "Abysses" and "Eternities," and other ornate vaguenesses and paraphrastic plurals of his middle period. Of all "the unveracities" which Mr. Carlyle used to denounce with so much vigour, it always seemed to me that the circumlocutions by which he himself avoided committing himself on the question whether the rule to which he was always exhorting us to submit was really the rule of wisdom or only the rule of brute necessities, were some of the worst;— for he knew very well that to such creatures as we are it makes the most enormous difference whether we be in truth guided by a divine mind which is infinitely above us, or only propelled by an undivine fate which has reached its *chef-d'œuvre* in ourselves. In one who has always been so bitter on what he calls juggles, who has insisted that man's religion "consists not of the many things he is in doubt of and tries to believe, but of the few he is assured of, and has no need of effort for believing," it was not surely a laudable practice to adopt as he did an ambiguous religious jargon, the meaning of which it was impossible to define. In his denunciations of Jesuitism, it always seemed to me that some of the sharpest blows really descended upon himself. For instance, Man's religion, he said in the *Latter-Day Pamphlets*, "whatever it may be, is a discerned fact and coherent system of discerned facts to him; he stands fronting the worlds and the eternities upon it: to *doubt* of it is not permissible at all! He must verify or expel his doubts, convert them into certainty of Yes or No, or they will be the death of his religion. But on the other hand, convert them into certainty of Yes *and* No; or even of Yes *though* No, as the Ignatian method is, and what will become of your religion?" Now the fault we have always been disposed to find with Mr. Carlyle's religious exhortations is precisely this, that he left us with the impression on our minds that his religious belief consisted of certainties of "Yes *and* No," or "Yes *though* No," rather than explicit beliefs and denials. What, for instance, does this dark saying about "Man fronting the worlds and the eternities" mean? Not clearly that he fronts God; nor that he fronts a yeast of fermenting forces of which he is the product; but rather that he fronts something ambiguous between the two, which the mystic meaning of the word 'Eternities' suggests as partaking of spiritual qualities, though Mr. Carlyle declined explicitly to affirm them. Is not that,—and the passage is an excellent specimen of a large part of Mr. Carlyle's prophecy,—as near to suggesting that the answer to the question 'Do you believe in God,' should be " Yes, *though* No," as Mr. Carlyle could go ? But I should not now have called attention to the elaborate disguises and ambiguities of Mr. Carlyle's religious prophecies of twenty years and more ago, if this last published letter of his had not been in a tone, as I think, so much simpler and higher. He is writing on the relations of labour and capital, and the little hope that political economy (Mr. Carlyle's ".dismal science") will ever adjust these relations rightly— (a state of mind, by the way, in which every reasonable man, economist or not, would, I believe, concur with Mr. Carlyle, for Political Economy has nothing to do with moral Economy, and does not pretend to explain what is just in action, but rather certain inevitable tendencies to action due to the pressure of human self-interests, the practical influence of which it is not only open to men to modify most seriously, but which they usually do modify most seriously, and always ought to modify most seriously on other than economical grounds) ; and he says : " The look of England is to me at this moment abundantly ominous, the question of capital and labour growing ever more anarchical, insoluble by the notions hitherto applied to it, pretty certain to issue in petroleum one day, unless some other gospel than that of the Dismal Science come to illuminate it. Two things are pretty sure to me. The first is, that capital and labour never can or will agree together till they both first of all decide on doing their work faithfully throughout, and, like men of conscience and honour, whose highest aim is to behave like faithful citizens of the universe, and obey the eternal commandment of Almighty God who made them. The second thing is, that a sadder object even than that of the coal strike, or any conceivable strike, is the fact that, loosely speaking, we may say all England has decided that the profitablest way is to do its work ill, slimly, swiftly, and mendaciously. What a contrast between now and, say, only one hundred years ago! At the latter date, or still more conspicuously for ages before it, all England awoke to its work with an invocation to the Eternal Maker to bless them in their day's labour, and help them to do it well. Now all England, shopkeepers, workmen, all manner of competing labourers, awaken as if it were with an unspoken but heartfelt prayer to Beelzebub, 'Oh! help us, thou great Lord of shoddy, adulteration, and malfeasance, to do our work with the maximum of slimness, swiftness, profit, and mendacity, for the Devil's sake.—Amen.'" I cannot say, however, that I accept Mr. Carlyle's history. If all England ever awoke daily with a real prayer to God in its heart to do its daily work well, I believe that that generation would have rendered the present generation, living within a hundred years of it, a very different thing from what it is. Nothing is more really unattainable than a true knowledge of the average moral condition of any age, even the present; and with respect to a past age, I believe such knowledge to be hopelessly beyond us. But whether England were ever before more genuinely in earnest than it now is, in its pious wish to do its work well, matters little, Mr. Carlyle's object being really only this, to persuade us that it is of the first moment that we should daily become more in earnest than we now are; and that without becoming so, the talk about rights and penalties, and strikes and lock-outs, will result in mere destructive passion,—petroleum and general chaos. There I sincerely hold Mr. Carlyle to be wholly in the right. And I believe that no advice can be wholesomer for the purpose of averting the chaos, than that all parties alike should look up from the scene of bitter contention and competition to "the eternal commandments of Almighty God who made them." There is nothing that makes men so reasonable as the disposition to take *themselves* more strictly to task than their antagonists for their shortcomings, and nothing which fosters that disposition like the faith that "Almighty God who made them" is expecting it of them. But I cannot help doubting if any sort of talk has done more to undermine this belief than Mr. Carlyle's old pantheistic practice of substituting 'the Immensities' and 'the Eternities' in the place of 'Almighty God.' I do not doubt that that practice was due to a certain sincerity in himself, though it produced on others the effect of that very ambiguousness and double meaning of which he was the bitterest denouncer. He did not, perhaps, *fully* believe in God,—the most difficult thing in the world, I admit, though the most necessary,—and he could not dismiss the thought of a personal ruler; so he invented an answer to the question "God, or no God?" which was in effect what he himself calls the answer "Yes, *though* No," "yes in one sense, no in another," in fact, an ambiguity, the true answer being evaded and deferred. And the effect of the Carlylian paraphrase for God was, in my opinion, much more disastrous to the numerous devotees of Mr. Carlyle, than a blank assertion that the truth was "unknown and unknowable." It enabled people to do exactly what Mr. Carlyle has always most severely condemned,—clothe themselves in an unreal costume of sentimental awe which was neither piety nor its negation. The great difference

I take it, between Pantheism and Theism is this,—that genuine Theism humbles the mind, while genuine Pantheism inflates it. You cannot believe that God exists for you; you know that, on the contrary, you exist through God and for God. But when you put the 'Eternities' and 'Immensities' and 'Abysses' in the place of God, you are very apt indeed to feel what a wonderful fellow you must be to "front the worlds and the eternities" in that grand way. There is nothing definite enough in the "Immensities" to humble you; on the contrary, they are a credit to you; they are grand ideal conceptions which add a certain distinction to your position on earth, and justify Hamlet's remark—"in form and moving how express and admirable, in action how like an angel, in apprehension how like a God." I believe that Mr. Carlyle in inventing, as he did, this compromise between faith in God and no faith, did very much indeed to smooth the way into that irreligious state of mind which instead of simply praying to do its work well, admires itself for the emotion with which it "fronts the world and the eternities," while it is doing its work ill. There is a kind of imaginative thought which is a fascinating substitute for the simplicity and humility of devotion, and I know no higher or more marvellous master in that kind than Mr. Carlyle. His writings are full of graphic power and moral passion. He sees the strength and weakness, the wisdom and folly, the good and evil of human life, with a power and a humour which gives the mere act of following in the track of his thought an intellectual charm of its own; and he has, moreover, an art of throwing a vague mystery over the whole, a splendid confusion of gorgeous tints and shadows, which makes his disciples feel as if their powers of insight and of moral passion had been indefinitely magnified during the time in which they are submitted to the spell of his genius. But all this is not only no substitute for religious faith : it is rather a gratifying stimulus which helps you to miss its absence less. It is therefore to my mind a most satisfactory thing to find Mr. Carlyle in his old age dismissing 'the Immensities' and 'the Eternities' altogether, and coming back to the simple advice to people inflated with the idea of the importance of their own rights, to pray to God that they may do their own work well. It is a sound, and in the most wholesome sense a humiliating bit of counsel, of quite an opposite tendency from the advice which we used to hear so frequently from him, to 'front the eternities' veraciously. Theism, and Christianity as the highest Theism, are sobering faiths of which humility is the first word though not the last. Pantheism—into whose scale Mr. Carlyle's influence had hitherto been thrown,—is an inebriating faith, of which vanity or sensationalism is apt to be the first word though not the last. It is compensation for much unwholesome teaching that Mr. Carlyle's latest and present vote is for the former faith, the faith which breeds sobriety and humility, and not that puffing-up of our mind with vain "Immensities," by which, as St. Paul once vividly remarked, "the foolish heart is darkened."

II

THOMAS CARLYLE

1881

FOR many years before his death last Saturday, Mr. Carlyle had been to England what his great hero, Goethe, long was to Germany,—the aged seer whose personal judgments on men and things were everywhere sought after, and eagerly chronicled and retailed. Yet it was hardly for the same reason. In Goethe's old age, the ripeness of his critical judgment, and the catholicity, not to say even the facility, of his literary taste, induced a sort of confidence that he would judge calmly and judge genially anything, whether in life or literature, that was not extravagant. Mr. Carlyle was resorted to for a very different reason. The Chelsea shrine, as was well known, gave out only one sort of oracles, and that sort was graphic and humorous denunciation of all conventional falsehoods and pretentiousness, or what was presumed to be conventional falsehood and pretentiousness;—and consequently recourse was had to that shrine only when some trenchant saying was wanted that might help in the sweeping-away of some new formula of the sentimentalists or of the panegyrists of worn-out symbols. His almost extravagant admiration for Goethe notwithstanding, Carlyle in his greatness was ever more disposed to sympathise with the great organs of destructive, than with those of constructive force. He sympathised with Cromwell for what he destroyed, with Frederick in great measure for what he destroyed, with Mirabeau and Danton for what they destroyed, and even with Goethe in large degree for the negative tendencies of his thought and criticism. With the constructive tendencies of the past he could often deeply sympathise,—as he showed in "Past and Present,"—but with those of the present, hardly ever. If we were asked what his genius did for English thought and literature, we should say that it did chiefly the work of a sort of spiritual volcano,—showed us the perennial fire subversive of worn-out creeds which lies concealed in vast stores beneath the surface of society, and the thinness of the crust which alone separates us from that pit of Tophet, as he would himself have called it. And yet, in spite of himself, he always strove to sympathise with positive work. His teaching was incessant that the reconstruction of society was a far greater work than the destruction of the worn-out shell which usually preceded it,— only, unfortunately, in his own time, there was hardly any species of reconstructive effort which could gain his acquiescence, much less his approval. He despised all the more positive political and philanthropic tendencies of his time; felt little interest in its scientific discoveries; concerned himself not at all about its art; scorned its economical teaching; and rejected the modern religious instructors with even more emphatic contumely than the "dreary professors of a dismal science." To Carlyle, the world was out of joint, and his only receipt for setting it right,—the restoration of " the beneficent whip " for its idlers, rogues, and vagabonds,—was never seriously listened to by thinking men. Consequently, all that he achieved was achieved in the world of thought and imagination. He did succeed in making men realise, as they never realised before, into what a fermenting chaos of passion human society is constantly in danger of dissolving, when either injustice or insincerity,—what Mr. Carlyle called a "*sham*,"—is in the ascendant, and rules by virtue of mere convention or habit. He did succeed in making men realise the wonderful paradox of all social order and discipline, in depicting to us the weakness and the hysterical character of much that is called patriotic and humane impulse, in making us see that justice and strength and a certain heroism of courage are all necessary for the original organisation of a stable society ; and that much sensibility in the body corporate, so far from making this organisation easier, is apt to make it both more difficult and more unstable. Carlyle's greatest power was the wonderful imaginative genius which enabled him to lift the veil from the strange mixture of convention, passion, need, want, capacity, and incompetence called human society, and make us understand by what a thread order often hangs, and how rare is the sort of genius to restore it when once it goes to pieces. No one ever performed this great service for the world as Carlyle has performed it in almost all his works,—notably in *The French Revolution* and *Sartor Resartus*, and this alone is enough to entitle him to a very high place among the Immortals of literature.

And he had all the gifts for this great task,—especially that marvellous insight into the social power of symbols which made him always maintain that fantasy was the organ of divinity.   He has often been called a prophet, and though I have too little sympathy with his personal conception of good and evil so to class him,—though religious seer as he was, he was in no sense Christ-like,—he certainly had to the full the prophet's insight into the power of parable and type, and the prophet's eye for the forces which move society, and inspire multitudes with contagious enthusiasm, whether for good or ill. He fell short of a prophet in this, that his main interest, after all, was rather in the graphic and picturesque interpretation of social phenomena, than in any overwhelming desire to change them for the better, warmly as that desire was often expressed, and sincerely, no doubt, as it was entertained.   Still, Carlyle's main literary motive-power was not a moral passion, but a humorous wonder.   He was always taking to pieces, in his own mind's eye, the marvellous structure of human society, and bewildering himself with the problem of how it could be put together again.   Even in studying personal character, what he cared for principally was this.   For men who could not sway the great spiritual tides of human loyalty and trust, he had—with the curious exception of Goethe—no very real reverence.   His true heroes were all men who could make multitudes follow them as the moon makes the sea follow her,—either by spiritual magnetism, or by trust, or by genuine practical capacity.   To him, imagination was the true organ of divinity, because, as he saw at a glance, it was by the imagination that men are most easily both governed and beguiled.   His story of the French Revolution is a series of studies in the way men are beguiled and governed by their imagination, and no more wonderful book of its kind has ever been written in this world, though one would be sorry to have to estimate accurately how much of his picture is true vision, and how much the misleading guesswork of a highly-imaginative dreamer.

It is in some respects curious that Carlyle has connected his name so effectually as he has done with the denunciation of Shams. For the passionate love of truth in its simplicity was not at all his chief characteristic. In the first place, his style is too self-conscious for that of sheer, self-forgetting love of truth. No man of first-rate simplicity—and first-rate simplicity is, I imagine, one of the conditions of a first-rate love of truth,—would express common-place ideas in so roundabout a fashion as he; would say, for instance, in recommending Emerson to the reading public, "The words of such a man,—what words he thinks fit to speak,—are worth attending to"; or would describe a kind and gracious woman as "a gentle, excellent, female soul," as he does in his *Life of Sterling*. There is a straining for effect in the details of Carlyle's style which is not the characteristic of an overpowering and perfectly simple love of truth. Nor was that the ruling intellectual principle of Carlyle's mind. What he meant by hatred of shams, exposure of unveracities, defiance to the "Everlasting No," affirmation of the "Everlasting Yea," and the like, was not so much the love of truth, as the love of divine force,—the love of that which had genuine strength and effective character in it, the denunciation of imbecilities, the scorn for the dwindled life of mere conventionality or precedent, the contempt for extinct figments, not so much because they were figments, as because they were extinct and would no longer bear the strain put upon them by human passion. You can see this in the scorn which Carlyle pours upon "thin" men,—his meagre reverence for "thin-lipped, constitutional Hampden," for instance, and his contempt for such men as the Edgeworth described in John Sterling's life, whom he more than despises, not for the least grain of insincerity, but for deficiency in *quantity* of nature, and especially such nature as moves society. Greatly as Carlyle despised "cant," he seems to have meant by cant not so much principles which a man does not personally accept, but repeats by rote on the authority of others, as principles which have ceased, in his estimation, to exert a living influence on society, whether heartily accepted by the individual or not. Thus, in his life of Sterling, he indulges in long pages of vituperation against Sterling for taking to the Church,—not that he believed Sterling to be insincere in doing so, but because what Carlyle called the "Hebrew old clothes" were to his mind worn out, and he would not admit that any one of lucid mind could honestly fail to see that so it was.

Carlyle, in short, has been the interpreter to his country, not so much of the "veracities" or "verities" of life, as of the moral and social spells and symbols which, for evil or for good, have exercised a great imaginative influence over the social organism of large bodies of men, and either awed them into sober and earnest work, or stimulated them into delirious and anarchic excitement. He has been the greatest painter who ever lived, of the interior life of man, especially of such life as spreads to the multitude, not perhaps exactly as it really is, but rather as it represented itself to one who looked upon it as the symbol of some infinite mind, of which it embodied a temporary phase. I doubt if Carlyle ever really interpreted any human being's career,—Cromwell's, or Frederick's, or Coleridge's,—as justly and fully as many men of less genius might have interpreted it. For this was not, after all, his chief interest. His interest seems to me always to have been in figuring the human mind as representing some flying colour or type of an Infinite Mind at work behind the Universe, and so presenting this idea as to make it palpable to his fellow-men. He told Sterling he did not mind whether he talked "pantheism or pottheism,"—a mild joke which he so frequently repeated as to indicate that he rather overrated its excellence,—so long as it was true; and he meant, I think, by being true, not so much corresponding to fact, as expressing adequately the constant effort of his own great imagination to see the finite in some graphic relation to the infinite. Perhaps the central thought of his life was in this passage from *Sartor Resartus*,—"What is man himself, but a symbol of God? Is not all that he does symbolical,—a revelation to sense of the mystic God-given power that is in him, a gospel of freedom, which he, the 'Messias of Nature,' preaches, as he can, by act and word? Not a hut he builds but is the visible embodiment of a thought, but leaves visible record of invisible things, but is, in the transcendental sense, symbolical as well as real." Carlyle was far the greatest interpreter our literature has ever had of the infinite forces working through society, of that vast, dim back-ground of social beliefs, unbeliefs, enthusiasms, sentimentalities, superstitions, hopes, fears, and trusts, which go to make up either the strong cement, or the destructive lava-stream, of national life, and to image forth some of the genuine features of the retributive providence of history.

III

CARLYLE'S REMINISCENCES [1]

1881

THERE can be no doubt as to the permanent vitality
of this book, or of the careless genius which produced
it after this random fashion, at an age when Carlyle
was looking back upon a long and laborious life.
But there may be, I think, much doubt as to the
manner in which Mr. Froude has exercised the
absolute discretion entrusted to him by Carlyle as to
the use he should make of these reminiscences. I
do not think that Carlyle, with his great pride and
his deep reserve, would ever have approved of the
inclusion in this book of all the constant references
to his wife, and to his love for her, poured out with
the freedom of a diarist, though of a diarist who has
formed for himself that semi-artificial manner which
suggests a consciousness of audience. The rhapsodies
on his "noblest," "queenliest," "beautifullest," and
so forth, natural enough to the old man in his desolation, should not, I think, have been given to the
world as they were written. What is the proper
sphere of privacy, if the half-remorseful self-reproaches

[1] *Reminiscences by Thomas Carlyle.* Edited by James
Anthony Froude. Two vols. 1881. London: Longmans.

of the tenderest love, accusing itself of inadequacy, are to be made public to all the world ?

However, I shall deal here only with the pleasanter and more brilliant characteristics of the book. And nothing contained in it is so affecting as the few pages devoted to the memory of James Carlyle. Carlyle speaks of himself, with a certain dignified pride, as "the humble James Carlyle's work"; and no doubt, there was much of the father in the son, though the stern, taciturn conciseness of the father was blended in the son with the artistic restlessness and discontent, which seek relief in words and cannot hold the mouth, as it were with a bridle, because it were pain and grief to do so. Here you see Carlyle's rich intellectual inheritance plainly enough :—

"None of us will ever forget that bold glowing style of his, flowing free from his untutored soul, full of metaphors (though he knew not what a metaphor was) with all manner of potent words which he appropriated and applied with a surprising accuracy you often would not guess whence—brief, energetic, and which I should say conveyed the most perfect picture, definite, clear, not in ambitious colours but in full white sunlight, of all the dialects I have ever listened to. Nothing did I ever hear him undertake to render visible which did not become almost ocularly so. Never shall we again hear such speech as that was. The whole district knew of it, and laughed joyfully over it, not knowing how otherwise to express the feeling it gave them; emphatic I have heard him beyond all men. In anger he had no need of oaths, his words were like sharp arrows that smote into the very heart. The fault was that he exaggerated (which tendency I also inherit), yet only in description, and for the sake chiefly of humorous effect. He was a man of rigid, even scrupulous, veracity. I have often heard him turn back when he thought his strong words were misleading, and correct them into mensurative accuracy."

All these qualities reappeared in Thomas Carlyle, even to the last feature,—the compunctious withdrawal of something which had overshot the mark, though often in Thomas Carlyle's case so reluctant a withdrawal that the withdrawal failed of its effect. But then Carlyle goes on to paint in his father a characteristic which he had absolutely failed to inherit:—nay, he had even fallen into something like an excess of the very weakness from which he declares his father so completely free :—

"A virtue he had which I should learn to imitate. He *never spoke of what was disagreeable and past.* I have often wondered and admired at this. The thing that he had nothing to do with, he did nothing with. His was a healthy mind. In like manner I have seen him always when we young ones, half roguishly, and provokingly without doubt, were perhaps repeating sayings of his, sit as if he did not hear us at all. Never once did I know him utter a word, only once, that I remember, give a look in such a case. Another virtue the example of which has passed strongly into me was his settled placid indifference to the clamours or the murmurs of public opinion. For the judgment of those that had no right or power to judge him, he seemed simply to care nothing at all. He very rarely spoke of despising such things. He contented himself with altogether disregarding them. Hollow babble it was for him, a thing, as Fichte said, that did not exist ; *das gar nicht existirte.* There was something truly great in this. The very perfection of it hid from you the extent of the attainment."

Carlyle, on the contrary, loved, like Hamlet, to "unpack his soul" with words, even when, like

Hamlet, he was profuse in his self-reproaches for the relief which that unpacking of his soul certainly gave him.   But even as regards this different temperament of the two men, it is clear that the father had something of that high-pressure of emotion in him which gave the literary writer his motive-power :—

"I have often seen him weep, too ; his voice would thicken and his lips curve while reading the Bible.   He had a merciful heart to real distress, though he hated idleness, and for imbecility and fatuity had no tolerance. Once—and I think once only—I saw him in a passion of tears.   It was when the remains of my mother's fever hung upon her, in 1817, and seemed to threaten the extinction of her reason.   We were all of us nigh desperate, and ourselves mad.   He burst at last into quite a torrent of grief, cried piteously, and threw himself on the floor and lay moaning.   I wondered, and had no words, no tears.   It was as if a rock of granite had melted, and was thawing into water.   What unknown seas of feeling lie in man, and will from time to time break through ! "

In painful contrast to this sketch of the strong peasant from whom Carlyle was so justly proud to be descended, is his sketch of the light literary men of the world, whom he felt (sometimes unjustly) to be writers and nothing more.   Take, for instance, a bitter, but I suppose substantially true, account of De Quincey, though it seems to me clear that Carlyle did not sufficiently appreciate that vivid *seeing* power in De Quincey which was his own greatest literary strength :—

"Jemmy Belcher was a smirking little dumpy Unitarian bookseller in the Bull-ring, regarded as a kind of curiosity and favourite among these people, and had seen me. One showery day I had took shelter in his shop; picked up a new magazine, found in it a cleverish and completely hostile criticism of my *Wilhelm Meister*, of my Goethe, and self, etc., read it faithfully to the end, and have never set eye on it since. On stepping out my bad spirits did not feel much elevated by the dose just swallowed, but I thought with myself, ' This man is perhaps right on some points ; if so, let him be admonitory ! ' And he was so (on a Scotticism, or perhaps two) ; and I did reasonably soon (in not above a couple of hours), dismiss him to the devil, or to Jericho, as an ill-given, unserviceable kind of entity in my course through this world. It was De Quincey, as I often enough heard afterwards from foolish-talking persons. ' What matter who, ye foolish-talking persons ? ' would have been my *silent* answer, as it generally pretty much was. I recollect, too, how in Edinburgh a year or two after, poor De Quincey, whom I wished to know, was reported to tremble at the thought of such a thing ; and did fly pale as ashes, poor little soul, the first time we actually met. He was a pretty little creature, full of wire-drawn ingenuities, bankrupt enthusiasms, bankrupt pride, with the finest silver-toned low voice, and most elaborate gently-winding courtesies and ingenuities in conversation. ' What wouldn't one give to have him in a box, and take him out to talk ! ' That was Her criticism of him, and it was right good. A bright, ready, and melodious talker, but in the end an inconclusive and long-winded. One of the smallest man figures I ever saw ; shaped like a pair of tongs, and hardly above five feet in all. When he sate, you would have taken him, by candlelight, for the beautifullest little child ; blue-eyed, sparkling face, had there not been a something, too, which said ' *Eccovi*—this child has been in hell.' After leaving Edinburgh I never saw him, hardly ever heard of him. His fate, owing to opium, etc., was hard and sore, poor fine-strung weak creature, launched *so* into the literary career of ambition and mother of dead dogs."

The graphic force shown in single sentences,—
frequently representative only of what Carlyle himself discerned, not of the reality behind what he
discerned, but still most telling, as showing what his
quick eye first lit upon,—is extraordinary. Thus
he describes John Stuart Mill's talk as "rather
wintry" and "sawdustish," but "always well-in-
formed and sincere." A great social entertainer of
those times—Lady Holland—he dashes off as "a
kind of hungry, ornamented witch, looking over at
me with merely carnivorous views,"—views, I suppose,
as to what she could make of him from the entertainer's point of view ; and he describes a speech of
the Duke of Wellington's on Lord Ellenborough's
"Gates of Somnauth," as "a speech of the most
haggly, hawky, pinched, and meagre kind, so far as
utterance and eloquence went, but potent for conviction beyond any other." No wonder that Irving,
who knew Carlyle so intimately, said of him to
Henry Drummond that "few have such eyes." Even
in describing scenes or incidents, the old man's
language beats in vividness the most vivid of our
modern describers. He dashes off a slight walking
tour with Irving, with all its joyous hilarity, in
lines so clear and strong, that we seem to have been
with him in his youth :—

" In vacation time, twice over, I made a walking tour
with him. First time I think was to the Trossachs, and
home by Loch Lomond, Greenock, Glasgow, etc., many
parts of which are still visible to me. The party generally was to be of four ; one Piers, who was Irving's
housemate or even landlord, schoolmaster of Abbotshall,
i.e. of ' The Links,' at the southern extra-burghal part of
Kirkcaldy, a cheerful scatterbrained creature who went
ultimately as preacher or professor of something to the

Cape of Good Hope, and one Brown (James Brown), who had succeeded Irving in Haddington, and was now tutor somewhere. The full rally was not to be till Stirling ; even Piers was gone ahead ; and Irving and I, after an official dinner with the burghal dignitaries of Kirkcaldy, who strove to be pleasant, set out together one grey August evening by Forth sands towards Torryburn. Piers was to have beds ready for us there, and we cheerily walked along our mostly dark and intricate twenty-two miles. But Piers had nothing serviceably ready ; we could not even discover Piers at that dead hour (2 A.M.), and had a good deal of groping and adventuring before a poor inn opened to us with two coarse, clean beds in it, in which we instantly fell asleep. Piers did in person rouse us next morning about six, but we concordantly met him with mere ha-ha's ! and inarticulate hootings of satirical rebuke, to such extent that Piers, convicted of nothing but heroic punctuality, flung himself out into the rain again in momentary indignant puff, and strode away for Stirling, where we next saw him after four or five hours. I remember the squalor of our bedroom in the dim, rainy light, and how little we cared for it in our opulence of youth. The sight of giant Irving in a shortish shirt on the sanded floor, drinking patiently a large tankard of 'penny whaup' (the smallest beer in creation) before beginning to dress, is still present to me as comic. Of sublime or tragic, the night before a mysterious great red glow is much more memorable, which had long hung before us in the murky sky, growing gradually brighter and bigger, till at last we found it must be Carron Iron- works, on the other side of Forth, one of the most im- pressive sights. Our march to Stirling was under pour- ing rain for most part, but I recollect enjoying the romance of it ; Kincardine, Culross (Cu'ros), Clackmannan, here they are then ; what a wonder to be here ! The Links of Forth, the Ochills, Grampians, Forth itself, Stirling, lion-shaped, ahead, like a lion couchant with the castle for his crown ; all this was beautiful in spite of rain. Welcome too was the inside of Stirling, with its fine warm inn and the excellent refection and thorough drying and refitting we got there, Piers and Brown looking pleasantly on. Strolling and sight-seeing, (day now very fine—Stirling all washed) till we marched for Doune in the evening (Brig of Teith, 'blue and arrowy Teith,' Irving and I took that by-way in the dusk); breakfast in Callander next morning, and get to Loch Katrine in an hour or two more. I have not been in that region again till August last year, four days of magnificently perfect hospitality with Stirling of Keir. Almost surprising how mournful it was to 'look on this picture and on that' at interval of fifty years."

But perhaps the most telling miniature in these *Reminiscences* is that of Jeffrey acting to Mrs. Carlyle and himself the various kinds of orators, "the windy-grandiloquent," "the ponderous stupid," "the airy stupid," and finally, "the abstruse costive," who is thus delineated :—

"At length he gave us the abstruse costive specimen, which had a meaning and no utterance for it, but went about clambering, stumbling, as on a path of loose boulders, and ended in total downbreak, amid peals of the heartiest laughter from us all. This of the aerial little sprite standing there in fatal collapse, with the brightest of eyes sternly gazing into utter nothingness and dumbness, was one of the most tickling and genially ludicrous things I ever saw ; and it prettily winded up our little drama. I often thought of it afterwards, and of what a part mimicry plays among human gifts."

It is rather remarkable in a man of Carlyle's birth, that there seems to have been an intolerable fastidiousness about him, not only in relation to people, but to sounds and sights, which must, we suppose, be ascribed to the artistic vein in his temperament. He says quite frankly:—"In short, as has been enough indicated elsewhere, I was advancing towards huge instalments of bodily and spiritual wretchedness in this my Edinburgh purgatory; and had to clean and purify myself in penal fire of various kinds for several years coming; the first, and much the worst, two or three of which were to be enacted in this once-loved city. Horrible to think of in part even yet! The bodily part of them was a kind of base agony (arising mainly in the want of any extant or discoverable *fence* between my coarser fellow-creatures and my more sensitive self), and might and could easily (had the age been pious or thoughtful) have been spared a poor creature like me. Those hideous disturbances to sleep, etc., a very little real care and goodness might prevent all that; and I look back upon it still with a kind of angry protest, and would have my successors saved from it." And in a later page he adds his confession that he liked, on the whole, social converse with the aristocracy best:—"Certain of the aristocracy, however, did seem to me still very noble; and, with due limitation of the grossly worthless (none of whom had we to do with), I should vote at present that, of classes known to me in England, the aristocracy (with its perfection of human politeness, its continual grace of bearing and of acting, steadfast 'honour,' light address and cheery stoicism), if you see well into it, is actually yet the best of English classes." That is a very curious testimony to the effect of Carlyle's artistic feeling in modifying his own teaching as to " the gospel of work." It was not the gospel of work which had made even the noblest of the aristocracy what they were.

After reading these *Reminiscences*, one cannot but

ask oneself in what respect was Carlyle really a great man, and where did he fall short of true greatness? I should say that he was really great in imagination,—very great in insight into the more expressive side of human character,—great in Scotch humour, though utterly unable to appreciate the lighter kinds of true humour, like Lamb's,—and very great, too, in industry, quite indefatigable in small painstakings, whenever he thought that the task to which he had devoted himself was worthy of him. But he was far from great, even weak in judgment, far from great, even narrow in sympathy, far from great, even purblind in his appreciation of the importance to be attached to the various mechanism of human life. It is singular that one who manifested his genius chiefly by history,—or should we rather say, by his insight into and delineation of some of the most critical characters in history, and some of the most vivid popular scenes in history?—should have been so totally devoid of what one may call the true historical sense,—the appreciation, I mean, of the inherited conditions and ineradicable habits of ordinary national life. There was something of the historical Don Quixote about Carlyle; he tilted at windmills, and did not know that he was tilting at windmills. He had so deep an appreciation of the vivid flashes of consciousness which mark all great popular crises, because they mark all great personal crises, that he wanted to raise all human life and all common popular life to the level of the high self-conscious stage. He never thoroughly appreciated the meaning of habit. He never thoroughly understood the value of routine. He never adequately entered into the power of tradition. He judged of human life as

if will and emotion were all in all. He judged of
political life as if great men and great occasions
ought to be all in all, and was furious at the waste
of force involved in doing things as men had been
accustomed to do them, wherever that appeared to
be a partially ineffectual way. And his error in
judging of peoples is equally traceable in his judgments on individuals. If a man had a strong interest in the routine and detail of life, he called him
"sawdustish." If he had a profound belief in any
popular ideas beyond those acknowledged by himself,
Carlyle probably called him moonshiny. Such men
as John Mill came under the one condemnation,
such men as Mazzini under the other. And yet
either John Mill or Mazzini may be said to have
applied a more effectual knowledge of men to the
historical conditions of their own time, than Thomas
Carlyle. Indeed, once go beyond the world of the
vivid personal and popular emotions and passions,
and Carlyle's insight seems to have been very limited,
and his genius disappears.

IV

THOMAS CARLYLE [1]

1882

MR. FROUDE takes credit to himself for being a true portrait-painter, a portrait-painter who abates nothing in his picture of the darker features of the man whom he has painted, and certainly he takes no credit in this respect to which he has not a just claim. The picture here given is strong but by no means idealised. Indeed, the gloomy impression left by the *Reminiscences* is rather deepened than softened by this portion of the Life. The stern gloom, contemptuousness, and cynicism of these earlier days are not even relieved, as they were in the *Reminiscences*, by the remorseful tenderness and grateful affection of the old man's feeling for his lost wife. It is only Carlyle's passionate devotion to his mother and father, to his brothers and sisters, which makes this part of his life even tolerable. That Carlyle was uniformly high-minded, so far as high-mindedness consists in a positive scorn for mean actions and ignoble ends, the

---

[1] *Thomas Carlyle: a History of the First Forty Years of his Life*, 1795-1835. By James Anthony Froude, M.A. 2 vols. With Portraits and Etchings. London: Longmans, Green, and Co.

reader never forgets ; that he thought much more of the welfare of his kith and kin than of his own welfare, you see constantly, with increasing admiration. But a man more absolutely destitute of that "charity" which, in St. Paul's words, "suffereth long and is kind, envieth not, vaunteth not itself, is not puffed up, doth not behave itself unseemly, seeketh not her own, is not easily provoked, thinketh no evil," cannot easily be imagined, and probably never yet lived, than the proud and scornful peasant of genius whom Mr. Froude's pages delineate. Carlyle writes to his mother in 1824, when he has just finished his *Life of Schiller :*—

"Sometimes of late I have bethought me of some of your old maxims about pride and vanity. I do see this same vanity to be the root of half the evil men are subject to in life. Examples of it stare me in the face every day. The pitiful passion, under any of the thousand forms which it assumes, never fails to wither out the good and worthy parts of a man's character, and leave him poor and spiteful, an enemy to his own peace and that of all about him. There never was a wiser doctrine than that of Christian humility, considered as a corrective for the coarse, unruly selfishness of man's nature."

But whatever Carlyle thought of the value of Christian humility "considered as a corrective for the coarse, unruly selfishness of man's nature," he never seems to have had any good opinion of it considered as a corrective for that irritable pride, and detestation of owing anything to the generosity of another, in which he indulged himself as if it were the highest of virtues. He is constantly comparing himself with people whom he denounces with a sort of contemptuous rage, rather than with those with whom he would desire to rank himself, if he could. Thus he writes to his mother :—

"I am in very fair health considering everything: about a hundred times as well as I was last year, and as happy as you ever saw me. In fact I want nothing but steady health of body (which I shall get in time) to be one of the comfortablest persons of my acquaintance. I have also books to write and things to say and do in this world which few wot of. This has the air of vanity, but it is not altogether so. I consider that my Almighty Author has given me some glimmerings of superior understanding and mental gifts; and I should reckon it the worst treason against him to neglect improving and using to the very utmost of my power these his bountiful mercies. At some future day it shall go hard, but I will stand above these mean men whom I have never yet stood *with*."

And this he writes without in the least explaining to what kind of mean men he refers, as if the class of men whom he denounces were always haunting his imagination, rather than the class of men of whose moral and spiritual position he could be really emulous. Except Goethe, who does not seem to me a very splendid object for moral emulation, it is wonderful how little Carlyle found among his contemporaries to appreciate and emulate. He can admire "heroes" of past ages, and can love his own family. But in relation to all his contemporaries,—and Goethe can be called a contemporary only in a very limited sense,—he finds hardly anything to emulate or admire. He loves Irving, but is never tired of girding at Irving's vanity and superstition. He despises, almost without exception, the literary men with whom he makes acquaintance. Here is

Carlyle's survey of literary London, when he first ventured into it :—

"Irving advises me to stay in London ; partly with a friendly feeling, partly with a half-selfish one, for he would fain keep me near him. Among all his followers there is none whose intercourse can satisfy him. Any other than him it would go far to disgust. Great part of them are blockheads, a few are fools. There is no rightly intellectual man among them. He speculates and speculates, and would rather have one contradict him rationally, than gape at him with the vacant stare of children viewing the Grand Turk's palace with his guards—all alive ! He advises me, not knowing what he says. He himself has the nerves of a buffalo, and forgets that I have not. His philosophy with me is like a gill of ditch-water thrown into the crater of Mount Ætna. A million gallons of it would avail me nothing. On the whole, however, he is among the best fellows in London, by far the best that I have met with. Thomas Campbell has a far clearer judgment, infinitely more taste and refinement, but there is no living well of thought or feeling in him. His head is a shop, not a manufactory ; and for his heart, it is as dry as a Greenock kipper. I saw him for the second time the other night. I viewed him more clearly and in a kindlier light, but scarcely altered my opinion of him. He is not so much a man as the editor of a magazine. His life is that of an exotic. He exists in London, as most Scotchmen do, like a shrub disrooted and stuck into a bottle of water. Poor Campbell ! There were good things in him too, but fate has pressed too heavy on him, or he has resisted it too weakly. His poetic vein is failing, or has run out. He has a Glasgow wife, and their only son is in a state of idiotcy. I sympathised with him, I could have loved him, but he has forgot the way to love. Procter here has set up house on the strength of his writing faculties, with his wife, a daughter of the Noble Lady. He is a good-natured man, lively and ingenious, but essentially a small. Coleridge is sunk inextricably in the depths of putrescent indolence. Southey and Wordsworth have retired far from the din of this monstrous city ; so has Thomas Moore. Whom have we left ? The dwarf Opium-eater, my critic in the *London Magazine*, lives here in lodgings, with a wife and children living, or starving, on the scanty produce of his scribble far off in Westmoreland. He carries a laudanum bottle in his pocket, and the venom of a wasp in his heart. A rascal (———), who writes much of the blackguardism in *Blackwood*, has been frying him to cinders on the gridiron of *John Bull*. Poor De Quincey ! He had twenty thousand pounds, and a liberal share of gifts from Nature. Vanity and opium have brought him to the state of 'dog distract or monkey sick.' If I could find him, it would give me pleasure to procure him one substantial beefsteak before he dies. Hazlitt is writing his way through France and Italy. The gin-shops and pawnbrokers bewail his absence. Leigh Hunt writes 'wishing-caps' for the *Examiner*, and lives on the lightest of diets at Pisa. But what shall I say of you, ye ———, and ———, and ———, and all the spotted fry that 'report' and 'get up' for the 'public press,' that earn money by writing calumnies, and spend it in punch and other viler objects of debauchery ? Filthiest and basest of the children of men ! My soul come not into your secrets ; mine honour be not united unto you ! 'Good heavens !' I often inwardly exclaim, 'and is this the literary world ?' This rascal rout, this dirty rabble, destitute not only of high feeling and knowledge or intellect, but even of common honesty ! The very best of them are ill-natured weaklings. They are not red-blooded men at all. They are only things for writing articles. But I have done with them for once. In railing at them, let me not forget that if they are bad and worthless, I, as yet, am nothing ; and that he who putteth on his harness should not boast himself as he who putteth it off. Unhappy souls ! perhaps they are more to be pitied than blamed. I do not hate them. I would only that stone walls and iron bars were constantly between us. Such is the literary world of London ; indisputably the poorest part of its population at present."

And again :—

"The people are stupid and noisy, and I live at the easy rate of five and forty shillings per week ! I say the people are stupid not altogether unadvisedly. In point either of intellectual and moral culture they are some degrees below even the inhabitants of the 'modern Athens.' I have met no man of true head and heart among them. Coleridge is a mass of richest spices putrefied into a dunghill. I never hear him *tawlk* without feeling ready to worship him, and toss him in a blanket. Thomas Campbell is an Edinburgh '*small*,' made still smaller by growth in a foreign soil. Irving is enveloped with delusions and difficulties, wending somewhat down hill, to what depths I know not ; and scarcely ever to be seen without a host of the most stolid of all his Majesty's Christian people sitting round him. I wonder often that he does not buy himself a tar-barrel, and fairly light it under the Hatton Garden pulpit, and thus once for all *ex fumo* giving *lucem*, bid adieu the gross train-oil concern altogether. The poor little ———. I often feel that were I as one of these people, sitting in a whole body by the cheek of my own wife, my feet upon my own hearth, I should feel distressed at seeing myself so *very* poor in spirit. Literary men ! The Devil in his own good time take all such literary men. One sterling fellow like Schiller, or even old Johnson, would take half-a-dozen such creatures by the nape of the neck, between his finger and thumb, and carry them forth to the nearest common sink. Save Allan Cunningham, our honest Nithdale peasant, there is not one *man* among them. In short, it does not seem worth while to spend five and forty shillings weekly for the privilege of being near such pen-men."

And you may say of the whole tone of his correspondence that his chief desire and resolve, as expressed in it, is to keep this "rabble rout" beneath his feet, rather than to attain to any height of intellectual or moral virtue which he has discerned in any living contemporary. With all his love for Irving, you never find a thought passing through Carlyle's mind that he, Carlyle, might with advantage emulate Irving's large and generous nature, and his eager spiritual faith. Nor do you find the character anywhere, unless it be within his own family, that Carlyle for a single moment sets before him as an ideal nobler than himself, to the elevation of which he would gladly aspire. His one ideal of life seems to be to tread down the "rabble rout," instead of to strain after any excellence above his own. Indeed, the thing which has struck me with most wonder in reading these letters, is that a man could *remain* so high-minded as Carlyle on the whole certainly did, and yet live so constantly in the atmosphere of scorn, —scorn certainly more or less for himself as well as every one else, but especially for every one else, his own clan excepted. He spends all his energies in a sort of vivid passion of scorn. He tramples furiously partly on himself and partly on the miserable generation of his fellow-men, and then he is lost in wonder and vexation that such trampling results in no great work of genius. It was not, of course, till he found subjects for genuine admiration,—which he seems to have been long in doing,—that he discovered subjects for his creative genius at all. You cannot make destructive fury serve you for a creative work, and it seems to me that Carlyle's vast waste of power in early life was greatly due to his giving up so large a portion of his mind and heart to the task of tearing to shreds the inadequate characters and aims which he found so richly strewn around him. The grim fire in him seems to have been in search of something to consume, and the following was the kind of fuel which, for the most part, it found. He is writing from Kinnaird, in Perthshire, where he was staying with Mr. and Mrs. Charles Buller, as tutor to that Charles Buller whose premature death some years later deprived England of a young statesman of the highest promise :

"I see something of fashionable people here (he wrote to Miss Welsh), and truly to my plebeian conception there is not a more futile class of persons on the face of the earth. If I were doomed to exist as a man of fashion, I do honestly believe I should swallow ratsbane, or apply to hemp or steel before three months were over. From day to day and year to year the problem is, not how to use time, but how to waste it least painfully. They have their dinners and their routs. They move heaven and earth to get everything arranged and enacted properly ; and when the whole is done, what is it ? Had the parties all wrapped themselves in warm blankets and kept their beds, much peace had been among several hundreds of his Majesty's subjects, and the same result, the uneasy destruction of half-a-dozen hours, had been quite as well attained. No wonder poor women take to opium and scandal. The wonder is rather that these queens of the land do not some morning, struck by the hopelessness of their condition, make a general finish by simultaneous consent, and exhibit to coroners and juries the spectacle of the old world of *ton* suspended by their garters, and freed at last from *ennui* in the most cheap and complete of all possible modes. There is something in the life of a sturdy peasant toiling from sun to sun for a plump wife and six eating children ; but as for the Lady Jerseys and the Lord Petershams, peace be with them."

No man not a man of genius could have written this, and much that is of the same type; but then, mere rage at the superficialities of the world was not enough for one whom it never could have contented to be a satirist. Carlyle had at least derived this from his father's education, that he was never content with raging at what was faulty and bad, unless he could find the means of suggesting something less faulty or even good to substitute for it; and the truth certainly is that during the early part of his life at all events, Carlyle never did find this, but gnawed his heart away in denouncing the follies and futilities—not always nearly so unmixed as his jaundiced eye persuaded him—which he did not know how to reform.

Unfortunately, as it seems to me, in the lady who became his wife, and whose mind he had a very great share in forming, he found a very apt pupil for this negative and contemptuous side of his own mind; and so, as Mr. Froude puts it, the sharp facets of the two diamonds, as they wore against each other, "never wore into surfaces which harmoniously corresponded." Mrs. Carlyle said, in the late evening of her laborious life, "I married for ambition. Carlyle has exceeded all my wildest hopes and expectations, and I am miserable." No wonder, when neither mutual love, nor even common love for something above themselves, but rather scorn for everything mean, was the only deep ground of their mutual sympathy. The wonder rather is that that scorn for what was mean should have remained, on the whole, so sound as it did, and should never have degenerated into a misanthropy at once selfish and malignant. Yet this certainly never happened. It is in the highest sense creditable both to Carlyle and his wife, that with all the hardness of their natures, and all the severe trials, which partly from health and partly from the deficiency in that tenderness which does so much to smooth the path of ordinary life, they had to undergo, they kept their unquestionable cynicism to the last free from all the more ignoble elements, and perfectly consistent with that Stoical magnanimity in which it began.

Still, say of it what you will, the spectacle of the life of this great genius is not, on the whole, a good, though it is in many respects a grand one. As for the prophetic message which Mr. Froude thinks that Carlyle had to deliver to the world, I hold that the more it is studied, and especially the more it is studied beside the life of him who promulgated it, the more it will be found to consist almost as much of a confession of its own insufficiency, and of the true cause of that insufficiency, as of the salutary warning and indignant denunciation. But to this message it is now time to refer.

The one thing upon which I differ more and more from Mr. Froude, the more I study all these strange records of a strange and even unique character, is his impression that Carlyle was really deeply possessed with a gospel or message that he was bound to deliver, that he was in this sense a veritable prophet, and one straitened in spirit till he had found a response in man. That one or two very important truths had gained a complete possession of his imagination is, of course, obvious. He saw with a vividness which hardly any of us, even with his help, realise, that almost all serious speech is a sort of venture, an attempt to embody something much deeper than itself, which at best it can only indicate, not adequately express. He saw with absolute insight the helplessness of mere institutions to cure evils which are deep-rooted in the characters of those who work the institutions. He felt, often with a humorous indignation, sometimes only with an indignant humour, the falsehood of the moral standards by which men measure each other; and he hated the conventional respectabilities at the bottom of middle-class morality, with a hatred almost too savage to be consistent with anything like a true perspective in his views of life. Further, he believed in the duty of doing thoroughly whatever you take in hand to do at all, as the first of human duties; and to this great article of his creed, he no doubt added, with profound confidence in the early part of his life, but with very much less distinctness, as it seems to me, towards its close, a faith in the providence of God, in the immortality of the human soul, and in the transcendental realities behind all the time-phenomena, as he called them, which are presented to us in history and in experience. But take all these beliefs together, and they form a very vague and ambiguous sort of gospel, almost all the elements of which, except, perhaps, the gospel of thoroughness in work, were embarrassed by all sorts of doubts, to which Carlyle found no answer; and yet of the embarrassment of these doubts he became more and more conscious as his life went on. For example, he never could get himself quite clear as to what he called his "creed of Natural Supernatur-alism." Late in his own life he declared, with a perfectly absurd dogmatism indeed, —at least, Mr. Froude asserts that he dogmatically laid it down,— that "it is as certain as mathematics, that no such thing" as the special miraculous occurrences of sacred history "ever has been, or can be." But when he came to work out what he meant by his own natural supernaturalism, he got quite out of his depth. "Is not every thought," he wrote, in his *Journal* in 1830, "properly an inspiration? Or how is one thing more inspired than another? Much in this." If there were really much in this, then surely all Carlyle's own teaching was wrong, for the Whigs and the fanatics, and the materialists and utilitarians, and all whom he denounced as the false teachers of the age, were, in that case, just as much speaking from inspiration, as he himself when he uttered the oracles of his own practical transcendentalism. Indeed, his whole early teaching really rested on the principle of the immutable hostility of good and evil, but what with his "natural supernaturalism," and his admiration for Goethe's calm indifference to the moral struggles of his age, he soon began to question whether there were not some common measure between sin and righteousness; and we find speculations like the following, not only scattered constantly through his journals, but bearing the most remarkable fruits in his later histories and moral essays:—

"What *is* art and poetry? Is the beautiful really higher than the good? A higher *form* thereof? Thus were a poet not only a priest, but a high priest. When Goethe and Schiller say or insinuate that art is higher than religion, do they mean perhaps this? That whereas religion represents (what is the essence of truth for man) the good as *infinitely* (the word is emphatic) different from the evil, but sets them in a state of hostility (as in heaven and hell), art likewise admits and inculcates this quite infinite difference, but *without* hostility, with peacefulness, like the difference of two poles which *cannot* coalesce, yet do not quarrel—nay, should not quarrel, for both are essential to the whole. In this way is Goethe's morality to be considered as a *higher* (apart from its comprehensiveness, nay, universality) than has hitherto been promulgated? *Sehr einseitig!* Yet perhaps there is a glimpse of the truth here." (Vol. II., pp. 93-4.)

This was written at the end of 1830. Again, at the end of 1831, we read :—

"This I begin to see, that evil and good are everywhere, like shadow and substance; inseparable (for men), yet not hostile, only opposed. There is considerable significance in this fact, perhaps the *new* moral principle of our era. (How?) It was familiar to Goethe's mind." (Vol. II., p. 228.)

And this thought certainly took more and more possession of Carlyle, touching with uncertainty half his most fiery moral judgments, and maturing ultimately, as we see in his Life of Sterling, into a "steady resolution to suppress" all discussions as to either the personality of God or the origin of moral evil, as "wholly fruitless and worthless." Indeed, the nearest approach to anything like a gospel on these deeper subjects, which Carlyle found himself able to preach in later life, is contained in the following ambiguous answer to a young man, the son of an old friend, who wrote to him on the subject of prayer :—

"Thomas Carlyle to George A. Duncan.

"Chelsea, June 9, 1870.

"Dear Sir—You need no apology for addressing me; your letter itself is of amiable, ingenuous character; pleasant and interesting to me in no common degree. I am sorry only that I cannot set at rest, or settle into clearness, your doubts on that important subject. What

I myself practically, in a half-articulate way, believe on it I will try to express for you. First, then, as to your objection of setting up *our* poor wish or will in opposition to the will of the Eternal, I have not the least word to say in contradiction of it. And this seems to close, and does, in a sense though not perhaps in all senses, close the question of our prayers being *granted*, or what is called ' heard ; ' but that is not the whole question. For, on the other hand, prayer is, and remains always, a native and deepest impulse of the soul of man ; and correctly gone about, is of the very highest benefit (nay, one might say, indispensability) to every man aiming morally high in this world. No prayer, no *religion*, or at least, only a dumb and lamed one ! Prayer is a turning of one's soul, in heroic reverence, in infinite desire and *endeavour*, towards the Highest, the All-Excellent, Omnipotent, Supreme. The modern Hero, therefore, ought *not* to give up praying, as he has latterly all but done. *Words* of prayer, in this epoch, I know hardly any. But the act of prayer, in great moments, I believe to be still possible ; and that one should gratefully accept such moments, and count them blest, when they come, if come they do—which latter is a most rigorous preliminary question with us in all cases. ' *Can* I *pray* in this moment' (much as I may *wish* to do so)? ' If not, then NO !' I can at least stand silent, inquiring, and *not* blasphemously *lie* in this Presence ! On the whole, Silence is the one safe form of prayer known to me, in this poor sordid era—though there are ejaculatory words, too, which occasionally rise on one, with a felt propriety and veracity ; words very welcome in such case ! Prayer is the aspiration of our poor, struggling, heavy-laden soul towards its Eternal Father ; and, with or without words, ought *not* to become impossible, nor, I persuade myself, need it ever. Loyal sons and subjects *can* approach the King's throne who have no ' request ' to make there, except that they may continue loyal. Cannot they ? "
(Vol. II., pp. 21-2.)

That seems to show that in spite of Carlyle's rough
way of treating Sterling's charge of Pantheism—
"Suppose it were Pottheism, if the thing is true !"—
he did to the last retain his belief in a Divine Will
higher than the human will, and quite distinct from
it. But gladly admitting and even maintaining this
as I do, it is clear enough that Carlyle's "gospel"
was overshadowed, even for himself, by such a
crowd of ambiguities and difficulties, by such con-
fusions between naturalism and supernaturalism,
between the lower and the higher nature, between
God and man, between morality and art, between
impulse and inspiration, between fate and free-will,
that he had very little heart left for genuine religious
appeal to any one, and could not even persuade himself to make much of an effort to rescue even his
most intimate friend, Edward Irving, from his
fanatical delusions about the gift of tongues. Once,
indeed, Carlyle seems to have told Irving his mind
pretty freely, but never again, even though he felt a
strong impulse at the last to make one more sally
against the superstitions in which he saw Irving more
and more involved.—Here, at least, it was not for
want of deep conviction, but probably for want of
confidence in his own power to express his too
negative convictions in any form which would persuade one who believed as fervently as Irving did in
the Christian revelation. Carlyle writes to his wife,
of a meeting with Irving in 1831, as follows :—
"The good Irving looked at me wistfully, for he
knows I cannot take miracles in ; yet he looks so
piteously, as if he implored me to believe. Oh dear,
oh dear ! was the Devil ever busier than now, when
the Supernatural must either depart from the world,
or reappear there like a chapter of Hamilton's

Diseases of Females?" But none the less, he spoke his mind freely to Irving only once, but never again took heart to preach his gospel,—if he had one,—to his old friend.

The more I study Carlyle, the less I believe that the word "prophet," and the language concerning a "message" which he had to deliver, in any proper sense describe him and his work. He knew very vaguely what he believed to be true, though he knew very vividly indeed what it was that he held to be utterly false, and from his heart repudiated. But even as to that perfectly distinct and negative part of his creed, even as to his hatred of what he persisted, with his usual unfortunate insistence on a humorous satirical expression of his own, in calling "gigmanity," —the morality, namely, of the class which believes in keeping a gig as a sign of respectability,—which he dubbed "gigmanity" by way of a joke, a joke well enough for once, but in oppressively bad taste when made to ring perpetually in all his friends' ears through years of private correspondence,—I do not believe that Carlyle's denunciations of woes represented a gospel at all. Doubtless, he detested the conventional conception of "respectability" as the characteristic of people who could make a show in the world. He looked upon that conception with supreme and absolute scorn, as well as with a certain indignant horror. But was his denunciation of it truly religious? Did he desire to denounce it, mainly *because* he wished to substitute in every human breast the higher and truer idea respecting moral worth? I doubt it. I do not in the least mean that he did *not* wish to substitute this. Of course he did. But what occupied him, what possessed his imagination, what fired his pen, was not, after all,

love of the true idea, but hatred of the false. He
shows not half so much trace of the desire to redeem
man by planting the true belief, as passionate possession with the miserableness and contemptibleness of
those who are deluded by the false belief. And how
do I judge of this? Why, thus: that hardly anywhere in all these letters and journals do we find
Carlyle fastening with delight on traces of the nobler
and truer standard of thought (at least outside his
own clan), while we constantly find him fastening
with a sort of fever of excitement on traces of the
ignoble and false standard. Where in the world
could Carlyle have found nobler evidence of this
higher standard of worth than in the works of the
great genius of his age, Sir Walter Scott? Yet, what
does he say of these works?—

"It is a damnable heresy in criticism to maintain
either expressly or implicitly that the ultimate object of
poetry is sensation. That of cookery is such, but not
that of poetry. Sir Walter Scott is the great intellectual
restaurateur of Europe. He might have been numbered
among the Conscript Fathers. He has chosen the worser
part, and is only a huge Publicanus. What are his
novels—any one of them? A bout of champagne, claret,
port, or even ale drinking. Are we wiser, better, holier,
stronger? No. We have been amused." (Vol. I., p.
371.) . . . "Walter Scott left town yesterday on his way
to Naples. He is to proceed from Plymouth in a frigate,
which the Government have given him a place in. Much
run after here, it seems; but he is old and sick, and
cannot enjoy it; has had two shocks of palsy, and seems
altogether in a precarious way. To me he is and has
been an object of very minor interest for many, many
years. The novelwright of his time, its favourite child,
and *therefore* an almost worthless one. Yet is there something in his deep recognition of the worth of the past,

perhaps better than anything he has *expressed* about it, into which I do not yet fully see. Have never spoken with him (though I might sometimes without great effort); and now probably never shall." (Vol. II., p. 208.)

It is curious by the way, that Carlyle, an immense reader, appears to have been wholly ignorant of the meaning of the word "publicanus," and to have confounded it with the English word "publican." But it is much more curious that he should have passed so grossly false a judgment on Sir Walter Scott. For if ever there were a man whose writings showed a profound appreciation of moral worth as distinct from conventional worth, it was Sir Walter Scott. Again, take the case of Wordsworth. If ever a man held and preached Carlyle's own transcendental doctrine, both as a creed and as a practical rule of life, it was Wordsworth. Wordsworth genuinely held and embodied in his own life the spiritual view of things, and he genuinely abhorred the life of luxury, and loved the life of "plain living and high thinking." In a word, Wordsworth was a poetical Carlyle, without Carlyle's full insight into the superficialities and conventionalities of bodies politic, but otherwise a genuine and powerful spiritual ally. But what does Carlyle think of Wordsworth? Instead of delighting to detect in him a kindred spirit, he writes of him in this way :—

"Sir Wm. Hamilton's supper (three nights ago) has done me mischief; will hardly go to another. Wordsworth talked of there (by Captain T. Hamilton, his neighbour). Represented verisimilarly enough as a man full of English prejudices, idle, alternately gossiping to enormous lengths, and talking, at rare intervals, high wisdom ; on the whole, endeavouring to make out a plausible life of *halfness* in the Tory way, as so many on all sides do. Am to see him if I please to go thither ; would go but a shortish way for that end." (Vol. II., pp. 338-9.)

And it is the same throughout. What Carlyle feels to be false, he denounces with all the eloquence of a great imagination. But the evidence that what he is driving at, is, not the dissemination of a gospel of new truth to his fellow-men, but rather the intellecual annihilation of an error for which he feels the utmost scorn, lies in the fact that he never seems to have felt the slightest affinity for those contemporaries who really held with him, but only a profound scorn for those contemporaries who lived in the mists of the illusions which he contemned.

On the whole, this picturesque life of Carlyle in his earlier years,—and a more vivid life I cannot imagine,—impresses me profoundly with the belief that the prophetic side of his mind hardly existed ; that he was a man of very rare genius, who had not so much a message to his fellow-men, which he was prompted by love for them to deliver, as a haunting vision of the exceeding emptiness of the commoner forms of human life, and who was brimful of the scorn which that emptiness deserved,—which scorn the intensity of his own imagination compelled him to embody in words. But of grave desire to redeem mankind by persuading them to accept even this message, of passionate craving to find others possessed with the same creed, of eager spiritual sympathy with those who preached anything at all analogous to it,—and there were many contemporaries who did so,—I can find no trace at all. Therefore I deny Carlyle the name of a prophet. His was the inspiration of genius, not the inspiration which comes of the love of God or man. He was, no doubt, "straitened" till his genius found utterance, as all men of genius are. But of the true preacher who yearns to see his truth conveying to other minds the illumination it has conveyed to his own, I can see no sign at all in these delightful and vivid volumes. Even to his wife, it is pretty clear that Carlyle failed altogether to convey any helpful sense of the divine character of the message which he supposed himself to have delivered to the world at large.

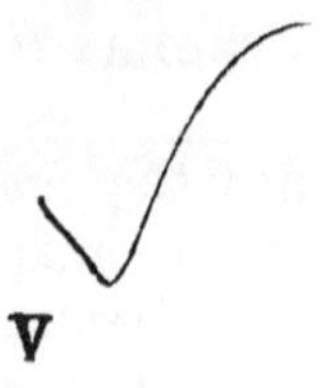

V

RALPH WALDO EMERSON

1882

THE great American thinker, who has been so often compared to Carlyle, and who in some respects resembles, whilst in many more he is profoundly different from him, and who has so soon followed him to the grave, will be remembered much longer, I believe, for the singular insight of his literary judgments, than for that transcendental philosophy for which he was once famous. It is remarkable enough that Carlyle and Emerson both had in them that imaginative gift which made them aim at poetry, and both that incapacity for rhythm or music which rendered their verses too rugged, and too much possessed with the sense of effort, to sink as verse should sink into the hearts of men. Carlyle's verse is like the heavy rumble of a van without springs; Emerson's, which now and then reaches something of the sweetness of poetry, much more often reminds one of the attempts of a seeress to induce in herself the ecstasy which will not spontaneously visit her. Yet the prose, both of Carlyle and of Emerson, falls at times into that poetic rhythm which indicates the highest glow of a powerful imaginative nature, though of such passages I could produce many more from Carlyle than from Emerson. I should say that a little of Emerson's verse is genuine poetry, though not of the highest order, and that none of Carlyle's is poetry at all; but that some of Carlyle's prose is as touching as any but the noblest poetry, while Emerson never reaches the same profound pathos. Nor is this the only side on which these two contemporary thinkers resemble each other. As thinkers, both were eager transcendentalists, and at the same time, rationalists too. Both were intended for divines, and both abandoned the profession, though Emerson filled a pulpit for a year or two, while Carlyle never even entered on the formal study of theology. Both, again, were in their way humourists, though Emerson's humour was a much less profound constituent of his character than Carlyle's. And finally, both would have called themselves the spokesmen of "the dim, common populations," the enemies of all selfish privilege, of all purely traditional distinctions between man and man, of all the artificial selfishness of class, of all the tyranny of caste, and the cruelty of custom.

Yet Emerson and Carlyle were in their way very remarkable contrasts. Emerson was as benignant and gentle as Carlyle was arrogant and bitter. Mr. Ruskin has asked, "What can you say of Carlyle, except that he was born in the clouds, and struck by lightning?" Of Emerson it might, perhaps, be also said that he was born in the clouds, but assuredly not that he was struck by lightning. There is nothing scathed or marred about him, nothing sublime, though something perhaps better, —a little of the calm of true majesty. He has the keen kindliness of the highest New-England culture,

with a touch of majesty about him that no other
New-England culture shows. He has the art of
saying things with a tone of authority quite unknown
to Carlyle, who casts his thunderbolt, but never
forgets that he is casting it at some unhappy mortal
whom he intends to slay. That is not Emerson's
manner; he is never aggressive. He has that regal
suavity which settles a troublesome matter without
dispute. His sentences are often like decrees. For
example, take this, on the dangers of the much-
vaunted life of action:—"A certain partiality,
headiness, and want of balance is the tax which all
action must pay. Act if you like, but you do it at
your peril;" or this, on the dangers of speculation,
—"Why should I vapour and play the philosopher,
instead of ballasting the best I can this dancing
balloon;" or this, on the dangers of hero-worship,
—"Every hero becomes a bore at last. We balance
one man with his opponent, and the health of the
State depends upon the see-saw;" or this, on the
Time-spirit,—"We see now events forced on which
seem to retard or retrograde the civility of ages.
But the World-spirit is a good swimmer, and storms
and waves cannot drown him." There is no thinker
of our day who, for sentences that have the ring of
oracles, can quite compare with Emerson. Mr.
Arnold, in a sonnet written near forty years ago, on
Emerson's essays, said,—

> " A voice oracular has pealed to-day ;
> To-day a hero's banner is unfurled."

And the first line at least was true, whatever may
be said of the second. No man has compressed
more authoritative insight into his sentences than
Emerson. He discerns character more truly than

Carlyle, though he does not describe with half the fervent vigour. Carlyle worships Goethe blindly, but Emerson discerns the very core of the poet. "Goethe can never be dear to men. His is not even the devotion to pure truth, but to truth for the sake of culture." And again,—Goethe, he says, "has one test for all men : *What can you teach me?*" Hear him of Goethe as artist,—"His affections help him, like women employed by Cicero to worm out the secrets of conspirators." Or take this, as summing up Goethe as a poet :—"These are not wild, miraculous songs, but elaborate poems, to which the poet has confided the results of eighty years of observation. . . . Still, he is a poet of a prouder laurel than any contemporary, and under this plague of microscopes (for he seems to see out of every pore of his skin), strikes the harp with a hero's strength and grace." There is something far more royal and certain in Emerson's insight, than in all the humorous brilliance of Carlyle.

Still, if I were to compare the two as transcendental thinkers, I should not hesitate to declare Carlyle much the greater of the two. Emerson never seems to me so little secure of his ground as he is in uttering his transcendentalisms,—Carlyle never so secure. Emerson on "Nature," Emerson on the "Over-soul," Emerson on the law of "Polarity," Emerson on "Intuition," does not seem to me even instructive. He takes no distinct aim, and hits only the vague. When he tells us, in his "Representative Men," that "animated chlorine knows of chlorine, and incarnate zinc of zinc," he attempts to state his peculiar pantheism in words which not only do not make it more intelligible, but rather illustrate the untruth of the general assertion that only like can perceive like. " Shall we say," he adds, " that quartz mountains will pulverise into innumerable Werners, Von Buchs, and Beaumonts, and that the laboratory of the atmosphere holds in solution I know not what Berzeliuses and Davys ? "—a question to which I, at least, should reply with a most emphatic " No," if, at least, the object be, as it no doubt is, to explain discoverers by their latent affinity with the thing discovered. Suppose I put it thus,—" Animated bacteria know of bacteria, incarnate lymph of vaccine : "—who would not see the absurdity ? Is there really more of the bacteria in Professor Pasteur or Professor Koch, than there is in the cattle inoculated by the former, or the consumptive patients who die from the presence of tubercular bacteria, according to the teaching of the latter, that Professors Pasteur and Koch discover their presence, while the patients themselves discover nothing of the nature of their own complaints ? Of course, Emerson would have said that he did not mean his statements to be thus carnally interpreted. Very likely not ; but have they any real meaning at all, unless thus carnally construed ? Emerson's transcendental essays are full of this kind of dark and vague symbolism, which carries weight only in proportion to the extent of our ignorance, not to the extent of our knowledge. Now, Carlyle, so far as he was a transcendentalist, stuck to the very truth and reality of nature. He showed us how small a proportion of our life we can realise in thought ; how small a proportion of our thoughts we can figure forth in words ; how immense is the difference between the pretensions of human speech and the real life for which it stands ; how vast the forces amidst which the human spirit struggles for its little modicum of purpose ; how infinite the universe, both in regard to space and time, on which we make our little appearances only to subside again before we can hope materially to change the great stream of tendencies which contains us ; and he made us feel, as hardly any other has made us feel, how, in spite of all this array of immensities in which we are hardly a distinguishable speck, the spirit whose command brings us into being requires of us the kind of life which defies necessity, and breathes into the order of our brief existence the spirit of impassioned right and indomitable freedom. This was but a narrow aim, compared with that of Emerson's philosophy, but it succeeded, while Emerson's did not. The various philosophic essays in which Emerson tried to assert the absolute unity of the material and spiritual laws of the Universe, have always seemed to me, though decidedly interesting, yet unquestionable failures. You can drive a coach and six through almost any one of the generalisations which pass for philosophy, in these vague and imaginative, but unreal speculations.

Inferior in genius,—as a man Emerson will compare favourably with Carlyle. He certainly possessed his soul in patience, which Carlyle never did. He had a magnanimity in which Carlyle was altogether wanting. He sympathised ardently with all the greatest practical movements of his own day, while Carlyle held contemptuously aloof. Emerson was one of the first to strike a heavy blow at the institution of slavery. He came forward to encourage his country in the good cause, when slavery raised the flag of rebellion. He had a genuine desire to see all men really free, while Carlyle only felt the desire to see all men strongly governed,—which they might be without being free at all. Emerson's spirit, moreover, was much the saner and more reverent of the two, though less rich in power and humour. His mind was heartily religious, though his transcendentalism always gave a certain air of patronage to his manner in speaking of any of the greater religions. One of his youthful sermons was thus described by a lady who heard it :—" Waldo Emerson came last Sunday, and preached a sermon, with his chin in the air, in scorn of the whole human race." That is caricature, but whenever Emerson spoke on any religion which claims a special revelation, even in later life, his chin seemed to be " in the air " still. He had the democratic transcendentalist's jealousy of any one who claimed to be nearer God than the race at large. He was contemptuous of the pretensions of special access to God, and this, to my ear at least, always spoils his tone, when he speaks of Christ and Christianity. But towards man, he is always reverent—which Carlyle seldom is—and he is always reverent, too, in relation to the Divine Mind itself. " I conceive a man as always spoken to from behind," he once wrote, " and unable to turn his head and see the speaker. In all the millions who have heard the voice, none ever saw the face. As children in their play run behind each other, and seize one by the ears, and make him walk before them, so is the Spirit our unseen pilot." Those are the words of a truly reverent mind, though of a mind as jealously devoted to a sort of false spiritual democracy, as it is reverent in its attitude and poetic in its inmost thought.

VI

EMERSON[1] AS ORACLE

1884

EMERSON was more of a great, though uncertain oracle, some of whose sayings ring for ever in the mind, while others only jingle there, than either a poet or a philosopher. There was too much strain in him for either. He rose too much on tiptoe for the poet, and was too broken in his insights for a philosopher's steady continuity of thought. I have read Mr. Joel Benton's little book on Emerson as a poet without any result, except, perfect concurrence with his remark,—aimed at "a critical English journal," which is very possibly the *Spectator*,—that "argument is as futile with this state of mental inaptitude as it is with the colour-blind. There is no delinquency of perception so unhelpable as that which discerns but one literary fashion." Only I deny that to reject Emerson's poetry as inadequate to the

[1] 1. *The Works of Ralph Waldo Emerson.* With an Introduction by John Morley. 6 vols. London : Macmillan.

2. *The Works of Ralph Waldo Emerson.* Riverside Edition. 8 vols. To be completed in 11 vols. London : Routledge.

3. *Emerson as a Poet.* By Joel Benton. New York : M. L. Holbrook and Co.

higher requirements of verse, implies limitation to one literary fashion. I find poetry of the truest kind at once in Isaiah and in Æschylus, in Shakespeare and in Shelley, in Tennyson and in Matthew Arnold, and surely these are not of one literary fashion. But Emerson's verse is laborious. It gives one that sense of uphill straining, as distinguished from flight, which is far removed from what seems to me of the essence of poetry, and though there are fine sayings in Emerson's verse which are near akin to poetry, there seems to me very little indeed of genuine poetic passion. This, perhaps, of all that Mr. Joel Benton quotes, comes nearest to it, but you could hardly rest the repute of a poet on this :—

> " The trivial harp will never please,
>   Or fill my craving ear ;
>   Its chords should ring, as blows the breeze,
>   Free, peremptory, clear ;
>   No jingling serenader's art,
>   Nor tinkle of piano-strings,
>   Can make the wild blood start
>   In its mystic springs.
>
> The kingly bard
> Must smite the chords rudely and hard,
>   As with hammer or with mace,
> That they may render back
> Artful thunder which conveys
> Secrets of the solar track,
> Sparks of the super-solar blaze."

I wholly agree with Mr. John Morley that Emerson's poems " are the outcome of a discontent with prose, not of that high-strung sensibility which compels the true poet into verse." His verse often attains the mystic dignity of gnomic runes, but seldom indeed embodies the passion of a poet's heart.

Emerson is a most stimulating writer,—one, however, who, like most stimulating writers, is apt sometimes to make you think that you have got hold of a real truth, only because he has put an old error into a novel and fascinating dress. If you would be stimulated by him to the best advantage, you must be stimulated to challenge his gnomic sayings, and to sift them through and through before you accept them. He has a genuine dignity in him which often gives a false air of authority to his announcements, and so takes in the unwary. It was he, I fancy, who introduced the unfortunate mistake, which has been followed by so many, of using imposing scientific terms, like 'polarity' or 'polarised,' for instance, in a hybrid popular sense, which makes them at once pretentious and misleading. "Let me see every trifle," says Emerson, "bristling with the polarity that ranges it constantly on an eternal law, and the shop, the plough, and the ledger referred to the like cause by which light undulates and poets sing." How the ledger is to be made to bristle with a polarity that ranges it constantly on an eternal law, Emerson, of course, never even suggested; but that grandiose mode of speaking of things takes hold of all his disciples. Mr. Joel Benton, in defending his poems, says, for instance,—"They are hints rather than finished statements. The words alone startle by their deep suggestion. Their polarised vitality, rich symbolism, and strong percussion, shock the mind, and celestial vistas or unfathomed deeps are opened." There, we venture to say that the metaphorical polarity of Emerson,—a very vague kind of polarity even in him, for it meant only the indication given by some detail of common life that that detail had its explanation in grander life beyond itself,—has fallen to a yet lower level of metaphorical emptiness. The "polarised vitality" of his poems can hardly be so explained as to give it any very distinct meaning. Polarised light is, I believe, light deprived of one set of its vibrations ; and polarised life ought, I suppose, by analogy, to mean life that does not show itself equally in all spheres,—life thinned off into what is spiritual only. If Mr. Benton means this by the "polarised vitality" of Emerson's poems, he certainly is using terms at once pedantic and ineffectual to convey a very simple meaning ; and this is just the fault into which Emerson not unfrequently fell himself, and almost always led his followers. There is a cant of scientific symbolism about their language which makes it at once obscure and affected.

What Emerson will always be remembered by is his noble and resonant depth of conviction, his pithy metaphor, and his keen, placid criticism. No one could give more perfect resonance to the convictions of the heart than he. One who was a boy forty years ago never forgot the impression made upon him by the last sentence of his address on the subject of slavery and our West India emancipation : —"The Intellect with blazing eye, looking through history from the beginning onwards, gazes on this blot and it disappears. The sentiment of right, once very low and indistinct, but ever more articulate, because it is the voice of the Universe, pronounces Freedom. The power that built this fabric of things affirms it in the heart, and in the history of the 1st of August has made a sign to the ages of his will." But even there, how strange is the assertion that "the sentiment of right" is "the voice of the

Universe!"   It is the voice of God, no doubt, but most certainly not the voice of the Universe, but a voice that overrules the many discordant voices of the Universe, some of which pronounce "slavery," and some "freedom."   Emerson's thin and curiously optimistic Pantheism seems to have derived hardly any verification from his intellect.   He assumed it as if it were the only intellectual assumption on which life to him was intelligible at all.

Emerson's pithy metaphor has a curious charm and sometimes a curious grandeur of its own:— "Man," he says, "is not a farmer, or a professor, or an engineer, but he is all.   Man is priest, and scholar, and statesman, and producer, and soldier. . . . But, unfortunately, this original unit, this fountain of power, has been so distributed to multitudes, has been so minutely subdivided and peddled out, that it is spilled into drops and cannot be gathered.   The state of society is one in which the members have suffered amputation from the trunk, and strut about so many walking monsters,—a good finger, a neck, a stomach, an elbow, but never a man." "The priest becomes a form; the attorney a statute book; the mechanic a machine; the sailor a rope of the ship."   Or again, how can you have a finer metaphor for the tendency of men to follow clearer minds than their own, than the following?—"The unstable estimates of men crowd to him whose mind is filled with a truth, as the heaped waves of the Atlantic follow the moon."   But I value Emerson most as a critic.   *Representative Men*, and the critical passages which abound in his book on the *Conduct of Life* and *English Traits*, seem to me his best literary achievements.

As Mr. Morley justly remarks, Emerson has a

marked dislike of disease in any form, and is helpless in dealing with "that horrid burden and impediment on the soul, which the Churches call sin, and which, by whatever name we call it, is a very real catastrophe in the moral nature of man." That is perfectly true, and by the way, I defy any one who wishes to call this phenomenon truly, to find a better name for it than the Churches have given. Sin would not be "a very real catastrophe," if it could be explained away into anything but sin,—that is, a conscious and voluntary revolt against a moral authority to which we owe obedience. Emerson lived in a pale moonlit world of ideality, in which there was little that was adapted to tame the fierce passions and appease the agonising remorse of ordinary human nature. He was a voice to the pure intellect and the more fastidious conscience of men, not a power of salvation for their wretchedness. But his gnomic wisdom will live long, and startle many generations with its clear, high, thrilling note.

VII

EDGAR POE[1]

1874

IT is pleasant to have Edgar Poe rescued from the reputation of something like infamy to which his first biographer had consigned him, even though it seems simply impossible to accept the vindication which Mr. Ingram has so successfully put forth for him without throwing upon his previous biographer, Mr. Rufus Wilmot Griswold, the responsibility not merely of misrepresentations which were very unpardonable in a biographer who should have taken, what certainly he did not take, the greatest pains to sift the truth of reports injuriously affecting the subject of his memoir, but the much more serious responsibility, if one may trust Mr. Ingram, of deliberate falsification of Mr. Poe's writings. Mr. Ingram (p. lxi. of the Memoir) criticises Mr. Griswold's account of one of Poe's literary quarrels, which he found untrue in almost every important respect, and especially in this, that the very editor who, according to Mr. Griswold, had refused to support Poe, on the ground that he

---

[1] *The Works of Edgar Allan Poe.* Edited by John B. Ingram. Vol. I. Memoir and Tales. Edinburgh : Adam and Charles Black.

was obviously in the wrong, had written in defence and praise of Poe's "honourable and blameless conduct"; but he does more—he states that though he was not at all surprised to find Mr. Griswold's whole account of the affair upset by his investigation of the facts, he *was* startled "to discover that the *whole of the personalities* of the supposed critique included in the collections of Poe's works, *edited by Griswold*, were absent from the real critique published in the 'Lady's Book.'" Of course, if Mr. Griswold, or his friends, cannot explain this strange appearance of direct fabrication, all belief in Mr. Griswold's veracity collapses at once. There would be no longer any reason to suppose that there was even a *foundation* in fact for a statement unfavourable to Poe, simply on the score that Mr. Griswold made it. And in point of fact, Mr. Ingram does seem to have refuted all the reasons for believing that there was anything whatever malign in Edgar Poe. That he led a restless and somewhat ungoverned life in his youth, and that in the unhappy days after he lost his wife he was occasionally intemperate,—though his was a physique overpowered by incredibly little wine,—seems to be true. But for the worse charges against him, for the insinuations repeated by Mr. Griswold that he was once guilty of an offence which it was not even possible to mention, for the charge that he was an ungrateful man towards those who had been good to him, for the stories of his inattention to business and neglect of his employers' interests, and for the assertion as to the reason why the engagement for his second marriage was broken off, there seems to be no foundation whatever,—nay, the best possible proof that the very reverse was true. Mr. Ingram has quoted the most convincing evidence of his fidelity to the interests of his literary employers, of the exactitude of his business accounts with them, of the regret with which they parted with him, and of the permanence of their esteem.   In short, he has proved that Edgar Poe was not only most faithful to his engagements, and a devoted husband and son-in-law, but that with the exception of one period of great misery, he led a most regular, industrious, and abstemious life, and was as earnestly loved as he was earnest in his own love.

All this will be a surprise to most of Edgar Poe's English readers, who have not unnaturally taken Mr. Griswold's statements without any distrust, and have discerned perhaps something in the rather revolting character of many of his tales, of a nature to support the assumption that there was a' sinister strain in his character.   But, in fact, though Edgar Poe is one of the greatest masters of the gruesome who ever lived, there seems to be no reason in that at all for making any kind of assumption as to his character. Curiously enough, one of the principal features of the most original among the American novelists has been a fascination for the gruesome.   The Hawthornes, father and son, are both great masters in it; Dr. Oliver Wendell Holmes made a study in this school the subject of the fiction by which he is best known, "Elsie Venner"; and Edgar Poe was but leading or following in the vein of some of his greater country-men, when he chose to devote himself to the working-up of weird and gruesome effects.   The contemplation of death, and of the earthly accompaniments of death, seems always to have had an overpowering fascination for him.   Indeed, his passion for producing that curdle of the blood with which the mind is apt to greet the close association of repulsive bodily conditions with intense ideal feelings,—either of love or scientific desire,—was almost the key-note of his imaginative genius. No writer was ever freer from a sensual taint. None was ever more constantly haunted by the corruptibility of the body, by what we may call the physical caprices of the soul in relation to that corruptibility, and by the vision of that spiritual clamminess which sometimes seems to spring out of tampering with questions too obscure for the intellect and at any rate depressing to the vitality of the whole constitution, or out of that morbid condition which insists on connecting with the mortal body what should be given only to the immortal spirit. These are the sort of themes on which Edgar Poe rings the changes till his stories seem to reek of the grave, and of the human affections which oppress "the portals of the grave" with their unhallowed pertinacity. I know nothing more gruesome in all fiction than such tales as *Ligeia* and *Morella* or that ghastly bit of fictitious science in which Edgar Poe gives the account of the mesmerising of a man *in articulo mortis*, and of its effect in preserving the body from decay for many months after death had occurred, without, however, depriving the separated soul of the power of occasionally using the tongue of the corpse. The atmosphere of thorough horror hanging round the realism of this little bit of morbid imagination is hardly to be conceived without reading it. And yet still more ghastly are such stories as *Ligeia*— the devoted wife who holds that Will ought to be able to conquer death, and who nevertheless dies of consumption, but apparently haunts her successor, the second wife, till she dies of the mere oppression on her spirits, and who then by a vast spiritual effort, the physical effects of the tentatives at which are described with hideous minuteness, enters the dead body of her rival, and brings back the exhausted organism to life in her own person. And yet perhaps even this morbid story is exceeded in the uncanniness of its effects by the brief story of *Morella,*—a wife who had pored over, or, shall we say, pried deeply into, all the forbidden lore of the mystical writers on personality and personal identity, till the subject seemed to have a kind of unholy fascination for both her husband and herself, and who in dying bears a daughter, into whom it soon becomes evident that the very personal soul of the mother had entered. It is not, however, the ghastliness of this fancy which chiefly gives its force to the tale. Possibly even more force is spent on the description of the woman herself,—which has nothing impossible or even improbable about it,—though the husband's impression of her is evidently a diseased one. Can what I have ventured to call spiritual " clamminess " be more powerfully conceived than in the following account of Morella ?—

" With a feeling of deep yet most singular affection I regarded my friend Morella. Thrown by accident into her society many years ago, my soul, from our first meeting, burned with fires it had never before known; but the fires were not of Eros, and bitter and tormenting to my spirit was the gradual conviction that I could in no manner define their unusual meaning or regulate their vague intensity. Yet we met; and fate bound us together at the altar; and I never spoke of passion nor thought of love. She, however, shunned society, and, attaching herself to me alone, rendered me happy. It is a happiness to wonder; it is a happiness to dream. Morella's erudition was profound. As I hope to live,

her talents were of no common order—her powers of
mind were gigantic. I felt this, and, in many matters,
because [? became] her pupil. I soon, however, found
that, perhaps on account of her Presburg education, she
placed before me a number of those mystical writings
which are usually considered the mere dross of the
early German literature. These, for what reason I could
not imagine, were her favourite and constant study—and
that in process of time they became my own, should be
attributed to the simple but effectual influence of habit
and example. In all this, if I err not, my reason had
little to do. My convictions, or I forget myself, were in
no manner acted upon by the ideal, nor was any tincture
of the mysticism which I read to be discovered, unless
I am greatly mistaken, either in my deeds or in my
thoughts. Persuaded of this, I abandoned myself implicitly to the guidance of my wife, and entered with
an unflinching heart into the intricacies of her studies.
And then—then, when poring over forbidden pages, I felt
a forbidden spirit enkindling within me—would Morella
place her cold hand upon my own, and rake up from the
ashes of a dead philosophy some low, singular words,
whose strange meaning burned themselves in upon my
memory. And then, hour after hour, would I linger by
her side, and dwell upon the music of her voice, until at
length its melody was tainted with terror, and there fell
a shadow upon my soul, and I grew pale, and shuddered
inwardly at those too unearthly tones. And thus, joy
suddenly faded into horror, and the most beautiful
became the most hideous, as Hinnon [? Hinnom] became
Ge-Henna. . . . But, indeed, the time had now arrived
when the mystery of my wife's manner oppressed me as
a spell. I could no longer bear the touch of her wan
fingers, nor the low tone of her musical language, nor the
lustre of her melancholy eyes. And she knew all this,
but did not upbraid ; she seemed conscious of my weakness or my folly, and, smiling, called it fate. She seemed
also conscious of a cause, to me unknown, for the gradual

alienation of my regard ; but she gave me no hint or token of its nature. Yet was she woman, and pined away daily. In time the crimson spot settled steadily upon the cheek, and the blue veins upon the pale fore-head became prominent ; and one instant my nature melted into pity, but in the next I met the glance of her meaning eyes, and then my soul sickened and became giddy with the giddiness of one who gazes downward into some dreary and unfathomable abyss."

It is very difficult to say where the genius of this kind of thing ends and the merely nervous horror of it begins. A good many of Edgar Poe's tales read as if they might have been suggested by a constant brooding over the conquests of the grave, in a state of health disordered by doses of opium. But that there is real literary power in the gruesome mixture of sweetness and moral clamminess in such a character as is here described, it is hardly possible to deny.

Perhaps a better measure of Edgar Poe's true literary power may be gained from stories in which he evidently intends to draw monomania, and draws it with a force that one would regard as implying a real experience of the confessions of a monomaniac. In these cases there is none of the gruesomeness on which I have been dwelling. The whole power is spent on delineating the almost diabolical possession of the mind by a single idea, and the rush with which this at last precipitates its victim into the fatal spring. "The Tell-tale Heart" and "The Imp of the Perverse" are two very fine illustrations of this power which Edgar Poe had of realising for us. what we may call moral "rapids," down which the will, if there be a will in such cases, is carried like a shallop down Niagara. Whatever may be said of his stories of corruption and sepulchral horrors, which no doubt owe a good deal of their appearance of power to their unnaturalness of conception, no one can doubt that such a description of monomaniac remorse as the following, implies very striking vigour. The hero of the story commits a murder by means which it is nearly impossible for any one to discover,—the manufacture of a poisoned candle, by which the victim reads at night in an ill-ventilated apartment, and of course is found dead in the morning; and the greatest delight he has is not the wealth he inherits, but the satisfaction he feels in his absolute security. This afforded him "more real delight than all the mere worldly advantages of his sin." But, at last he caught himself repeating to himself "I am safe," just as the words of a song, which have somehow caught the fancy, go round continually like a mill-wheel in the head :—

"One day whilst sauntering along the streets, I arrested myself in the act of murmuring half-aloud these customary syllables. In a fit of petulance I re-modelled them thus: —'I am safe—I am safe—yes, if I be not fool enough to make open confession!' No sooner had I spoken these words than I felt an icy chill creep to my heart. I had had some experience in these fits of perversity (whose nature I have been at some trouble to explain), and I remembered well that in no instance I had successfully resisted their attacks; and now my own casual self-suggestion that I might possibly be fool enough to confess the murder of which I had been guilty confronted me, as if the very ghost of him whom I had murdered—and beckoned me on to death. At first I made an effort to shake off this nightmare of the soul. I walked vigorously, faster, still faster, at length I ran. I felt a maddening desire to shriek aloud. Every succeeding wave of thought overwhelmed me with new terror, for, alas! I well, too well, understood that to *think* in my situation was to be lost. I still quickened my pace. I bounded like a madman through the crowded thoroughfares. At length the populace took the alarm and pursued me. I felt *then* the consummation of my fate. Could I have torn out my tongue I would have done it—but a rough voice resounded in my ears—a rougher grasp seized me by the shoulder. I turned—I gasped for breath. For a momet I experienced all the pangs of suffocation ; I became blind, and deaf, and giddy ; and then some invisible fiend, I thought, struck me with his broad palm upon the back. The long-imprisoned secret burst forth from my soul. They say that I spoke with a distinct enunciation, but with marked emphasis and passionate hurry, as if in dread of interruption before concluding the brief but pregnant sentences that consigned me to the hangman and to hell."

" The Tell-tale Heart " shows power of the same kind, but in a still higher degree.

But I have not yet mentioned one of the most distinctive features of Poe's literary power, his delight in the exercise of that sort of skill which consists in the nice and delicate appraising of circumstantial evidence. Poe was very fond of decyphering cyphers, and proved, it is said, to many who brought him puzzles of this kind that there was no cypher which human art could invent, that human art could not also unriddle. He has explained in the story of *The Gold Beetle* (or *Gold Bug*, as they call it in America) the principles on which one simple specimen of a cypher can be decyphered, but he himself surmounted the difficulties of far more complicated problems. This, however, was only one department of the field of circumstantial evidence of which he was so fond. In the case of a New York murder, he seems to have really detected the secret which had baffled the police, and all his discussions of the value to be assigned to circumstantial indications of human motives are very keen. Indeed, in his tales of this kind, he shows that minute practical ingenuity which seems to be one of the chief marks of American life, as strongly as he elsewhere shows that curiosity to explore the influence of the body on the mind which is another of those marks. Circumstantial evidence seems to have been the concrete region in which Edgar Poe sought relief from the lurid and gruesome dreams of his imagination. Nor is it the first time that the piecing together of an almost mechanical puzzle has been a vast relief to a mind oppressed by dreary phantoms.

Of Edgar Poe's poems,—except *The Raven*, which will always owe a certain popularity to the skill with which rhyme and metre reflect the dreary hopelessness and shudderiness, if I may coin a word, of the mood depicted—it is impossible to speak very highly. His imagination was not high enough for the sphere of poetry, and when he entered it he grew mystical and not a little bombastic. Yet his criticisms of poetry were very acute and almost always worthy of an imaginative man. Indeed, he had imagination enough for criticism, but hardly enough for successful poetic creation. On the whole, while I should place him on a level far below Hawthorne,—on the level of great but, in almost all creative regions, essentially sickly power,—I do not doubt that Edgar Poe will have a permanent and a typical name in the history of American literature; and I rejoice heartily that Mr. Ingram has vindicated his memory from aspersions so terrible, and apparently so unscrupulous and unjust, as those deliberately cast upon him by his previous editor and biographer.

VIII

DEMOCRACY: AN AMERICAN NOVEL[1]

1881

THIS is a very brilliant little book, of the authorship of which we have no knowledge whatever. Its chief object is, of course, to attack the corruptions of American democracy, but there is truly marvellous skill in the literary form which, without including anything even verging on a political dissertation, without even a tendency to injure the lightness and brilliancy of a novelette, yet contrives to produce, in a very much more telling shape than any political dissertation could supply, the impression of the leaden monotony, the deadly inertia, the vulgar self-interest, the sodden complexity of the moral influences which, according to the author, determine all the secondary agencies in the legislative and administrative policy of the great Republic. I do not for a moment mean to say that the picture thus given us produces a just impression. Indeed, it is obvious enough that wherever any issue of the first magnitude is present to the mind of the country, these corrupt secondary influences are compelled to act within very closely

---

[1] *Democracy: an American Novel.* New York: Henry Holt and Co.

circumscribed limits, and never dispose of the greater questions at all. But however untrue the general effect may be, what the anonymous author meant to paint, he has painted with extraordinary force and vividness, and without for a moment dropping the interest of his little story. Those who used to admire the late Lord Beaconsfield's success in grafting political interests on a romance, would find the same thing done with far greater skill and delicacy of touch in the present story, the author's object being to dismay his readers with the utter dreariness and vulgarity of the politics he intends to portray, while never for a moment relaxing his hold of their sympathies for the heroine of his tale. So far as I can judge, the writer of this little tale has no latent sympathy with monarchy or aristocracy. Whenever he glances at either of these, it is with something very like a sneer. But what he desires to depict in American democracy is the flagrant vulgarity and coarseness of the individual self-interests which battle with, and override, the interests of the whole community. He evidently holds that in the American democracy at least there are no characters pre-eminent enough in nobility of purpose, popular influence, or political knowledge, to command the respect of the whole people in defeating the cunning conspiracies of the Party wire-pullers. One would suppose that such a thesis would be irrelevant and tedious in a novelette. On the contrary, the whole interest of the novelette is made to depend upon it, and is made all the keener for the coarse political by-play with which it is bound up.

Mrs. Lightfoot Lee is a young and restless widow, who, after losing a husband and baby to whom she was devotedly attached, plunges first into philanthropy, and then into politics, in the hope of winning back some intellectual interest in life which may fairly fill up the void in her heart. She goes to Washington, to gain some insight, if she can, into the springs of popular power. "What she wished to see, she thought, was the clash of interests, the interests of forty millions of people and a whole continent, centring at Washington; guided, restrained, controlled, or unrestrained and uncontrollable by men of ordinary mould, the tremendous forces of government, and the machinery of society, at work." She had rejected the idea of Swift, that he who made two blades of grass grow where only one grew before, deserved better of mankind than the whole race of politicians. "She could not find fault with the philosopher," she said, "had he required that the grass should be of an improved quality." But she remarked, "I cannot honestly pretend that I should be pleased to see two New York men, where I now see one; the idea is too ridiculous; more than one and a half would be fatal to me."

So to Washington Mrs. Lee goes, and there studies the problem of democracy in the particular form of the character of Mr. Silas P. Ratcliffe, the Senator for Illinois, otherwise called the "Peonia Giant," whose is the one master-mind of the Republican organisation, and who holds the key of all the party combinations of the capital. In her desire to see something of the sources of political power, she discovers a good deal of its hollowness. She hears the whole correspondence between the wire-pullers on one side, and the new President on the other, "with Sam Grimes, of North Bend." At last, she reaches the inmost altar of the god of Democracy. Nothing is more spirited than the account of the amazement, and even terror, with which Mrs. Lee observes the

first evening reception of the new President,—" Old
Granite," as his friends call him, " Old Granny," as
he is nicknamed by his foes,—and anticipates that
in· this mechanical worship of Democracy, the new
age will find its euthanasia:—

' " Then, Madeleine found herself before two seemingly
mechanical figures, which might be wood or wax, for any
sign they showed of life. These two figures were the
President and his wife ; they stood, stiff and awkward,
by the door, both their faces stripped of every sign of
intelligence, while the right hands of both extended themselves to the column of visitors, with the mechanical action
of toy dolls. Mrs. Lee for a moment began to laugh, but
the laugh died on her lips. To the President and his
wife, this was clearly no laughing matter. There they
stood, automata, representatives of the society which
streamed past them. . . . What a strange and solemn
spectacle it was ! and how the deadly fascination of it
burned the image upon her mind ! What a horrid warning to ambition ! And in all that crowd, there was no
one besides herself who felt the mockery of this exhibi-
tion. . . . She groaned in spirit. ' Yes, at last I have
reached the end ! We shall grow to be wax images, and
our talk will be like the squeaking of toy dolls. We shall
all wander round and round the earth, and shake hands.
No one will have any other object in this world, and there
will be no other. It is worse than anything in the
" Inferno." What an awful vision of eternity ! ' "

Mrs. Lee further forms a friendship with Lord Skye,
the British Minister, and discovers that " a certain
secret jealousy of the British Minister is always lurk-
ing in the breast of every American Senator, if he is
truly democratic ; for democracy, rightly understood,
is the Government of the people, by the people, for
the benefit of Senators, and there is always a danger

that the British Minister may not understand this political principle as he should."

One very skilful touch among the early pictures of Mrs. Lee's life in Washington, is the discovery quickly made by her that the most cultivated Americans in Washington feel the same sort of delicacy in talking freely of the democratic principle, which cultivated Englishmen so often feel in talking freely of the religious principle.   Mr. Gore, a historian, and candidate for the post of American Minister to Madrid, is one of the first to encourage Mrs. Lee to believe in the Illinois Senator—to whom, indeed, he looks for support in his candidature—but when challenged as to how far he accepts that fundamental principle of democracy of which Mr. Ratcliffe is the most effective representative, he replies, " These are matters about which I rarely talk in society ; they are like the doctrines of a personal God, of a future life, of revealed religion ; subjects which one naturally reserves for private reflection."   And as that is the attitude of the acuter and more refined minds towards democracy,—which they regard as a " universal postulate," too awful, deep, and far-reaching for ordinary discussion,—of course its consequences, or what are supposed to be its consequences, are accepted with a sort of fatalist resignation, even when they are wholly pernicious and corrupting.   Mrs. Lee falls under the spell of Mr. Silas P. Ratcliffe, the powerful, coarse, unscrupulous Senator from Illinois, and is very near being drawn by him into the muddy whirlpool of Washington politics, and turned, against her will, into one of the chief social springs of the lobbying in Washington.   The story of this danger is made the main thread of the novel, and most admirably is the interest kept up, so as neither to merge the novel in political life, nor to lose sight for a moment of the social aspect of Washington politics. The interest of the struggle for Mrs. Lee is very powerful, and the side-portraits are all so skilful, from Sibyl, the pretty and practical sister of Mrs. Lee, and Mr. Carrington, the dejected Virginian barrister, who is Mr. Ratcliffe's chief rival, down to Miss Victoria Dare, who affects a little stammer when she is saying anything more than usually impudent, the Voltairian minister from Bulgaria, and the miserable President and his wife, that the story grows quite dramatic. Mrs. Lee becomes the pet detestation of the new President's wife, who cannot endure a refined woman who knows what dress means ; and so soon as it is rumoured that Mr. Silas P. Ratcliffe,—the great Peonia Giant,—is bent on making her his wife, all the political eddies of Washington seem to be intent on sucking her into the maelstrom. Victoria Dare retails to Mrs. Lee the choicest bits of gossip about her. "Your cousin, Mrs. Clinton, says you are a ca-ca-cat, Mrs. Lee."— "I don't believe it, Victoria. Mrs. Clinton never said anything of the sort."—"Mrs. Marston says it is because you have caught a ra-ra-rat, and Senator Clinton was only a m-m-mouse." Carrington, who has some knowledge of the disreputable political intrigues in which Mr. Silas P. Ratcliffe has been involved, and who is himself in love with Mrs. Lee, does all in his power to open her eyes to the true character of Mr. Silas P. Ratcliffe, and the kind of ambition to which she will surrender herself, if, in her passion for self-sacrifice, she chooses to be absorbed into his political career. Long the struggle remains doubtful, and the author with great subtlety uses the various vicissitudes of the battle to give one picture after another of the political intrigues of democratic life. At length the crisis comes, in a grand ball given by the British Minister to a Royal princess of his Sovereign's own family, who, with her husband, the Grand Duke of Saxe-Baden-Hombourg, comes on a tour of pleasure. The scene of this ball, in which there is a dais for the President and his wife, and another dais for the Grand Duke and Duchess, while Mrs. Lee is used by the Grand Duchess—who is dressed, by the way, in an ill-fitting black silk, with false lace and jet ornaments, and makes herself extremely unpleasant—as a sort of amulet with which to keep off the approaches of the President's wife, for whom she has conceived the most deadly disgust, is admirably painted, and is painted too with that exactly balanced disgust for Royalty and Democracy which seems to indicate the universal political pessimism of the author. After the departure of the Princess, Mr. Silas P. Ratcliffe seizes his opportunity to make a bid for the great prize at which he has so long been aiming. And in the story of how he is foiled, the author strikes his final blow at the corruption of Democracy. I will not attempt to diminish the interest of the reader by giving extracts from the tale —which is so short that it may be read in two or three hours without losing any of its points. But this I will say, that blank and pessimist as its political doctrine appears to be, the literary skill with which it is executed suggests the touch of a master-hand. Whose that master-hand is, I have no guess, but not often before have I read a political novel in which the political significance has been so perfectly blended with literary interest, as to create a lively and harmonious whole.

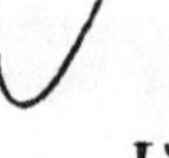

IX

LONGFELLOW

1882

"THE fact is, I hate everything that is violent," said
the poet whom the world lost last week, to some
friend who had been with him during a thunderstorm,
and to whom he was excusing himself for the care
with which he had endeavoured to exclude from his
house the tokens of the storm ; and one sees this in
his poetry, which is at his highest point when it is
most restful, and is never so happy in its soft radiance
as when it embodies the spirit of a playful or childlike humility. I should not claim for Longfellow
the position of a very great or original poet ; it was
his merit rather to embody in a simple and graceful
form the gentleness and loveliness which are partially
visible to most men's eyes, than to open to our sight
that which is hidden from the world in general. To
my mind, *Hiawatha* is far the most original of his
poems, because the happy nature-myths which best
expressed the religious genius of the American Indians
appealed to what was deepest in himself, and found
an exquisitely simple and harmonious utterance in
the liquid accents of his childlike and yet not
unstately verse. His material in *Hiawatha* was

so fresh and poetical in itself, as well as so admirably suited to his genius, that in his mind it assumed its most natural form, and flowed into a series of chaunts of childlike dignity and inimitable grace.   The story of Nature has never been told with so much liquid gaiety and melancholy,—so much of the frolic of the childlike races, and so much of their sudden awe and dejection,—as in *Hiawatha* which I, at least, have never taken up without new delight in the singular simplicity and grace, the artless art and ingenuous vivacity, of that rendering of the traditions of a vanishing race.   How simple and childlike Long-fellow makes even the exaggerations so often found in these traditions, so that you enjoy, where you might so easily have sneered !   How spontaneously he avoids anything like dissertation on the significance of the natural facts portrayed, leaving us the full story and poetry of impersonation, without any attempt to moralise or dilate upon its drift !   How exquisitely the account of the first sowing and reap-ing of the Indian corn, of Hiawatha's revelation of agriculture to his people, is told in his three days' wrestling with Mondamin, in his conquest over him, and the sowing of the bare grain, that the green and yellow plumes of Mondamin may wave again over his grave !   And how eerie is the tale of the first warning of spiritual truths, the return of spectres from beyond the grave to warn Hiawatha that for him, too, there are secrets which it will need a higher revelation than his to reveal :—

> " One dark evening, after sun-down,
> In her wigwam Laughing Water
> Sat with old Nokomis, waiting
> For the steps of Hiawatha
> Homeward from the hunt returning.

On their faces gleamed the fire-light,
Painting them with streaks of crimson,
In the eyes of old Nokomis
Glimmered like the watery moonlight,
In the eyes of Laughing Water,
Glistened like the sun in water ;
And behind them crouched their shadows
In the corners of the wigwam,
And the smoke in wreaths above them
Climbed and crowded through the smoke-flue.

Then the curtain of the doorway
From without was slowly lifted ;
Brighter glowed the fire a moment,
And a moment swerved the smoke-wreath,
As two women entered softly,
Passed the doorway uninvited,
Without word of salutation,
Without sign of recognition,
Sat down in the farthest corner,
Crouching low among the shadows.

From their aspect and their garments,
Strangers seemed they in the village ;
Very pale and haggard were they,
As they sat there sad and silent,
Trembling, cowering with the shadows.

Was it the wind above the smoke-flue,
Muttering down into the wigwam ?
Was it the owl, the Koko-koho,
Hooting from the dismal forest ?
Sure a voice said in the silence :
‘ These are corpses clad in garments,
These are ghosts that come to haunt you,
From the kingdom of Ponemah,
From the land of the Hereafter !’

Homeward now came Hiawatha
From his hunting in the forest,
With the snow upon his tresses,
And the red deer on his shoulders.

At the feet of Laughing Water
Down he threw his lifeless burden ;
Nobler, handsomer she thought him,
Than when first he came to woe her ;
First threw down the deer before her,
As a token of his wishes,
As a promise of the future.

Then he turned and saw the strangers,
Cowering, crouching with the shadows ;
Said within himself, ' Who are they ?
What strange guests has Minnehaha ? '
But he questioned not the strangers,
Only spake to bid them welcome
To his lodge, his food, his fireside.

When the evening meal was ready,
And the deer had been divided,
Both the pallid guests, the strangers,
Springing from among the shadows,
Seized upon the choicest portions,
Seized the white fat of the roebuck,
Set apart for Laughing Water,
For the wife of Hiawatha ;
Without asking, without thanking,
Eagerly devoured the morsels,
Flitted back among the shadows
In the corner of the wigwam.

Not a word spake Hiawatha,
Not a motion made Nokomis,
Not a gesture Laughing Water ;
Not a change came o'er their features ;
Only Minnehaha softly
Whispered, saying, ' They are famished ;
Let them do what best delights them ;
Let them eat, for they are famished.'

    .   .   .   .   .

Once at midnight Hiawatha,
Ever wakeful, ever watchful,
In the wigwam dimly lighted

By the brands that still were burning,
By the glimmering, flickering fire-light,
Heard a sighing, oft repeated,
Heard a sobbing, as of sorrow.

From his couch rose Hiawatha,
From his shaggy hides of bison,
Pushed aside the deer-skin curtain,
Saw the pallid guests, the shadows,
Sitting upright on their couches,
Weeping in the silent midnight.

And he said : 'O guests ! why is it
That your hearts are so afflicted,
That you sob so in the midnight ?
Has perchance the old Nokomis,
Has my wife, my Minnehaha,
Wronged or grieved you by unkindness,
Failed in hospitable duties ? '

Then the shadows ceased from weeping,
Ceased from sobbing and lamenting,
And they said, with gentle voices :
' We are ghosts of the departed,
Souls of those who once were with you.
From the realms of Chibiabos
Hither have we come to try you,
Hither have we come to warn you.

Cries of grief and lamentation
Reach us in the Blessed Islands ;
Cries of anguish from the living,
Calling back their friends departed,
Sadden us with useless sorrow.
Therefore have we come to try you ;
No one knows us, no one heeds us.
We are but a burden to you,
And we see that the departed
Have no place among the living.

Think of this, O Hiawatha !
Speak of it to all the people,
That henceforward and for ever

> They no more with lamentations
> Sadden the souls of the departed
> In the Islands of the Blessed.'"

There you see Longfellow at his best, rendering with a singular mixture of simplicity and dignity legends of which the very essence is a mixture of simplicity and dignity, yet a mixture so rare, that the least false note would have destroyed the whole poetry of the tradition.

But Longfellow, singularly happy as he was in catching the spirit of the American-Indian nature-myths, could yet render with hardly less success,—though here he shared his success with scores of other poets not less skilful,—the grace and culture of a thoughtful criticism of the past. Many have equalled, I think, though few have surpassed, the beauty of such a sonnet as this on Giotto's famous tower, for the thought it expresses was one so deeply ingrained in Longfellow's own mind, that he seemed to be breathing out the very heart of his own Christian humility in thus singing the glory of the incomplete :—

> " How many lives, made beautiful and sweet
>> By self-devotion, and by self-restraint,
>> Whose pleasure is to run without complaint
>> On unknown errands of the Paraclete,
> Wanting the reverence of unshodden feet,
>> Fail of the nimbus which the artists paint
>> Around the shining forehead of the saint,
>> And are in their completeness incomplete !
> In the old Tuscan town stands Giotto's tower,
>> The lily of Florence blossoming in stone,—
>> A vision, a delight, and a desire,
> The builder's perfect and centennial flower,

> That in the night of ages bloomed alone,
> But wanting still the glory of the spire."

Longfellow certainly, though often inaffective and common-place in his treatment of a subject, had a true genius for touching the subject of humility in any form, and is never more successful than when relating the legend how Robert, King of Sicily, was taught the truth of those words in the " Magnificat " —" He hath put down the mighty from their seat, and hath exalted the humble and meek ; " or when finding in the midnight chimes of the belfry of Bruges, —heard fitfully in sleep,—the best type of the sort of half-accidental power which the poet exerts over the careless and preoccupied spirit of man :—

> " But amid my broken slumbers
> Still I heard those magic numbers
> As they loud proclaimed the flight
> And stolen marches of the night ;
> Till their chimes in sweet collision
> Mingled with each wandering vision.
> Mingled with the fortune-telling
> Gipsy-bands of dreams and fancies,
> Which amid the waste expanses
> Of the silent land of trances
> Have their solitary dwelling.
> All else seemed asleep in Bruges,
> In the quaint old Flemish city.
>
> And I thought, how like these chimes
> Are the poet's airy rhymes,
> All his rhymes and roundelays,
> His conceits, and songs, and ditties,
> From the belfry of his brain,
> Scattered downward, though in vain,
> On the roofs and stones of cities !

> For by night the drowsy ear
> Under its curtains cannot hear,
> And by day men go their ways,
> Hearing the music as they pass,
> But deeming it no more, alas!
> Than the hollow sound of brass.
>
> Yet perchance a sleepless wight,
> Lodging at some humble inn
> In the narrow lanes of life,
> When the dusk and hush of night
> Shut out the incessant din
> Of daylight and its toil and strife,
> May listen with a calm delight
> To the poet's melodies,
> Till he hears, or dreams he hears,
> Intermingled with the song,
> Thoughts that he has cherished long ;
> Hears amid the chime and singing
> The bells of his own village ringing,
> And wakes, and finds his slumbrous eyes
> Wet with most delicious tears."

I cannot particularly admire the pieces which one oftenest hears quoted from Longfellow,—"Excelsior," "A Psalm of Life," "The Light of Stars," and so forth, all of which seem to express common-place feelings, with a certain picturesque and conventional eloquence, but without anything of individual or unique power.   Longfellow is too apt to take up the conventional subjects of poetry, and deck them out with a pretty patch of colour that does not redeem them from common-placeness, but does make their common-placeness agreeable to the popular mind; and when he does this, though we perfectly understand why he is so popular, we also perfectly understand why so many of the poets think of him as

falling short of the true poetic standard.   But though
I cannot feel any enthusiasm for the remark that,

> "—Our hearts, though stout and brave,
>   Still like muffled drums are beating
> Funeral marches to the grave,"

I do hold that Longfellow was not only a poet, but
a poet whom the critics will appreciate better the
more they turn their attention away from the pieces
which, by a sort of trick of sentimental metaphor,
have caught hold of the car of the public, to those
which are less showy and more restful.

It has been said, and truly said, that there was
very little of the local genius of the New World in
Longfellow's poetry ; that he was as Conservative at
heart as a member of the oldest European aristocracy,
that even the form of his poetic thought was not
bold, or striking, or unique.   And this is undoubtedly
true ; but after the first period of *ad captandum* writing,
which almost every young man of talent passes
through, he gained that singular grace of perfect
simplicity,—simplicity both instinctive and cultivated,
—which rejects everything adventitious with a sure
and steady antipathy ; and this it was which enabled
him, when he had secured a fine subject, to produce
such a poem as "Hiawatha," or, again, so graceful
and tragic a picture as that embodied in the following
verses :—

"KILLED AT THE FORD.

He is dead, the beautiful youth, ·
The heart of honour, the tongue of truth,
He, the life and light of us all,
Whose voice was blithe as a bugle-call,
Whom all eyes followed with one consent,
The cheer of whose laugh, and whose pleasant word
Hushed all murmurs of discontent.

Only last night, as we rode along
Down the dark of the mountain gap,
To visit the picket-guard at the ford,
Little dreaming of any mishap,
He was humming the words of some old song :
' Two red roses he had on his cap,
And another he bore at the point of his sword.'

Sudden and swift a whistling ball
Came out of a wood, and the voice was still ;
Something I heard in the darkness fall,
And for a moment my blood grew chill ;
I spake in a whisper, as he who speaks
In a room where some one is lying dead ;
But he made no answer to what I said.

We lifted him up to his saddle again,
And through the mire and the mist and the rain
Carried him back to the silent camp,
And laid him as if asleep on his bed,
And I saw by the light of the surgeon's lamp
Two white roses upon his cheeks,
And one, just over his heart, blood-red !

And I saw in a vision how far and fleet
That fatal bullet went speeding forth
Till it reached a town in the distant North,
Till it reached a house in a sunny street,
Till it reached a heart that ceased to beat
Without a murmur, without a cry ;
And a bell was tolled in that far-off town,
For one who had passed from cross to crown,—
And the neighbours wondered that she should die."

It would be hard, we think to convey better the
strange contrast between the gay and picturesque
courage of youth, and the sudden sentence which
absolutely ended the story of life and love, than it is
conveyed in these few stanzas ; their simplicity has

no nakedness in it; it is the simplicity which avoids
detail, because detail only obscures the effect, not
the simplicity which says a thing crudely or poorly.
Longfellow, like all poets who had not any great
originality of initiative, was singularly dependent on
his subjects for his success; but when his subject
suits him, he presents it with the simplicity of a
really great classic, with all its points in relief, and
with nothing of the self-conscious or artifical tone of
one who wants to draw attention to the admirable
insight with which he has grasped the situation.
He can be very conventional, when the subject is
conventional. When it is not, but is intrinsically
poetical, no one gives us its poetry more free from
the impertinences of subjective ecstasy than he. He
was not a great poet, but he was a singularly restful,
singularly simple-minded, and—whenever his subject
suited him, as in one very considerable and remarkable instance it certainly did—a singularly classical
poet, who knew how to prune away every excrescence
of irrelevant emotion.

X

THE GENIUS OF DICKENS

1874

LORD DERBY not long ago recalled to one of his audiences at Liverpool the old definition of Genius, that it is only a power of taking much greater pains about a certain class of subjects than it is in other people to take. In other words, genius, so defined, flows from the labour and concentration of attention, though the taste or predisposition which renders that labour and concentration possible because delightful, may fairly be regarded as the ultimate root of it. That is a very good definition of a good deal of what the world calls genius. But it would be difficult to imagine any definition which would be further from the mark of the kind of genius which must be ascribed to Dickens. At least, if the great humourist's genius is to be brought within this definition at all, we must describe all the brightness and truth of momentary flashes of perception, and equally momentary humourous combinations, to a power of *taking pains*, which would certainly be a very eccentric and forced construction of the term. Indeed, it can hardly be said that in any intellectual way Dickens *had* much power of taking pains in the common sense of that term. It has been observed that if he went down a street, he had more power of telling you what he had seen in that street than all the rest of the passers-by in the whole day would have made out amongst them. He caught character, so far as it could be caught in a glance of the eye, as no other Englishman probably ever yet caught it. Mr. Forster, who in his new volume resents warmly a criticism of Mr. Lewes's on the want of true individual characteristics in Dickens's set types of character,—such as Pecksniff, who is pure humbug; Micawber, who is " always confident of something turning up, always crushed and rebounding, and always making punch;" Mrs. Gamp, who is always referring to "sicking," and "monthlying," and so forth,—Mr. Forster, we say, rashly maintains that there is nothing of this sort in the earlier tales, especially *Pickwick* and its immediate followers. Surely Mr. Wardle's fat boy, Sawyer late Knockemorf, Mr. Jingle, Mr. Tupman, Mr. Winkle, Mr. Pickwick himself, Mr. Weller, senior, nay, we will say even the great Sam Weller himself, are all types made in keeping with one ruling feature, though Dickens's wonderful fancy and curious store of miscellaneous observations enabled him so to vary the appropriate illustrations of that ruling feature, that something which looked like the variety and ease of life resulted from the variation. It seems to us almost absurd to deny that the power of kaleidoscopic variation and multiplication of the same general characteristic, is the main key to Dickens's humour and power. Even in *Oliver Twist*, where Nancy and Sykes at least seem to reach a stage of individualisation beyond anything that can be thus accounted for, by far the greater part of the book is occupied with sketches which fall under the same general rule, such as those of Noah Claypole, of the Dodger, and Flash Toby Crackit. But not the less do I quite agree with Mr. Forster that Mr. Lewes's mode of explaining Dickens's popularity as the result of a kind of glamour of enthusiasm which he threw over his figures, like that which the child throws over a wooden horse, till it really represents to him an actual horse, is a mere blunder. I should say, on the contrary, that that popularity is due to the wonderful breadth of real life which Dickens was able to lay under contribution for the illustration of his various types, and that he had little or no power of throwing a deceptive glamour of enthusiasm over inadequate descriptions, All that could be known by the help of astounding capacity for swift, sudden, and keen vision, and through that large sense of humour which brings an indefinite range of analogy and contrast within the field of view at any one moment, Dickens knew and painted. The result was that he easily divined the secret of almost every crotchety and superficial vein of character that came within his view. Every one tells you that they have met with a real Mrs. Nickleby and with a real Mr. Micawber, and ·I could quote sayings of a person known to me, far more Micawberish than Micawber's own. So all the secrets of any professional life with which he was familiar, were made by Dickens completely his own. Nothing so perfect as his pawnbrokers and his undertakers, his beadles and his matrons, his boarding-housekeepers and his bone-articulators, his dolls' dressmakers, his Yorkshire schoolmasters, his travelling players, and his wax-work men, his fire-eating editors and his Yankee rogues, were ever produced for us before. But then all these characters are photographs from a superficial stratum of real life, which he hardly ever goes beneath, and where, if he does go beneath it, he is apt to fail. While he sticks to his local colour, only varying it as his extraordinary experience in the varieties of local colour taught him to do, he is a wonder and a delight to his readers. Directly he tries to create anything in which his swift decisive knowledge of detail does not help him, anything in which a general knowledge of the passions and heart and intellect of man is more needed than a special knowledge of the dialect of a profession or the habits of a class, he too often loses all his certainty of touch, and becomes a painful mannerist. Compare Nicholas and Kate Nickleby with their mother and little Miss La Creevy. The former are nobodies, the latter great successes. Compare Mr. Brownlow, or Rose Maylie, or any of the ordinary human beings in *Oliver Twist* or even Oliver himself when he has ceased to be the terrified little boy, with any of the thieves or scoundrels in that delightful book. Compare the merely human beings in *Martin Chuzzlewit* with the typical beings, and it is always the same. Directly the shaft is sunk beneath the characterising stratum of some particular type of manners, the fountain no longer seems bubbling-up with life. It does not follow that Dickens did not produce a vast number of really life-like figures. It rather follows that he did. Not only do eccentricities, who really are moulded on the type of a few remarkable traits, actually exist, but characters so much moulded by class as to breathe, at first at least, all the class-flavour, all the professional bouquet which Dickens attributes to them, actually exist. Sam Weller is hardly more than the distilled life of a sharp, cockney servant, a wit of the lower class, who knows London trickery well, and never loses his temper; but then such characters, no doubt, have existed; and the only defect about Sam Weller is one which no one would feel who had not known such a person intimately enough to find out that he had passions and superstitions and affections of his own which would not completely fit into the typical framework, which were apt sometimes to break through it. Dickens seems to me never to fail in this kind of typical sketch, unless he prolongs his story so as to exhaust his stock of illustrations for it, and then he often does fail by harping monotonously on the fundamental string. Every one is sick of Carker's teeth and Susan Nipper's pertness long before the end of *Dombey*. Even Toots's pack of cards, "for Mr. Dombey, for Mrs. Dombey, for Miss Dombey," pall upon us. Honest John Browdie's loud Yorkshire jollity grows tiresome before *Nicholas Nickleby* is at au end, and Lord Frederick Verisopht only regains a gleam of individual character at the moment of his death. John Willett's stupid study of the Boiler in *Barnaby Rudge* is exhausted almost before it is begun, and even Miss Miggs's malice and hypocrisy are worked a little too hard before the tale is out. As for the good characters,— the young lady who "points upwards," for instance, in *Copperfield*,—they are hardly ever tolerable after their first appearance. Dickens had no special store of experience from which to paint them, and his general knowledge of the human heart and mind was by no means profound.

Indeed this is a natural result of his biographer's admission that Dickens had no refuge within himself, no "city of the mind" for inward consolation.

Without that it would have been hardly possible for him to gain the command of the deeper secrets of human emotion and passion. No author indeed could draw more powerfully than he the mood of a man haunted by a fixed idea, a shadowy apprehension, a fear, a dream, a remorse. If Dickens had to describe the restlessness of a murderer, or the panic of a man apprehending murder, he did it with a vigour and force that make the blood curdle. But there, again, he was studying in a world of most specific experience. He was a vivid dreamer, and no one knew better the sort of supremacy which a given idea gets over the mind in a dream, and in those waking states of nervous apprehension akin to dreams. Where he utterly fails is in giving the breadth of ordinary life to ordinary characters. He never drew a *mere* artisan, or a mere labourer or labourer's wife, or a mere shopkeeper, or a mere gentleman or lady, or a mere man or woman of rank. Without something to render such characters peculiar and special, he made the most wooden work of them, simply because he had no field of special experience upon which to draw for their delineation.

But after all, wonderful as are the riches of the various specific worlds which Dickens ransacked for his creations, there is nothing in him, as the most realistic and picturesque of describers, to equal his humour. The wealth and subtlety of his contrasts, the fine aim of his exaggerations, the presence of mind (which is the soul of wit) displayed in his satire, the exquisitely professional character of the sentiments and metaphors which fall from his characters, the combined audacity and microscopic delicacy of his shading in caricature, the quaint flights of his fancy in illustrating a monstrous absurdity,

the suddenness of his strokes at one moment, the
cumulative perseverance of his touches at another,
all make him such a humourist as many centuries
are not likely to reproduce. But then humour of
this kind is not necessarily connected with any deep
knowledge of the heart and mind of man, and of
such a knowledge I can see little trace in Dickens.
He had a memory which could retain, and an imagination which could sublimate, and a fancy which
could indefinitely vary almost any trait which had
once fixed itself in his mind ; but the traits which
did so fix themselves, were almost always peculiarities,
and his human figures are only real so far as they
reproduce the real oddities of life, or what to a man
in Dickens's rank and class seemed real oddities ;
and of course, while there are many real oddities in
the world, these are not the staple of our average
life,—with which indeed Dickens's genius never
dealt either willingly or successfully.

XI

CHARLES DICKENS'S LIFE[1]

1874

WE have here a melancholy close to a book which,
in spite of the many traits of astonishing perceptive
power, and prodigal generosity, and unbounded
humour, contained in it, will certainly not add to the
personal fascination with which Dickens is regarded
by so many of his countrymen. The closing volume
contains more evidence than any of the others of the
very great defect of character which seems to have
grown from the very roots of Dickens's genius. Mr.
Forster himself admits it fully enough, though he
hardly seems to be aware what an admission it is.
"There was for him," says his biographer, "no 'city
of the mind' against outward ills for inner consolation
and shelter." In other words, Dickens depended
more than most men on the stimulus which outer
things provided for him; first, on the excitement
caused by the popularity of his books, and on that
which he drew from his own personal friends' private
appreciation; then on the applause which attended
his actings and readings, the intensity of the eagerness

[1] *The Life of Charles Dickens.* By John Forster. London :
Chapman and Hall.

to hear him and the emotion he excited ; and lastly, on the triumph excited by the counting-up of the almost fabulous sums which the readings produced. These were evidently the moral drams without security for which his life would have lost all its spring and interest, and it is clear that as his productiveness as an author began to fail, he grasped eagerly at the quasi-theatrical powers displayed in his readings to fill up the blank he was beginning to feel, and to compensate him for the restlessness and almost despair which the consciousness that his genius was on the wane began to produce in him. The painful story of his estrangement from his wife, which Mr. Forster has told at once with judicious candour and equally judicious reticence is evidently closely connected with this dependence of his on the stimulus of external excitement. There would indeed have been no reason for any public reference to that story at all, but for the inexcusable intolerance of public censure which made Dickens, when he was contemplating his first course of public readings, insist on publishing a defence of himself against the false and slanderous rumours which were abroad. He did not see apparently that this proceeding was a cruel injustice to the lady whose name was thus dragged into print, without its being within her power in any way to give her own view of what had occurred ; he only thought of the imperious need he felt for an explanation which would secure the possibility of a cordial good-will between him and his public. His last will betrays the same ungenerous desire to clear himself with the public from any charge of want of generosity, and to impress upon men his own case, though he must have known that just so far as he succeeded, the one concerned equally with himself, who was not famous and not popular, would inferentially suffer in public estimation. Yet the public neither knows nor can know anything of the faults or faultlessness of the two parties in a quarrel thus indelicately dragged into the light. And if they are just, they must sum up the whole matter in their own minds by saying, "Here was a case in which a magnanimous man, even if wholly in the right, would have borne in silence false rumours of a very painful kind rather than defend himself publicly, when that defence was necessarily at the cost of one whose mouth was shut, and who had no door of escape into the excitements of public applause and unbounded popularity."

The volume before me, so far as it illustrates Dickens's moral qualities at all, may be said to be one long chronicle of his craving for these delights of popular applause,—sometimes outweighing, as in the case to which I have alluded, what the least modicum of magnanimity would have enforced upon him,—at other times, extinguishing all the sense of personal dignity which might have been expected in an author of so much genius,—and finally overpowering the commonest prudence, and leading directly, no doubt, to his premature death. Mr. Forster, by giving so much prominence to the certainly extraordinary and marvellous popularity of the public readings, and recording, at excessive length, Dickens's unbounded triumph in the enthusiasm and numbers and reckless prodigality of his audiences, has given to this craving of his hero's a somewhat needless emphasis, and has, moreover, extended his already very big book beyond reasonable limits. Nobody wants to hear how the people at Tynemouth did exactly what the people at Dover did; how Cambridge and Edinburgh behaved in exactly the same manner as Dublin and Manchester, and so forth. There is something a little ignoble in this extravagant relish of a man of genius for the evidence of the popularity of his own writings. Dickens must have known that theatrical effects are by no means the best gauge of the highest literary fame. He must have been well aware that no one could have produced with scenes from Shakespeare or from Scott ànything like the intensity of superficial excitement which he himself produced with the death of little Paul Dombey or the pathetic life of Tiny Tim ; and whether the difference were due to something of melodrama in him or something of deficiency in the greater masters, must, at least, have been a question on which his mind could hardly have been definitely made up in his own favour. I by no means deny the value of the test to which his readings subjected the literary power of his writings. Undoubtedly it demonstrated very great qualities. I believe that it also demonstrated some great defects ; and certainly the passion with which he gave away his very life to producing these popular emotions, pointed to a grave want of that higher life in himself which could not have been compatible with such constant superficial strains on his nervous energy. It would have added to the literary worth of the book, and certainly not have diminished the reader's admiration, if Mr. Forster had curtailed greatly the tiresome redundancy of Dickens's own gratitude for the popular enthusiasm with which he was received.

Mr. Forster notes another quality besides this absence in Dickens of any inner life in which he could take refuge from the craving for external excitement,—a quality which, while it very much increased the danger of this dependence on the stimulus of bursts of popular favour, was also inseparable from his greatest qualities. There was "something of the despot, seldom separable from genius," says Mr. Forster, in Dickens. No doubt there was, but I should say that genius is quite as often found without it as with it; that it was the peculiarity of Dickens's own genius, and closely connected with his highly-strung nerves, rather than the token of genius in general. There are many types of genius which are too largely tolerant, like Scott's or Thackeray's, for this kind of disposition ; many, too, which are too purely receptive, too sensitive to external influences, for anything like despotism. But Dickens's genius was of neither kind ; he hardly seems to have enjoyed his visions merely as intellectual perceptions, as food for his own reflection. He enjoyed them chiefly as materials for sensation, as the means of producing an intense effect on the world without. " I wish," said Landseer of him, " he looked less eager and busy, and not so much out of himself or beyond himself. I should like to catch him asleep and quiet now and then." But that was not in him. Never was there a genius so little contemplative. Never had a man of such wonderful powers so little of—

> "The harvest of a quiet eye,
> That broods and sleeps on his own heart."

His mind was always trying to "work up" even the most idle and worthless fancies and situations into pictorial effects. Mr. Forster's chapter called " Hints for Books Written and Unwritten " seems to me much more of an evidence of weakness in this respect than of power. The forced and extravagant suggestions which Dickens sets down for himself as possible hints for future works are far more numerous than those of

real power or promise. In fact, what even his marvellous humour lacks is repose. Often he cannot leave
even his most humourous things alone, but must tug
and strain at them to bring out their full effects, till
the reader is nauseated with what was, in its first
conception, of the richest and most original kind.
Dickens was too intensely practical, had *too much* eye
to the effect to be produced by all he did, for the
highest imagination. He makes you feel that it is
not the intrinsic insight that delights him half so
much as the power it gives him of moving the world.
The visible word of command must go forth from
himself in connection with all his creations. His
imagination is not of the ruminating kind. He uses
his experience before it is mellow, in the impatience
of his nervous haste. But on the whole, while
the absolute deficiency of an inner life, and the want
of magnanimity it sometimes entailed, comes out more
powerfully in this volume of Mr. Forster's than in its
predecessors,—the despotic imperiousness of Dickens's
nature does not perhaps show quite so strongly. He
does not at least assert himself with the same passion
as in the earlier part of his life.

The new volume, of course, contains very fine
illustrations of the perceptive power and the exquisite
humour of Dickens. Nothing, perhaps, shows the
full *abandon* with which he entered into children's
natures more delightfully than this conversation with
a little boy of his Dublin landlord's, during his
"readings" in Dublin in 1858 :—

"Within the hotel, on getting up next morning, he
had a dialogue with a smaller resident, landlord's son he
supposed, a little boy of the ripe age of six, which he
presented, in his letter to his sister-in-law, as a colloquy
between Old England and Young Ireland inadequately

reported for want of the 'imitation' it required for its
full effect. 'I am sitting on the sofa, writing, and find
him sitting beside me. *Old England.* Halloa old chap.—
Young Ireland. Hal—loo!—*Old England* (in his delightful way). What a nice old fellow you are. I am very
fond of little boys.—*Young Ireland.* Air yes? Ye'r right.
—*Old England.* What do you learn, old fellow?—*Young
Ireland* (very intent on Old England, and always childish
except in his brogue). I lairn wureds of three sillibils—
and wureds of two sillibils—and wureds of one sillibil.—
Old England (cheerfully). Get out, you humbug! You
learn only words of one syllable.—*Young Ireland* (laughs
heartily). You may say that it is mostly wureds of one
sillibil.—*Old England.* Can you write?—*Young Ireland.*
Not yet; things comes by deegrays.—*Old England.* Can
you cipher?—*Young Ireland* (very quickly). Whaat's that?
—*Old England.* Can you make figures?—*Young Ireland.*
I can make a nought, which is not asy, being rocnd.—*Old
England.* I say, old boy! Wasn't it you I saw on Sunday
morning in the Hall, in a soldier's cap? You know!—In
a soldier's cap?—*Young Ireland* (cogitating deeply). Was
it a very good cap?—*Old England.* Yes.—*Young Ireland.*
Did it fit ankommon?—*Old England.* Yes.—*Young
Ireland.* Dat was me!'"

And nothing indicates the delicacy of his perception
more wonderfully than this exquisite criticism in
1855 on the acting of Frédéric Lemaître :—

'Incomparably the finest acting I ever saw, I saw last
night at the Ambigu. They have revived that old piece,
once immensely popular in London under the name of
Thirty Years of a Gambler's Life. Old Lemaître plays his
famous character, and never did I see anything, in art, so
exaltedly horrible and awful. In the earlier acts he was
so well made up, and so light and active, that he really
looked sufficiently young. But in the last two, when he
had grown old and miserable, he did the finest things, I

really believe, that are within the power of acting. Two
or three times, a great cry of horror went all round the
house. When he met, in the inn yard, the traveller
whom he murders, and first saw his money, the manner
in which the crime came into his head—and eyes—was
as truthful as it was terrific. This traveller, being a good
fellow, gives him wine. You should see the dim remem-
brance of his better days that comes over him as he takes
the glass, and in a strange dazed way makes as if he were
going to touch the other man's, or do some airy thing
with it ; and then stops and flings the contents down his
hot throat, as if he were pouring it into a lime-kiln.
But this was nothing to what follows after he has done
the murder, and comes home, with a basket of provisions,
a ragged pocket full of money, and a badly-washed bloody
right hand—which his little girl finds out. After the
child asked him if he had hurt his hand, his going aside,
turning himself round, and looking over all his clothes
for spots, was so inexpressibly dreadful that it really
scared one. He called for wine, and the sickness that
came upon him when he saw the colour, was one of the
things that brought out the curious cry I have spoken of,
from the audience. Then he fell into a sort of bloody
mist, and went on to the end groping about, with no
mind for anything, except making his fortune by staking
this money, and a faint dull kind of love for the child.
It is quite impossible to satisfy one's-self by saying enough
of such a magnificent performance. I have never seen
him come near its finest points, in anything else. He
said two things in a way that alone would put him far
apart from all other actors. One to his wife, when he
has exultingly shown her the money and she has asked
him how he got it—' I found it '—and the other to his
old companion and tempter, when he charged him with
having killed that traveller, and he suddenly went head-
long mad, and took him by the throat and howled out,
' It wasn't I who murdered him,—it was Misery ! ' And
such a dress ; such a face ; and, above all, such an

extraordinary, guilty wicked thing as he made of a knotted branch of a tree which was his walking-stick, from the moment when the idea of the murder came into his head ! I could write pages about him. It is an impression quite ineffaceable. He got half-boastful of that walking-staff to himself, and half-afraid of it ; and didn't know whether to be grimly pleased that it had the jagged end, or to hate it and be horrified at it. He sat at a little table in the inn-yard, drinking with the traveller ; and this horrible stick got between them like the Devil, while he counted on his fingers the uses he could put the money to."

On the whole, I cannot deny either that Mr. Forster's biography was a very difficult book indeed to write, or that it has been well done. It has painted for us a picture morally much more disappointing than was expected, and it has perhaps dwelt on some of the most disappointing features at unnecessary length, and with a certain awkward air of half-admission, half-deprecation. There is far too much criticism on individual works of Dickens, to some of which Mr. Forster recurs repeatedly ; and it does not appear to me that the criticism is always sound. His attack on Mr. Lewes in the present volume is very fierce, but by no means as effective as it is fierce, and though I cannot pretend to accept Mr. Lewes's judgment,—I believe Dickens to be certainly the greatest humourist of his nation, while Mr. Lewes appears to give him credit only for fun, —Mr. Forster quite fails to make good against Mr. Lewes the largeness and wholeness of the humanity in Dickens's creations. But with all these faults and shortcomings, Mr. Forster's life of Dickens will always be eagerly read as long as Dickens himself is eagerly read ; and that will be as long as Englishmen retain their delight in English literature.

XII

THE FUTURE OF ENGLISH HUMOUR

MR. AINGER'S " CHARLES LAMB "

1882

THE publication of Mr. Ainger's little book on Charles Lamb, one of the truest and most unique of all the great English humourists, has set people talking, as people always will talk, of the superiority of the past over the present, and the gradual decay of the forms of life which make the past so fascinating. 'Will there ever be such another humourist as Charles Lamb?' said one literary man, during the present week, to another. 'Is there not a tendency at work in our modern life to the *pettification* of everything, till the highest form of humour which the public will enjoy is the form given in Mr. Gilbert's operettas and Mr. Burnand's "Happy thoughts"?' The interlocutor interrogated wisely reserved judgment, thinking reserve wise, as the Judges do on great occasions, and suspecting that pessimism is always apt to be out in its reckoning; moreover, that it is rather a hasty thing to assume that because our cleverest operettas and contributions to *Punch* may leave something in the way of largeness to be desired, largeness of humour is dying out in the world.   And, indeed, if we only consider what stores of fun Hood, who was one of Lamb's youngest friends, produced ; then that before Lamb's death, the greatest English humourist of any age—Shakespeare himself not excepted—was beginning to try his wings ; further, that one of the greatest of Dickens's contemporaries, Thackeray, though much more of a satirist than a humourist, was still a humourist of a very high order ; moreover, that while both of them were in the maturity of their powers, a totally new school of humour of the most original kind sprang into existence on the other side of the Atlantic, of which the present American Minister to this country is the acknowledged master,—the *Biglow Papers* having scarcely been surpassed in either kind or scale of humour since the world began ; and finally, that to prove that very true humour of slighter calibre is plentiful enough, we have the extraordinary popularity and originality of such books as *Alice in Wonderland* on this side of the Atlantic, and of trifles like Artemus Ward's various lectures, Hans Breitmann's ballads, and Bret Harte's "Heathen Chinee," on the other side of the Atlantic, to bring up in evidence,—I suspect that it would be much more plausible, looking at the matter from the point of view of mere experience, to argue that English humour is only in its infancy, and that we are likely to have an immense multiplication of its surprises, rather than that it is already in the sere and yellow leaf.   The truth is, no doubt, that as human competition increases, there is a tendency to refine and subdivide and think more exclusively about a succession of trifles, which is not favourable to the larger humour ; but then this very tendency drives men into opposition to it, makes them eager to steep themselves, as Charles Lamb steeped himself, in the dramatic life of a more spontaneous age, and the contrast brings to light ever new forms of that grotesque and conscious inconsistency and incompatibility between human desire and human condition, on which the sense of humour feeds. When Charles Lamb called Coleridge "an archangel,—a little damaged," he painted this contrast between human ideals and human experience in its most perfect form. But every new generation is probably richer in suggestions of that kind than all the preceding generations put together, for this, if for no other reason,—that whether we still believe in the ideals of the past or not, as future realities, we never cease to yearn after them, and to yearn after them all the more that they excite less active hope, while the accumulating experience of centuries brings us face to face with the oddest and most grotesque forms of disappointment and disillusion. No contrast could have been more striking, for instance, than that between Coleridge's eloquent expositions of divine philosophy and faith, and his own helpless life, sponging on the hospitality of Good Samaritans, and leaving his family to the generosity of friends. And no condition of the world can be reasonably expected in which contrasts of that pathetic kind will not be multiplied rather than diminished in number, or in which it may not reasonably be expected that the eye to discern and the power to make us feel these contrasts will be multiplied at the same time.

In some respects, though in some only, Charles Lamb's humour anticipates the type of humour which we now call, in the main, American. When, for instance, he gravely narrated the origin of the Chinese invention of roast pig, in the burning down of a house,—when he told a friend that he had moved just forty-two inches nearer to his beloved London, —and again, when he wrote to Manning in China that the new Persian Ambassador was called "Shaw Ali Mirza," but that the common people called him "Shaw Nonsense," we might think we were listening to Artemus Ward's or Mark Twain's minute and serious nonsense.   But for the most part, Charles Lamb's humour is more frolicsome, more whimsical, and less subdued in its extravagance ; more like the gambolling of a mind which did not care to conceal its enjoyment of paradox, and less like the inward invisible laughter in which the Yankees most delight. Lamb dearly loved a frisk.   And when, for instance, he blandly proposed to some friend who offered to wrap up for him a bit of old cheese which he had seemed to like at dinner, to let him have a bit of string with which he could probably "*lead* it home," there was certainly nothing in him of the grim impassiveness of Yankee extravagance.

It might be asserted, perhaps, that even if the prospect of a great future for English humour is good, there is still reason to fear that it must dwindle in largeness of conception, so that such massive forms of humour as we find, for instance, in *Gulliver's Travels* are not likely to return.   But even this I greatly doubt.   As I noticed just now, Dickens, who, as a humourist was probably not inferior in conception, and certainly more abundant in creation, than any humourist in the world—is wholly modern, and yet he has by no means exhausted the field even of that sort of humour in which he himself was most potent.   The field of what we may call idealised vulgarities, which includes sketches of the abstract

monthly nurse whose every thought and action
breathe the fawning brutalities of the Mrs. Gamp
species,—of beadles who incarnate all beadledom,—
of London pickpockets who have assimilated all that
is entertaining in the world of professional slang and
nothing that is disgusting,—of boarding-house keepers
whose whole mind is transformed into an instrument
for providing enough food and gravy and amusement
for their commercial gentlemen,—of water-rate col-
lectors glorified by one ideal passion for the ballet,
—of rascally schoolmasters whose every action betrays
the coward and the bully,—or of hypocrites who
secrete airs of pretentious benevolence as an oil-gland
secretes oil, is by no means exhausted, hardly more
than attacked. And yet it promises a sort of
humour particularly well adapted to this period of
at once almost sordid realism and ingenious abstraction. Nor can it be denied that, *Alice in Wonderland*, especially such plaintive ballads as that of the
walrus and the carpenter, provide us with a type of
grotesque fancy almost cut free from the realities of
life, and yet quaintly reproducing all the old human
tendencies under absurdly new conditions ; nor that
this promises well for the infinite flexibility of the
laughing faculty in man.

I quite admit that we never expect to see the
greater types of Transatlantic humour reproduced on
this side of the Atlantic. These, for the most part,
imply a rare faculty for turning the mind aside from
the direct way of saying a thing to one that is so
indirect as to lead you travelling on a totally opposite
track, as, for example, when Bret Harte declares that
one of his rowdies,—

"Took a *point of order* when
A chunk of old red sandstone hit him in the abdomen,

And he smiled a kind o' sickly smile, and curled up on
    the floor,
And the subsekent proceedings *interested him no more ;* "

or when the American blasphemer retorted that if
his censor had but " jumped out of bed on to the
business end of a tin-tack, even he would have cursed
some."   This wonderful power of suggesting misleading analogies taken from the very province which
would seem to be least suggested either by·analogy
or contrast, seems to be, in some sense, indigenous
in the United States, and no one is so great a master
of it as Mr. Lowell himself, who has made the sayings
of John P. Robinson and of Bird-o'-freedum Sawin
famous all over the world, for their illustration of
this very power of interlacing thoughts which are
neither mental neighbours nor mental contrasts, but
simply utterly unlikely to suggest each other.   To
give one instance of this, I will recall Bird-o'-freedum
Sawin's comment on the powerfully persuasive
influence of being tarred and feathered, and taken
round the village astride of a rail, on your opinions,
where he remarks that,—

        " Riding on a rail
Makes a man feel unanermous as Jonah in the whale."

Why the United States should seem to have a very
special affinity for this species of humour it may seem
difficult to divine.   Perhaps it is that amongst our
kinsmen there the principle of utility has gained
what we may call a really imaginative ascendancy
over all minds, to a degree to which it has never yet
touched the imagination of Europe, and that this
has resulted not only in the marvellous inventiveness
which Americans have always shown in the small
devices of practical life, but in the discovery of an

almost new class of mental associations,—such as that which distinguishes the head of the nail from the point as sleeping and working partners in the same operation, or such as that which suggested to a reader of the story of Jonah, that if the prophet had had to pass resolutions as to the desirability of getting out of the whale's belly, he would certainly have passed them with something very much like the unanimity of an assembly in which the completeness of the concord is caused by stress of circumstances.   The humour of the United States, if closely examined, will be found to depend in great measure on the ascendancy which the principle of utility has gained over the imaginations of a rather imaginative people.   And utility is a principle which has certainly not yet completed its career, even in the way of suggesting what seems to us the strangest and quaintest of all strange and quaint analogies.

XIII

MR. FITZJAMES STEPHEN'S CREED[1]

1874

MR. FITZJAMES STEPHEN has added a preface to the second edition of his *Liberty, Equality, Fraternity,*[2] in answer to some criticisms passed upon his work by Mr. Morley and Mr. Harrison. As I do not, except on one point, very materially differ from Mr. Stephen on the subject of his controversies with these two critics, so far, at least, as he answers them in this preface, but am inclined to think he has the best of the argument, I should not notice this further explanation of his views, but for the opportunity it gives me for referring to a subject on which, when I reviewed Mr. Stephen's book in June last, I had no space to comment adequately,—I mean, on Mr. Stephen's somewhat remarkable type of moral and religious creed. He says, in a very brief reference to my criticism, "Of this critic, I will only say that he and I write different languages, so far as the fundamental terms employed are concerned,"—a fact of which I sufficiently showed that I, too, was aware in my reviews of Mr. Stephen's book. And since the

---

[1] Now Sir James Fitzjames Stephen.
[2] Smith, Elder, and Co.

illustration which Mr. Stephen gives of this extraordinary difference between us in our fundamental conceptions of morals, religion, and their intellectual conditions, will introduce very well what I have to say of Mr. Stephen's form of creed, I will presently quote it. In the substance of his work Mr. Stephen had laid it down that all actions are 'free,' of which hope is the motive, and that all are done under compulsion or omitted under restraint, of which fear is the motive. It appeared and appears to me that a definition wider of the commonest and also the deepest meaning of the word ' free' could not possibly be given,—first, because fear and hope are often only different modes of describing the same motive. Mr. Stephen, for instance, says that if a woman marries "from the ordinary motives" she does it freely, but if she submits "in order to avoid a greater evil," she acts under compulsion, and not freely. But how are you to distinguish between the woman who marries from the hope of comfort or luxury, and from the fear of the poverty and discomfort she escapes? It is quite clear that the two motives are identical, though looked at from different points of view. I had spoken of an act as 'free' "if it proceeds from the deliberate and rational act of the mind itself," on which Mr. Stephen comments:—"So that if a man gives up his purse to a robber, he does it freely, provided only that the robber gives him time to consider deliberately the alternatives, ' Your money or your life?'" I should answer that, as between these two alternatives of death or surrender of the purse, the choice is free, on the condition stated, and that there is no paradox in saying so. Of course, you are not left free to retain both money and life. The robber puts that out of the question by his alternative, but within the range left to you, you are free, if you are left time to choose deliberately. To call a man free who turns Queen's evidence on the promise of a pardon, and to say that he acts under compulsion if he turns Queen's evidence under the fear of death, seems to me to be playing with words, and not using them, as Mr. Stephen in one of his chapters finely says that all words on the highest subjects must be used as "signals" made by "spirits in prison" to each other, "with a world of things to think and to say which our signals cannot describe at all." I hold that the word 'free' is a sign of a great deal in the world of things "which our signals cannot describe at all," and that it becomes a mere false sign when it is made to stand for an act done under an impulse of hope, and not under one of fear. We fear for the loss of our hopes as we hope for the loss of our fears, so that the two motives are the same from different points of view. 'Freedom' and 'free' seem to me to be words as old as any civilised language, with a meaning far less open to juggling than this, and always to have had more or less reference to the exercise, or the opportunity for the exercise, of rational volition. A slave may, under conditions of martyrdom, prefer his own highest mind to his master's will. A free man has thousands of opportunities for the exercise of this voluntary energy, to every one of the slave's.

But this strange obtuseness of Mr. Stephen's to the higher and positive implications of the word 'liberty' seems to me characteristic of one of the most curious aspects of his creed, which condenses in itself a strong and manly, though wonderfully maimed religion,—a religion breaking down suddenly into the most unexpected and abrupt chasms, misshapen here, stunted there, and elsewhere again exhibiting the most massive and even pathetic grandeur. For instance, this blunt and, as it seems to me, almost supercilious refusal to see any question at all in the freedom of the will, might be expected *a priori* to go with an equally contemptuous view of the mystery of personality and personal identity. Certainly I should have said that if there is one experience more than another by which the "I" is known, and known as something not to be explained by "a series of states of feeling," it is the sense of creative power connected with the feeling of effort, the consciousness that you can by a heave of the will alter your whole life, and that that heave of the will, or refusal to exert it, is not the mere resultant of the motives present to you, but is undetermined by the past,—is *free*. This view Mr. Stephen not merely rejects, but regards as unmeaning; he quotes concerning it Locke's unintelligent remark that "the question whether the will is free, is as unintelligible and as insignificant as to ask whether a man's virtue is square." One might have thought, therefore, that he would go on with Locke as he began, and accept Locke's equally superficial judgment on "personal identity," which makes it to consist solely in the continuous series of conscious memories, and which would deny personal identity to two different parts of the same life, supposing the tie of memory between them was irrevocably dissolved. That, however, is clearly not Mr. Stephen's view at all. He has the deepest sense of the identity of the "I" as one of the inexplicable facts at the basis of the expectation of immortality. He reproaches Mr. Mill for not putting explicitly enough the fair inference from the sense of fixity belonging to the "I am." "All human language," says Mr. Stephen, "all human observation, implies that the mind, the 'I,' is a thing in itself, a fixed point in the midst of a world of change, of which world of change its own organs form a part.   It is the same yesterday, to-day, and to-morrow.   It was what it is, when its organs were of a different shape, and consisted of different matter from their present shape and matter.   It will be what it is, when they have gone through other changes.   I do not say that this proves, but surely it suggests, it renders probable, the belief that this ultimate fact, this starting-point of all knowledge, thought, feeling, and language, this 'final inexplicability' (an emphatic, though a clumsy phrase,) is independent of its organs; that it may have existed before they were collected out of the elements, and may continue to exist after they are dissolved into the elements.   The belief thus suggested by the most intimate, the most abiding, the most widespread of all experiences, not to say by universal experience, as recorded by nearly every word of every language in the world, is what I mean by a belief in a future state, if indeed it should not rather be called a past, present, and future state, all in one, a state which rises above and transcends time and change.   I do not say that this is proved, but I do say that it is strongly suggested by the one item of knowledge which rises above logic, argument, language, sensation, and even distinct thought, that one clear instance of direct consciousness in virtue of which we say 'I am.'   This belief is that there is in man, or rather that man is that which rises above words and above thoughts, which are but unuttered words; that to each one of us, 'I' is the ultimate central fact which renders thought and language possible." Now that passage goes as far beyond Locke's thin and meagre view of personal identity, as our belief in the freedom of the will goes beyond either Locke's or Mr. Stephen's view of the will. And yet, while I heartily agree, and more than agree, with every word in that passage, I should have said that the one central fact which makes this sense of the 'I' so unequivocal, is the consciousness of being able to put out on occasions, or to refuse to put out, free, undetermined effort, and that it is in virtue of this fact that we recognise that self goes deep beneath, or rises high above, the world of determined change in which it lives. Mr. Stephen, however, characteristically as I think, has the most profound feeling of the depth and the mystery of the self, but not the least feeling of the one central and characteristic fact about it,—its qualified liberty.

Equally strong, vivid, and curiously stunted with Mr. Stephen's sense of the personal self, is also his view of human ethics. He holds that all men act, and must act with a view to their own happiness ; that rational considerations show how closely the happiness of one man is bound up with that of another ; that without any belief in a revealed law of God or in immortality, this community of interests would only affect a man's own actions so far as his affections compelled him to rate others' happiness as part of his own, or again, so far as prudential considerations showed what he must concede to them, in order to get them to concede what he needed to him ; but that, with a belief in a revealed law of God and in immortality, men may find it their interest and therefore their duty to do much that is not for their own happiness, though it is for other people's, and this during a whole life-time, with a view to forming a character that, in conformity with God's law, will much more conduce to their own happiness during the life to come.   For all disinterested actions which are not in some remote sense interested, either as required by the personal affections for others, or as enjoined by God, who has power to reward and punish, Mr. Stephen has a great contempt; and even for some which are required by what he deems a morbid and unhealthy affection for the human race in general, he expresses a very deep scorn.   As far as any religion forbids, under pains and penalties, actions hurtful to others which we should otherwise like to do, Mr. Stephen thinks it not only right for those who hold such a religion to abstain, but,—and this it is that puzzles me—he also *admires* those who abstain, for some strange reason, for their abstinence.   He admires them apparently because he thinks the type of character which postpones present to future enjoyments stronger and manlier than that which takes no heed to threats or promises affecting only a far-off future.   He calls the constitution of mind which habitually has regard to these distant considerations "conscience," speaks of it as one of the most personal and deep-rooted of the mental faculties, and altogether holds it in high honour, though, failing any presumptive belief in immortality and a personal God whose moral will is revealed, he hardly admits that such a faculty exists.   Here, again, I regard with wonder not so much Mr. Stephen's negative views, which are common to him with the Benthamites, but his profound positive reverence for the "prudent, steady, hardy, enduring race of people, who are neither fools nor cowards, who have no particular love for those who are, who distinctly know what they want, and are determined to use all lawful means to get it,"—

the type of character this form of creed tends, in his opinion, to perpetuate. What I find it difficult to understand is the hearty warmth with which Mr. Stephen says that "the class of pleasures and pains which come from virtue and vice respectively, cannot be measured against those" of health and disease,— a statement which seems to me a rare paradox as coming from one who not only admits, but maintains, that the difference between the two classes is one which might totally disappear if we were all to die at twenty, instead of to be immortal. In that case, says Mr. Stephen, health and disease and moderate wealth would be of infinitely more importance than virtue and vice ; but if we are to be immortal, they are infinitely less important ; and if we were to live 1000 years and no more, then, apparently, some mean would have to be discovered between virtue as calculated for immortality, and the health and moderate wealth which is the most reasonable aim for men living a short life. I am struck with the strongest sense of incongruity at these statements. Sometimes Mr. Stephen speaks as if virtue, even as we know it, were an experience wholly different in kind and infinitely higher than any other human experience. In the next breath he speaks of it as a pleasure which would vanish altogether if the belief in immortal *consequences* of pleasure and pain were to disappear. Such views are not a morality : they are a sort of torso of morality, with some of the finest portions of the figure wanting.

And so of Mr. Stephen's conception of God. He speaks of him as a being above all moral attributes, to whom it is unmeaning to ascribe justice, for instance. " I think of him as conscious, and having will, as infinitely powerful, and as one who, whatever he be in his own nature, has so arranged the world or worlds in which I live as to let me know that virtue is the law which he has prescribed to me and to others.   If still further asked, 'Can you love such a Being?' I should answer, Love is not the word I should choose, but awe.   The law under which we live is stern and, as far as we can judge, inflexible, but it is noble," [why noble?] "and excites a feeling of awful respect for its Author and for the constitution established in the world which it governs, and a sincere wish to act up to it and carry it out as far as possible."   Now I can't understand that.   If the law-giver is incapable of moral attributes, and the only sense of 'virtue' is the law which his will has established amongst us, why is there anything 'noble' in its sternness and inflexibility?   Is a law of the Medes and Persians 'noble,' apart from its morality, simply for its sternness, because it altereth not?   Mr. Stephen's religion, like his morality and his moral psychology, consists of one or two fine, but rugged fragments. . He believes in the 'I,' but not in its only striking characteristic; he believes in the infinitely deeper joy of virtue than of any other mental experience, but thinks there would be no such distinction to a being of definitely limited hopes; he believes in the nobility of God's law, but not in the righteousness of God.   In fact, Mr. Stephen's creed consists of a few huge, almost Cyclopean, masses of moral conviction, impressive and striking enough, but broken off just at the most critical points, and as striking from their apparently almost wilful insufficiency and isolation, as from their solidity and strength.

XIV

MR. STEPHEN [1] ON LIBERTY, EQUALITY, FRATERNITY [2]

1873

THERE is certainly a quality in books, even of pure discussion like the present, which makes them strong or weak quite independently of the amount of just intellectual discernment they embody. This is a very strong book, the expression of a very strong character, but it is a book so limited in its power of apprehension and judgment, even in relation to the subjects to which it is devoted, that there is something almost grotesque in the general intellectual effect produced by its collective teachings, when we grasp them in a single whole. Mr. Stephen has been graphically described as a Calvinist with the bottom knocked out, and it is difficult to describe him better. Before touching on the main subject of which he treats, in the heterogeneous conclusions of which I find both much to differ from and much to agree with, it may be just as well to group together the main positive features of Mr. Stephen's philosophical faith, so as to obtain as complete a picture as possible

[1] Now Sir James Fitzjames Stephen.
[2] *Liberty, Equality, Fraternity.* By James Fitzjames Stephen, Q.C. London : Smith, Elder, and Co.

of the quaint, and as it seems to me, very ill-assorted details of his creed.

Mr. Stephen is a utilitarian in this sense, that he believes that the only ultimate test of right is the tendency of actions to produce happiness, though he admits that men have a derivative conscience, as a result of which they pass, at least as soon as their character is formed, very strong moral judgments on their own actions and those of others, without having verified for themselves the issues in happiness or unhappiness which those actions are likely to have.   Moreover, Mr. Stephen, if I understand him aright, is a utilitarian of Bentham's own school, and not of Mr. Mill's ; that is, he thinks every man always acts with a view to his own happiness and his own happiness solely, and that every other view is simply unthinkable.   "When, and in so far as we seek to please others," he says, "it is because it pleases us to give them pleasure" (p. 273), and he maintains that acts of self-sacrifice are mere misnomers, and do not mean acts of self-sacrifice at all (self-sacrifice being inconceivable) ; but what they do mean is, acts of an exceptionally constituted person, in which " the motives which have reference to others immediately and to self only mediately, happen to be stronger than the motives which have immediate reference to self and only a mediate relation to others."   Mr. Stephen illustrates his meaning by saying that in ordinary society politeness is not self-sacrifice, because it has become much pleasanter to almost all men to consider others before themselves in trifling matters ; but that if a man gives up a marriage on which he had set his heart in order to provide for destitute and disagreeable relations, that is called self-sacrifice, not because he really sacrifices himself, any more than the man who gives up the best seat to a lady, but because he is peculiarly constituted, and finds his pleasure more in acts which please him only through the pleasure they give to others, than ordinary men.   Men call such acts acts of self-sacrifice—so I infer from Mr. Stephen—because if such acts were ever performed at all (which they never can be) by the majority of men, in them they *would* be self-sacrifice.   A taste so peculiarly formed as to suggest to ordinary men the notion that the doer prefers somebody else to himself,—an assumption, as Mr. Stephen thinks, simply irrational, —is the sole origin of the term.   "That any human creature ever, under any conceivable circumstances, acted otherwise than in obedience to that which for the time being was his strongest wish, is to me an assertion as incredible and as unmeaning as that on a particular occasion two straight lines enclosed a space."   So far Mr. Stephen's philosophy is very simple, very old, and about as false and contrary to the testimony of human experience as extremely simple theories of human nature usually are.

But here comes grotesque inconsistency number one.   Having made it clear that men are always and everywhere driven hither and thither by their strongest wishes, and that such a thing as a will, in the sense of an independent source of force in human nature, does not exist, Mr. Stephen is compelled to testify to a truth utterly inconsistent with his fundamental principle, which he does in the following fine passage.   After quoting a characteristic passage from Carlyle about the transcendental self within the body,—the eloquence of which, only half veracious and very self-conscious as it seems to me, I confess I think Mr. Stephen overrates,—Mr. Stephen continues thus :—

" I know of no statement which puts in so intense and impressive a form the belief which appears to me to lie at the very root of all morals whatever—the belief, that is, that I am one ; that my organs are not I ; that my happiness and their well-being are different and may be inconsistent with each other ; that pains and pleasures differ in kind as well as in degree ; that the class of pleasures and pains which arise from virtue and vice respectively cannot be measured against those say of health and disease, inasmuch as they affect different subjects or affect the same subjects in a totally different manner. The solution of all moral and social problems lies in the answer we give to the questions, what am I ? How am I related to others ? If my body and I are one and the same thing—if, to use a phrase in which an eminent man of letters once summed up the opinions which he believed to be held by an eminent scientific man—we are all 'sarcoïdous peripatetic funguses,' and nothing more, good health and moderate wealth are blessings infinitely and out of all comparison greater than any others. I think that a reasonable fungus would systematically repress many other so-called virtues which often interfere with health and the acquisition of a reasonable amount of wealth. If, however, I am something more than a fungus—if, properly speaking, the fungus is not I at all, but only my instrument, and if I am a mysteriously permanent being who may be entering on all sorts of unknown destinies—a scale is at once established among my faculties and desires, and it becomes natural to subordinate, and if necessary to sacrifice, some of them to others. To take a single instance. By means which may easily be suggested, every man can accustom himself to practise a variety of what are commonly called vices, and, still more, to neglect a variety of what are generally regarded as duties, without compunction.

Would a wise man do this or not ?   If he regards himself as a spiritual creature, certainly not, because conscience is that which lies deepest in a man."

If every man always acts from the strongest wish, or complex combination of wishes, impressed upon him at the moment, and can no other, where the room may be for this spiritual individuality and the power of choice which Mr. Stephen assigns to it, it is hard to see. Admitting there is a higher and lower class of pleasures, how can the former belong more to the essence of the man than the latter unless they actually conquer ? Is it not self-contradiction itself to say that that which is vanquished and subdued is more of the essence of a necessary being, —which man not only is, but is by the very laws of thought itself, according to Mr. Stephen,—than that which vanquishes and subdues it ? Surely the question of essence, in a necessary being, must be judged by the result ? If the pleasures of virtue are more of the essence of the man, they will come out in the man, and triumph over the lower pleasures. If, on the contrary, the pleasures of vice are more of the essence of the man, they will triumph over the higher pleasures. Whether " conscience is that which lies deepest in a man " can only be proved,— if man be a necessary being,—by the result. It is most inconsistent first to lay it down that a man from moment to moment is the mere victim of the strongest motive acting upon him, and then to speak of the conscience as that which is more of his essence than his other desires. If it conquers his other desires, doubtless so it is. If not, then it is not so. Mr. Stephen may assert an indestructible essence of higher desires for those whose higher desires get the victory, if he pleases. But he has no business at all to say that the higher desires are of the essence of the man of conscience, unless he also says that the lower desires are of the essence of the man of sense. He should stick to his Calvinistic scheme, in spite of the loss of its religious basis, if he would be consistent with himself, and assert boldly that 'the elect' are those who have a spiritual essence, while 'the damned' are those who have a sensual or unspiritual essence. And in both cases the essence is not to be considered as 'will,' but simply as a constitution of latent properties which is developed under the fitting external conditions, so as to display what was from the first implicitly contained in it.

Again, when Mr. Stephen asserts that "right and wrong depend upon the tendency of actions to produce happiness," and then goes on to tell us that we are to decide for men what sort of happiness they *ought* to desire, and to promote that, and that only, he is guilty of one of the most extraordinary of philosophical inconsistencies, . explicable only by reference to that broken-down Calvinism to which we have before referred. He tells us :—

"For these reasons I should amend Mr. Mill's doctrine thus :—The utilitarian standard is not the greatest amount of happiness altogether (as might be the case if happiness was as distinct an idea as bodily health), but the widest possible extension of the ideal of life formed by the person who sets up the standard. . . . A friend of mine was once remonstrating with an Afghan chief on the vicious habits which he shared with many of his countrymen, and was pointing out to him their enormity according to European notions. 'My friend,' said the Afghan, 'why will you talk about what you do not understand ? Give our way of life a fair trial, and then you will know something about it.' To say to a man who is grossly sensual, false all through, coldly cruel and ungrateful, and absolutely incapable of caring for any one but himself,—'We, for reasons which satisfy us, will in various ways discourage and stigmatise your way of life, and in some cases punish you for living according to your nature,'—is to speak in an intelligible, straightforward way. To say to him,—'We act thus because we love you, and with a view to your own happiness'—appears to me to be a double untruth. In the first place, I for one do not love such people, but hate them. In the second place, if I wanted to make them happy, which I do not, I should do so by pampering their vices, which I will not."

In other words, Mr. Stephen thinks that the test of a true moral rule is *not* its tendency to promote the actual happiness even of whole races for long periods of time, but to promote a type of character to which he knows (by secret criteria of his own), that a higher kind of happiness must ultimately belong. Well, but this is not utilitarianism in any sense whatever, unless he is willing to admit that the revealed will of God, accompanied by a revelation of the happy consequences of obedience and the unhappy consequences of disobedience, is the basis of this secret knowledge. If that be so, why, of course, Mr. Stephen is still a good utilitarian, going, like Paley, on the basis of an explicit revelation. If not,—and he sedulously hides from his readers whether there really be such a thing, in his opinion, as a revelation or not,—nothing can be more absurdly inconsistent than his claim for the moralist of the right to impose on men, out of his own self-consciousness, rules of conduct which he admits will not promote their happiness, or that of even their immediate descendants, and the origin of which can only be a sort of absolute caprice,—for he will not admit an original

moral faculty apart from the calculation of happiness ;
—so that men are to be compelled to do what will
make them and their posterity unhappy or far less
happy than they might be, on the strength of the
ipse dixit of a person who first tells you that happiness
is the true test of morality, and then enjoins you to
prefer an indefinitely lesser happiness attained by
a particular set of rules, to an indefinitely greater
amount attained by another set of rules.   Is it not
perfectly evident that in his heart Mr. Stephen
assumes that he knows a shorter cut to the highest
moral type of man, than can be found by any elaborate calculation of happiness ?   Yet if he does, he is
either not a utilitarian at all, but a man who holds
that the conscience is ultimate,—which he denies,—
or he is a utilitarian only because he believes that
God has revealed that certain modes of life will result
in certain eternal consequences, which far outweigh
the temporary consequences ; but if he believes that,
he should confess it, and base his moral principles at
once upon revelation, as lying at their very root.
But Mr. Stephen throughout his book, while most
eloquent on the *hypothetical* importance of Revelation
to human morality, elects to leave the truth of the
hypothesis perfectly open.   There, again, his system
is Calvinistic, minus its foundations.   It relies on
the threat of damnation for its moral power, but
declines to say whether that threat is true or false.

Once more, Mr. Stephen is always urging that
morality must, in a large degree, depend on religious
belief.   He holds the theological creed to be the basis
of conduct in a sense specially appropriate to the
utilitarian, who, as we have seen, can only overrule
the conclusions to be derived from definite calculations of human happiness by a divine revelation as to

some otherwise unknown results of those actions. He therefore argues, and argues most eloquently, that if States are to have any regard at all for morality, or the type of character which they should aim at producing, they must more or less assume the truth of some creeds and the falsehood of others :—

"The object of forbidding men to deny the existence of God and a future life would be to cause those doctrines to be universally believed, and upon my principles this raises three questions—1. Is the object good? 2. Are the means proposed likely to be effective? 3. What is the comparative importance of the object secured and of the means by which it is secured? That the object is good if the doctrines are true, admits, in my opinion, of no doubt whatever. I entirely agree with the common-places about the importance of these doctrines. If these beliefs are mere dreams, life is a very much poorer and pettier thing ; men are beings of much less importance ; trouble, danger, and physical pain are much greater evils, and the prudence of virtue is much more questionable than has hitherto been supposed to be the case. If men follow the advice so often pressed upon them, to cease to think of these subjects otherwise than as insoluble riddles, all the existing conceptions of morality will have to be changed, all social tendencies will be weakened. Merely personal inclinations will be greatly strengthened. Men who say 'to-morrow we die,' will add 'let us eat and drink.' It would be not merely difficult, but impossible in such a state of society to address any argument save that of criminal law (which Mr. Mill's doctrine about liberty would reduce to a minimum) to a man who had avowed to himself that he was consistently bad. A few people love virtue for its own sake. Many have no particular objection to a mild, but useful form of it, if they are trained to believe that it will answer in the long run ; but many, probably most of them, would like it dashed with a liberal allowance of vice, if they thought that no

risk would be run by making the mixture. A strong
minority, again, are so viciously disposed that all the
considerations which can be drawn from any world, present
or future, certain or possible, do not avail to hold them
in.   Many a man too stupid for speculative doubt or for
thought of any kind says, 'I've no doubt at all I shall
be damned for it, but I must, and I will.'   In short, all
experience shows that almost all men require at times both
the spur of hope and the bridle of fear, and that religious
hope and fear are an effective spur and bridle, though some
people are too hard-mouthed and thick-skinned to care
much for either, and though others will now and then take
the bit in their teeth and rush where passion carries them,
notwithstanding both.   If, then, virtue is good, it seems
to me clear that to promote the belief of the fundamental
doctrines of religion is good also, for I am convinced that
in Europe at least the two must stand or fall together."

I confess that seems to me quite unanswerable, as far
as it goes.   Why should not polygamy, or polyandry,
or any other such institution, be legalised, if there be
no moral evil involved in it?   But the most that
Mr. Stephen does assume in this book is *not* that any
religious creed whatever is true,—not even the faith
in a God who has proclaimed a simple moral code,
and one in which the obedience to that code is to
work happiness and disobedience unhappiness,—but
only that in all probability one or two creeds,—
especially, one might infer, Roman Catholicism,
Mahometanism, and Hindooism,—are false.   But how
will the assumption that Roman Catholicism or any
other religion is false help Mr. Stephen in his legislation on moral questions?   Roman Catholicism and
Mahometanism may clearly be false, and all the Ten
Commandments fictions also.   There is nothing in
the falsehood of any of these religions to offer any
presumption of the truth of Christian morality,—

rather the reverse. Mr. Stephen tells us explicitly that there are races which, in his opinion, won't be made any happier by our European morality. How, then, can we be justified in imposing upon them our morality, unless we are sure that it does represent God's eternal laws? Here, again, his view breaks down entirely, in consequence of the bottom being lost out of his Calvinism. He believes in no intuitive morality to embody in legislation; he is dependent for his justification of any morality on the evidence that it will promote human happiness. He wants, nevertheless, to embody the law of our own social state in our legislation for lower races, but he is quite uncertain whether, after all, it is a divine law. Nothing would suit him better than Calvin's conception of what law ought to be as embodied in his Genevan legislation,—only Mr. Stephen has lost his grasp of Calvin's faith. He wants the State to be placed on a religious basis, if only he knew which religion were true. As he does not, he is content with pleading feebly that one or two religions are certainly false, and they may be discouraged. Grant it. How will that justify what is being continually done in India,—which Mr. Stephen seems to admit is not for the happiness of the natives in any sense in which we can make it clear even to ourselves that it is so,—and which assumes a definite morality to be obligatory even in case it does *not* conduce to the happiness of the present or any very near generation? From the beginning to the end of his book Mr. Stephen writes on the basis of belief in a hypothetical creed,—a creed of pitiless necessarianism garnished by threats and bribes which serve to discriminate the elect from the damned,—which he wishes he held, but is tolerably well aware he does not hold. And

this gives a most ludicrous air of intellectual helplessness, and sometimes almost intellectual imbecility, to
one of the strongest books by one of the strongest
men of our day.

Mr. Stephen is not only a necessarian as regards
the doctrine of motives, but, characteristically enough,
he regards the free-will doctrine as not a doctrine at
all, but simply an inconceivable confusion of ideas.
Mr. Stephen is not only a utilitarian, but, again
characteristically enough, regards the doctrine that
any disinterested action is possible to men as a mere
confusion of ideas, a muddle-headed way of saying
that peculiar people have peculiar pleasures, which,
viewed from the point of view of the majority of
mankind, *look* like disinterested actions,—just as fox-
hunting would look like self-sacrifice to a book-worm,
or reading would appear the most heroic kind of
voluntary martyrdom to a prize-fighter. Of course
with such a philosophy Mr. Stephen sees no magic
in the idea or the word 'liberty.' 'Liberty' to
him only means freedom from constraint, and
constraint only means the introduction of threats, or
other modifications of the principle of fear, into the
motives of our voluntary actions. Here is his statement of the case :—

" All voluntary acts are caused by motives. All
motives may be placed in one of two categories—hope
and fear, pleasure and pain. Voluntary acts of which hope
is the motive are said to be free. Voluntary acts of which
fear is the motive are said to be done under compulsion,
or omitted under restraint. A woman marries. This in
every case is a voluntary action. If she regards the
marriage with the ordinary feelings and acts from the
ordinary motives, she is said to act freely. If she regards
it as a necessity, to which she submits in order to avoid

greater evil, she is said to act under compulsion and not freely."

I should have thought that Bishop Butler had exposed the utter unsoundness of saying that any one of the acts which springs from the primary impulses and instincts, is done from either hope or fear. If a man kills another in revenge, or in a fit of jealousy, it is untrue to say that his motive is the desire of any pleasure or dread of any pain. It is conceivable, and no doubt often true, that men who have experienced these and other passions frequently, and reflected on the emotions which succeed their satisfaction or mortification, may act from the desire of the pleasure or the fear of the pain which followed the satisfaction or mortification. This is indeed the precise difference between the man who acts on self-conscious calculation, and the man who acts on impulse, and the difference is so great as to alter the whole mould of the character. But not only does it seem totally false that the only motives of voluntary actions are hope or fear, but I believe it to be also quite false that, even of those actions which are governed by hope and fear, 'voluntary actions of which hope is the motive' are necessarily at all more free than those of which fear is the motive. The identification of liberty with liking is a fallacy as old as Hobbes. An action is free if it proceeds from the deliberate and rational act of the mind itself, and that deliberate and rational act may be prevented as completely by the sudden and violent action of a hope as by the sudden and violent action of a fear. A faint and long-pondered fear interferes far less with moral freedom than a violent and sudden hope. A statesman who stifles his conscience to seize a great prize suddenly placed within his grasp, may be far less morally free than one who stifles his sense of public duty and retires from public life under the influence of a faint but long-pondered fear of death as likely to result earlier from his over-exertion. According to my view, moral freedom depends on the controlling power which the mind has over its own motives. According to Mr. Stephen, there is no such power at all, either actual or conceivable. He holds that *all* the power of the mind is the power of its own motives, either open or in disguise, and that the only difference is between motives which attract and motives which repel. This appears to me so monstrously inconsistent with all the facts of human consciousness and the consequent usages of human language, that studying the writings of a man who holds it is rather like reading a message sent in a cypher, where every word means something quite different from that attached to it in the ordinary tongue, so that you have to translate by substituting at every step for a commonly accepted meaning, one which is wholly foreign to that meaning. Mr. Stephen himself is not consistent with himself. Indeed no writer so forcible as he, *could* be consistent with such a false and artificial theory as is here given. He tells us (p. 99), "The essence of life is force, and force is the negation of liberty." Now it is hard to say which is the falser of the two propositions,— "voluntary actions of which hope is the motive are said to be free," and "the essence of life is force, and force is the negation of liberty,"—but while both are false, they are also quite inconsistent with each other. There is just as much force, I suppose, in fascination as in repulsion. If "the essence of life is force," the essence of life is, I suppose, strong hope as well as strong fear. But according to Mr. Stephen, strong hope is *not* the negation of liberty, though strong fear is.   Hence you might have the essence of life without the negation of liberty. The truth is, Mr. Stephen's psychology is not his strong point. There is a sense in which force is the negation of liberty, but it is in the sense in which force means a violent intrusive constraint, acting against the grain of any man's judgment, and reason, and conscience; and in that sense certainly it is not the essence of life. Again, constraining force may sometimes, as Mr. Stephen truly points out, elicit a very strong force of reaction and resistance from strong minds; "coercion and restraint," he says (p. 44), "are necessary astringents to most human beings, to give them the maximum of power" they are capable of attaining. But then in this case force is not the negation, but a stimulus to the assertion of liberty. It is worth noting that Mr. Stephen is so little influenced by his own avowed system of thought, that he hardly sticks to it in any of his more powerful passages at all.

My readers will now understand pretty well how and why I differ from the main doctrine of Mr. Stephen's book about Liberty, which is most tersely stated in the following passage :—

"To me the question whether liberty is a good or a bad thing appears as irrational as the question whether fire is a good or a bad thing? It is both good and bad according to time, place, and circumstance, and a complete answer to the question, In what cases is liberty good and in what cases is it bad? would involve not merely a universal history of mankind, but a complete solution of the problems which such a history would offer. I do not believe that the state of our knowledge is such as to enable us to enunciate any 'very simple principle as entitled to govern absolutely the dealings of society with the individual in the way of compulsion and control.' We must proceed in a far more cautious way, and confine ourselves to such remarks as experience suggests about the advantages and disadvantages of compulsion and liberty respectively in particular cases. The following way of stating the matter is not and does not pretend to be a solution of the question, In what cases is liberty good? but it will serve to show how the question ought to be discussed when it arises. I do not see how Mr. Mill could deny its correctness consistently with the general principles of the ethical theory which is to a certain extent common to us both. Compulsion is bad—1. When the object aimed at is bad. 2. When the object aimed at is good, but the compulsion employed is not calculated to obtain it. 3. When the object aimed at is good, and the compulsion employed is calculated to obtain it, but at two great an expense. Thus to compel a man to commit murder is bad, because the object is bad. To inflict a punishment sufficient to irritate but not sufficient to deter or to destroy for holding particular religious opinions is bad, because such compulsion is not calculated to effect its purpose, assuming it to be good. To compel people not to trespass by shooting them with spring-guns is bad, because the harm done is out of all proportion to the harm avoided. If, however, the object aimed at is good, if the compulsion employed is such as to attain it, and if the good obtained overbalances the inconvenience of the compulsion itself, I do not understand how, upon utilitarian principles, the compulsion can be bad."

Now I differ from that, because it entirely denies what seems to us the central fact of human morality, —that man rises in the scale of being in proportion as, instead of being driven about by hopes and fears of which he is the shuttlecock, he shapes his own course by lending the whole force of his will to the

pursuit of the nobler aims of life.   Free choice of the
good is a higher thing than even the fascination of
desire for what is good.   Liberty of action, therefore,
is morally desirable *on its own account.*   It is much
higher for men to be free to choose between evil and
good, and some to choose good and some evil, than
for men not to be free to choose, even though the
result were that the compulsion to which they were
subjected ended in their all attaining the seeming
equivalent for good.   Good chosen has so much more
of good in it than good enforced, that it leaves room
for a considerable margin of evil chosen, before any
wise man would think of wishing to interpose constraints.   This is where I differ from Mr. Stephen.
It seems to me the end of all legislation, spiritual,
moral, and political, to enlarge the sphere of true
moral liberty,—in the existence of which we believe,
and Mr. Stephen does not believe at all.   I should,
therefore, add to the canons which he lays down in
the above passage that all true liberty is always good,
the highest good, but that you may often protect the
liberty of the many by interfering with the liberty
of the few.   Criminal law, for instance, is certainly adapted and intended to put theft and,
murder, and many other acts out of the category of
those which ordinary men feel they have a real option
of committing.   When these acts are punished as
they are by the criminal law, the majority of men
feel that the threats it enforces are so strong, that it
takes these crimes away out of the region of open
questions altogether, and so to some extent narrows
the sphere of vulgar men's field of moral trial.   And
this is advisable, because there is a solidarity amongst
men living in society which makes it impossible for
the higher fields of morality to be seriously entered

upon by the majority, while the lower fields are still open ; and when, therefore, the conscience of any society is virtually unanimous up to a certain point, it is a guarantee for the exercise of moral liberty in a higher field, that the lower field should as far as possible be excluded by common consent from any competition with it. I should add, therefore, to Mr. Stephen's list of cases in which compulsion is bad, the following, as the most important of all :—Compulsion is bad whenever it really interferes with the free action of the conscience and the will, on subjects on which there is danger of a conventional as distinguished from a real moral conviction. Of course, this might come under Mr. Stephen's third principle, as a case in which the moral cost of applying the compulsion is too great; but I see no sign that Mr. Stephen really means to reckon this as one of the greater dangers, nor can he do so, because he does not recognise moral liberty as one of the characteristics of man at all, still less as one which, even when exercised amiss, points to a far higher nature and far higher possibilities than any moral constitution determined only by overwhelming constraints to what is good, could suggest. Of course, this fundamental difference from Mr. Stephen affects profoundly my estimate of his practical application of the theory of Liberty. He thinks nothing of liberty except as a means to an end. "To me the question whether liberty is a good or a bad thing appears as irrational as the question whether fire is a good or a bad thing. It is both good and bad, according to time, place, and circumstance." To me that reply appears much more irrational than the statement that happiness is neither a good nor a bad thing, but both good and bad, according to time, place, and circumstance. Indeed, to my mind, man lives much more for the sake of learning to be truly free, than for the sake of learning to be truly happy. Liberty is only a bad thing where it is not really liberty, where the mind appears to have a liberty it has not really,—as where you leave to a child to choose what it has not the mental or moral experience adequate to enable it to choose with discrimination. And of course, therefore, I do not go with Mr. Stephen in his apparent longing for the restoration of something very like persecution of those religions which he holds to be false. Even the moral law should not be embodied in legislation based upon a moral standard higher than that of the average conscience of the community, or this legislation will stifle more liberty than it will protect. The object is to get the largest possible amount of free co-operation with the moral law; and that can not be attained except where its threats are needed only for the few, where to the many it represents their own inward sense of right and shame. As for religion, it seems to me a strange mistake to found morality upon it, as Mr. Stephen does. It is much truer to say that morality is the foundation of religion, that religion is the highest point of morality, —and that any coarse interference with it by threats and penalties only corrupts it. Mr. Stephen is compelled by his common-sense to see this as to a great number of religious beliefs, though his theory does not teach it him; but why he stops short where he does is a mystery :—

"When you persecute a religion as a whole, you must generally persecute truth and goodness as well as falsehood. Coercion as to religion will therefore chiefly occur in the indirect form, in the shape of treating certain parts—vital parts, it may be—of particular systems as mischievous and possibly even as criminal falsehoods when they come in the legislator's way. When priests, of whatever creed, claim to hold the keys of heaven and to work invisible miracles, it will practically become necessary for many purposes to decide whether they really are the representatives of God upon earth, or whether they are mere impostors, for there is no way of avoiding the question, and it admits of no other solution."

And of course Mr. Stephen means that the State should decide them to be "impostors," and so treat them. I maintain, on the contrary, that no line of action could be sillier or more fatal. The real question is, 'as a matter of fact, *are* priests in general impostors? Do those who know them usually find them interested, insincere, full of trickery and conscious insincerity, or more or less average men, not immaculate, but often possessed of the highest enthusiasm, and generally perhaps of more disinterestedness, if perhaps less manliness, than other human beings of their class?' If the latter is true by the testimony of those who know them, what is the use of setting up a fictitious morality, and saying, 'Their religion is false, and *therefore* they are impostors?' Is it not a great deal easier to judge whether they are impostors or not, directly, than indirectly as an inference from their religion? Do we not know hosts of people whose religion must be false,—if more than one religion cannot be true,—and who are yet at the furthest possible extreme from impostors?

The whole system of Mr. Stephen's book is artificial. His utilitarianism is artificial. His notion of liberty is wholly artificial. His idea of morality as a mere derivative from creed is most artificial of all. I maintain that morality lies at the root of religion and is its base rather than its superstructure;

that men are much more agreed about the former than they are about the latter; that in choosing the latter the exercise of the most delicate and the highest kind of liberty is needed, and that to interfere with that exercise by pains and penalties, on an abstract theory that this or that is 'imposture,' is to mar what we shall never mend. Mr. Stephen's theory tramps over the most delicate blossoms of human life and character with a heavy elephantine tread. There is one view, and but one, which would justify him;—if religious truth were, as he seems to think, absolutely unattainable by any exercise of intellectual liberty, he might perhaps justify the manufacture of a sort of coarse substitute for it, to act as stays to the human conscience, which has an indestructible longing for truth. Indeed, Mr. Stephen glances once longingly at this notion; but is obliged to dismiss it with some reluctance as intrinsically hopeless,—in which I hold him to be right.

XV

MR. LESLIE STEPHEN AND THE
SCEPTICISM OF BELIEVERS

1877

MR. LESLIE STEPHEN is a powerful writer, but he would be more, not less powerful, if there were less of the sneering tone in his writings, and more anxiety to do justice to the views of his opponents. The first position Mr. Stephen takes up in his paper on "the Scepticism of Believers" in the September *Fortnightly* is not only true, but so obviously true, that he need hardly have laboured it as he has done. It is, that just as the sceptic is a doubter as to the religious creeds which he rejects, so the believer is a doubter of the sceptical creeds which he in his turn rejects,—that there is as much scepticism of the adequacy of the sceptic's creed in the religious believer, as there is scepticism of the adequacy of the Christian's creed in the sceptic. That is perfectly true, and hardly needed stating. The man who believes in miracle is a sceptic as to the absolute uniformity of physical order. The man who believes in revelation is a sceptic as to the mere humanity of the conscience and of the spiritual affections of man. The man who believes in immortality is a sceptic as to the extinction of the person with the dissolution of the visible body. All this is self-evident. And it is self-evident, too, that Mr. Stephen is right in assuming that if scepticism is to be saddled with a reproachful meaning at all, the greatest scepticism should be defined as the scepticism which resists the greatest weight of evidence, so that a believer who believes something arbitrarily and against all sound reason is, in this sense, as true a sceptic as any one who rejects something arbitrarily and against all sound reason. So far I go entirely with Mr. Leslie Stephen, and only wonder that he should have taken so much pains to establish what is so obvious. If it would please anybody to invert the names ordinarily in use, and to call one who believes in the separableness of the mind and body, a sceptic of physiological psychology,—or one who believes in God, a sceptic of humanism,—or one who believes in miracle a sceptic of naturalism,—there could be no objection, and no further difficulty about the matter than the difficulty of getting the new language properly popularised and understood. But all this would change nothing in reality. It would soon be ascertained that it was the unbeliever in the finality of death who had the most belief in the moral and spiritual individuality of man; that it was the unbeliever in the self-sufficiency of humanity, who trusted in God; that it was the unbeliever in the self-evolution of nature who had the most belief in it as the creation of divine thought. Nothing is affected by showing that from an eccentric point of view you may find some sort of justification for a topsy-turvy use of human language. After all, language can be nothing but short-hand notes of the facts it describes. And however true it is that belief is unbelief in unbelief,—and that unbelief is belief in that unbelief, the multitude will class as believers those who ascribe their existence and its conditions to a spirit mightier than their own, and as unbelievers those who find no traces in themselves of a guidance that is of diviner origin, or that points to a greater destiny than anything which they can identify in germ.

This being premised, I am not only willing but eager to plead guilty to the main charge of scepticism which Mr. Leslie Stephen brings against all theological belief,—the scepticism, I mean, as to the sufficiency of what he calls the scientific or, more barbarously, the "sociological" basis, for the explanation of our moral nature.   Mr. Leslie Stephen clearly sees the vital connection between the absolute and inexplicable "imperative" in all the phenomena of moral obligation, and theological belief.   He sees and is most anxious to clear it away.   He declares that there is nothing supernatural about the origin of morality; that the human race has learnt that murder is injurious to its welfare "by trying the experiment on a large scale"; that the moral code, so far as it is generally accepted, is the formulated result of this kind of practical experience; that a disregard of morality is nothing "but a disregard of the conditions of social welfare"; that if any one asks *why* he is bound to regard the conditions of social welfare, you can say no more than that he recognises in himself that he does owe allegiance to the society to which he . belongs, and that all the theological sanctions you discover or invent, only give articulate expression to that sense of allegiance, without either making it more sacred or more intelligible.   Mr. Stephen then goes on to explain that this mysterious impulse of allegiance to the claims of society on the part of the individual heart, is quite sufficiently gratified by the performance of very minute services to a very finite thing. "The planet itself will ultimately, we are told, become a mere travelling gravestone, and before that time comes, men and their dreams must have vanished together. Our hopes must be finite, like most things. We must be content with hopes sufficient to stimulate action. We must believe in a future harvest sufficiently to make it worth while to sow, or in other words, that honest and unselfish work will leave the world rather better off than we found it."

Now I not only admit, but am willing even to boast that this kind of exposition of the meaning and force of moral obligation, which we have had in abundance lately from men as able as Professor Clifford and Mr. Leslie Stephen, does awaken in us the most absolute and hopeless scepticism. And I notice, in the first place, that it is not those external things, of the social mischief of which men are said to have had so much experience, namely, slaughter, or error, or the false relations of the sexes, which appeal to the moral faculty of man at all, but very different things,—things of which the hidden motive is the very essence,—namely, *murder*, which may be committed in the heart without taking the form of slaughter at all, while slaughter may and does happen probably a hundred thousand times for every true murder,—and again, *lying*, which is as distinct from mischief-making error as slaughter is from murder, —and lastly, impurity, which is as distinct from mere evil relations of the sexes, such as are often to be found among savages or half-civilised peoples without any impurity, as error is from lying; these are the things which conscience forbids, and haunts us with perpetual remorse for committing, not the external acts, the evil of which, we are told, society has learned purely by experience. Will Mr. Stephen allege that it is solely as the spring and fertile source of mischief-making and society-marring acts, that these interior motives are searched out and condemned and forbidden by the secret conscience? Will he say that, except in relation to the conduct of which they might be the causes, it would be a pure superstition to condemn them,—that, for example, for an unbeliever in human immortality who is to die in an hour, to try and resist a vengeful or an impure thought would be fatuity? If he does make this latter assertion, I should certainly reject his analysis of the facts as the most utterly incompatible with our moral nature as it is, that I ever heard of. Yet it is the very boast of his " sociological " method that, rejecting all irrelevant hypotheses which go outside human nature, it does account for our moral nature as it is. And judging it therefore even by its own claims, the thorough-going scepticism I acknowledge concerning it would be amply justified.

In the next place, as to Mr. Stephen's assertion that "a disregard of morality is nothing but a disregard of the conditions of social welfare," I feel a scepticism at least equally profound. The late Mr. Bagehot, in his striking little book on *Physics and Politics*, showed, I think with great force, that for long ages of the world that which is of the very essence of modern progress would have been most detrimental to social welfare,—that in those ages, the problem was much rather how to subdue the disintegrating impulses of men, and get them to hold together, though even by a rough and bad method, than how to give them true ideas of their best relations to each other. Socrates, for instance, was very probably put to death for " disregard of the conditions of social welfare " as they applied to the Athens in which he lived. Now, assuming this to have been so, would Mr. Stephen maintain that this was really equivalent to disregard of morality ? Is the individual man so merged in the society to which he belongs, that he must strangle his own highest nature because it undermines the morality of his age ? Above all, does such a view represent the facts of moral experience ? Is a man who—even hopelessly —breaks with the society in which he lives, under the constraint of a far more advanced morality, conscious of sin in so doing ? The statement is absurd. Nothing can be less true to the facts of human nature than that " the disregard of morality is nothing but a disregard of the conditions of social welfare." So far is this from being true, that we attach a conception of the highest heroism to many acts of " disregard of the conditions of social welfare," if they have been the acts of one who had a heart or mind too large for the society in which he lived. But if this be so, there must be something in morality beyond its ordinary tendency to contribute to the welfare of society. In other words, the moral problem is deeper than the social problem ; morality cannot be defined as that which ensures the welfare of society ; indeed, we cannot determine what constitutes the welfare of society without assuming many of the principles of morality.

Finally, when Mr. Stephen admits that he can assign no reason why a man should sacrifice himself to society, except that he recognises the virtuousness of the impulse which urges him to do so, he throws up his case altogether for an empirical morality, and becomes a transcendentalist—a theologian even—without admitting it. All that, even in his view, experience can teach, is that society *will* benefit by a man's self-sacrifice, if wisely made after a study of social laws; but certainly not that he is bound to confer on society that benefit. If the man himself desires to benefit society more than he desires his own happiness, well and good,—he will, we suppose, do as he desires. But if he does not,—if he desires his own happiness most,—how can he say that experience teaches him that he is *bound* to sacrifice himself? Experience could not by any possibility teach him anything of the kind, for it is the very contention of the philosophy of Mr. Stephen that moral obligation is only a name for the teaching of experience as to the laws of cause and effect in human conduct; and clearly no empirical evidence as to the laws of cause and effect in human conduct, can prove that I am "bound" to do what is not for my own happiness and what I dislike. If, therefore, Mr. Stephen says that it is "virtuous" to do so against one's wishes, he assumes an ultimate claim on the will which is absolutely independent of mere knowledge, and different in kind from anything which knowledge conveys. And then Mr. Stephen goes on, with his usual courage, to confess and even maintain that this tremendous and inexplicable obligation is imposed on us only in virtue of our anticipation of the modicum of blessing we may thus render to a society which, in a few thousand years at most, must die out, and leave the earth a mere revolving "gravestone,"—the mere monument of all its perished joys and sorrows. Well, the more perishable, petty, and uncertain the result, as compared with the certain dictates of imperious desire in the present,—the more mysterious is this 'categorical imperative' of which Mr. Stephen confesses that his scepticism gives us no account. And in fact the authority and urgency and the complete indifference to apparent results, which is of the very essence of moral obligation, always has been and always will be a rock confronting scepticism of Mr. Stephen's type, and driving it to hopeless and final defeat. It is the moral experience of man, witnessing to the independence of the moral element in our nature of all time-considerations, and to the close affinity of that part of us with a nature purer and holier than our own, standing far above temporary circumstances, which teaches us the reality of the spiritual world.

In a word, I am not at all afraid of the charges of scepticism correlative with our faith, which Mr. Leslie Stephen brings against us. I cordially admit them, and should be quite as willing to take the issue on the ground of those scepticisms as on the ground of faith. Indeed, you hardly see the full strength of the case for faith, till you look into the recriminations of so able a writer as Mr. Leslie Stephen on the "scepticism of believers." Most of his accusations seem to me accusations of indulging freely in sobriety of judgment and in a considerate intellectual temper which cannot ignore spiritual things only because they are not visible.

MR. LESLIE STEPHEN'S "SCIENCE OF ETHICS." [1]

1882

THIS is an able book, and extremely fair in its endeavour to state those views which Mr. Stephen rejects, but it is hardly necessary to say that Mr. Stephen's view of the "Science of Ethics" ignores altogether, in my opinion, the most distinctive quality of moral obligation. Mr. Leslie Stephen's view is that morality arises out of the indisputable fact that certain instincts and modes of conduct are essential to social vitality, and that other impulses and modes of conduct are pernicious to social vitality. Those men who instinctively desire to have the social vitality strengthened, and who discriminate truly,—whether consciously or unconsciously,—how it can best be strengthened, and act upon this desire and discrimination, are good men. Those men who either do not desire this, or do not desire it so strongly as they desire other ends inconsistent with this, or even, if I rightly understand Mr. Stephen's drift, who, though they desire the strengthening of the social vitality

[1] *The Science of Ethics.* By Leslie Stephen. London: Smith, Elder, and Co.

more than they desire personal ends inconsistent
with it, still discriminate wrongly what is and what
is not for the advantage of society, and embark on a
wrong tack for its reform) are not good men, but bad
in proportion to the efficiency of their disorganising
influence over the society to which they belong.   Mr.
Stephen rejects entirely the purely selfish theory of
human nature.   He not only holds indeed, but
maintains, that every human action follows the law
of least resistance, that we do at any moment what,
under the influence of the complex feelings which
solicit or deter us, it is easiest, or least difficult for
us to do.   But he affirms resolutely that it is by no
means always easiest for us to do that which will
most certainly contribute to our own sum-total of
happiness; that it may be much easier for a man to
do that which involves the sacrifice of his own
happiness to the happiness of his fellow-creatures;
and if it is the easier for him so to do, then he is, in
Mr. Leslie Stephen's sense, a man of the virtuous
type, one of those whom the selective influence of the
competition between different races has so far moulded
into the right shape, that his feelings impel him to care
more for the good of his fellow-men than he can care
for his own enjoyment.   From this brief statement
it will be evident that Mr. Leslie Stephen, though
he is a strict " determinist," and though he rejects a
conscience or distinctive moral faculty of any kind,
is not in the least disposed to adopt the "selfish
system " of Hobbes.   Perhaps, indeed, one of the
greatest advantages of the new insight to which Mr.
Darwin's instructive teaching as to the involuntary
adaptation of species to the outward conditions of
their existence, has led us, is this,—that it has
become almost impossible for any wise man to think

of any moral agent as always acting from one and
the same conscious motive. The number of really
unconscious influences by which Mr. Darwin has
shown that all living organisms are induced to act in
this way or that, is so great, that it has become quite
impossible to regard "the selfish system," or any
other system which reduces all the principles of action
to a single conscious motive, as in any degree tenable.
An organised being whose life is made what it is by
so many instincts of which he neither knows the
origin, nor understands the exact significance, is but
little likely when he comes to consciousness to find
that he has but one and the same conscious motive
for action, in which the differences are only differences of degree, and not of kind. In some sense, it
may be truly said that the "selfish system" is now
not merely gone out of fashion, but that it has
become obsolete, through the wealth of discoveries
recently made in relation to the organic structure
and the various origin of the instincts and impulses
which beset us. A nature moulded by so many
subtle influences into grooves and habits of its own,
inexplicable to its owner, and yet rich in significance,
is not the sort of nature to disclose one dead-level of
uniformity in relation to all those springs of action
of which man is clearly conscious. In recognising
the simple disinterestedness, as Bishop Butler termed
it, or as Mr. Leslie Stephen prefers to call it,—not we
think, very wisely,—the genuine "altruism," of many
of the human sympathies and passions, he opens
the way for that portion of the Science of Ethics, in
which, so far as I can judge, he is on the right track.

This book has one great evidence of candour
about it,—that Mr. Stephen never seems to satisfy
himself with his own discussion of any part of the

subject, but rather pursues his ethical questions through one phase after another of constantly changing form, till he leaves, as it seems to me, the most important of them not only unanswered, but with something like the impression that they are unanswerable, at the close.   Through the whole book we seem to be interrogating a sort of Proteus, who is always changing his shape, but who escapes from us without giving his reply, even at the last.   For instance, the questions soon arise—Is there such a thing as human volition ?   Is there such a thing as moral obligation ?   Is there any power by which a bad man can become good, or any reason which you can expect him to recognise why he should become good ?   If all these questions cannot be answered explicitly, and answered in the affirmative, I should have said that there is no proper ethical science, though there may be an explanation of the distinction between good and bad, just as there is an explanation of the distinction between wise and foolish, or between beautiful and ugly.   Mr. Leslie Stephen seems to reply to the first two questions with a direct negative, though he himself probably would not acquiesce in that statement.   To the third I understand him to reply that a bad man who is also sensible, and a man of some force of character, might easily find very good selfish reasons for bringing himself up to the average moral standard of his age and class, if he could but find the means for effecting this change in himself, but that it is almost impossible to assign any selfish reason why a man not already virtuous should even wish to be better than the average moral standard of his day, the standard that the class to which he belongs would be apt to require ; and that even a highly virtuous man,

who, being virtuous, would be, of course, rendered
to a certain extent miserable by falling below his
own standard, might, nevertheless, succeed in very
effectually stilling his own remorse, and in persuading
himself that he had chosen rightly, in choosing not
to sacrifice life and happiness and every pleasant
prospect to an ideal martyrdom. For the rest, Mr.
Leslie Stephen holds that there will be martyrs in
the good cause all the same ; and that they will only
be the better and truer martyrs for having no
command of what he evidently deems that moral
sleight-of-hand by which religious people first take
credit for virtue, as if it were purely disinterested,
and then claim all the advantages of the so-called
selfish system, by parading the rewards of another
life for what they have disinterestedly done.

In order to review this book with any profit, one
must keep very close to one or two main questions
which it raises.   And first, I will deal with one which
arises as follows :—Mr. Leslie Stephen regards the
Moral Law as enjoining those qualities which are
found to tend to the health and strength of the
society to which those who possess them belong.
He admits, and, indeed, maintains, that this is not
the uniform or, usually, the explicit reason given for
admiring those qualities. On the contrary, as the
swifter birds gain an advantage by their swiftness, of
which they probably never know the magnitude,
and as the caterpillars marked like the leaves on
which they feed, gain a protection from their markings, of which they are quite unconscious, so he
holds that courage and temperance and truthfulness,
and justice and pity, add so much to the moral
stamina of the race in which those qualities are
developed, that numberless individuals in whom these

virtues are inbred, are quite unaware of the grounds
of their own preference for them.   Granted ; but it
is obvious, and Mr. Leslie Stephen no doubt admits,
that any one who accepts this mode of defining the
moral virtues as qualities tending to the health and
strength of a society, must not import into the
meaning of the words "the health and strength of
society" the many qualities which he proposes to
explain as the *means* to this health and strength.
When you speak of the length of a bird's wing as
being an advantage to it, or of the spots on a caterpillar or grub as preserving it from destruction, you
mean, of course, that these qualities are physical
advantages, that they save it from physical danger.
So, too, you must mean by the qualities which
minister to the health and strength of society,
qualities which save it from danger or death as a
society, which give it cohesion, which enable it to
hold together when assailed by force, or conquered,
or tempted by influences which have disintegrated
other societies.   The moral qualities are, in Mr.
Stephen's view, means to this quasi-physical end,—
antiseptics preventing the decay of the social
cohesion.   These qualities come to be valued in the
end so highly as they are,—come, in short, to be
esteemed moral qualities,—because they keep up this
vitality, this cohesion.   If lying, instead of truthfulness, could be essential to this social cohesion and
vitality, lying instead of truthfulness would, so I
understand Mr. Stephen, become one of the features
of the Moral Law.   Well, that being so, what I want
to ask is this,—how is it that qualities which come
into such high repute because they tend to social
cohesion, ever lead us to put a much higher value on
themselves than on the social vitality and cohesion

to which they are subordinate ? Supposing the bird
came to know the importance of his greater swiftness
of flight in preserving his race, would he ever think
of putting the means above the end, and preferring
to hold fast by his swiftness of flight, even though
it should threaten the existence of his race ? Supposing a caterpillar could foresee that his markings,
instead of preserving his life, would, by some sudden
change in the environment, become the chief cause
of risk, would not the caterpillar at once sigh for the
power of changing his dangerous markings for other
safer markings ? If this be so, I want to know why
it is that the moral qualities which, according to Mr.
Leslie Stephen, have come to be so valuable to us only
as protective of the cohesion and vitality of society,
should ever be valued very much more than we value
the cohesion and vitality of the society which they
protect ? And especially I want to know how Mr.
Leslie Stephen explains, what he never discusses in
this book, how it happens that a change in the conditions of life which obviously leads to the disintegration of society in a given time and place, can seem
to be not only right, but morally obligatory on an
ordinary human mind—on a mind, that is, which cannot, of course, venture to anticipate, without the
teaching of experience, that this disintegration will
tend to form a new and stronger society, in another
time and another place ? I understand antiseptics for
society. But how are antiseptics, the first effect of
which is profoundly disintegrating to society, to be
justified ; and how, especially, are we to justify these
on the basis of a pure experience-philosophy, like Mr.
Leslie Stephen's ?

My first criticism on this book is, then, the following. I hold that, as a matter of fact, men have a

great deal more direct insight into moral laws than
they have either implicit or explicit apprehension of
the principles which tend to the health and vitality
of society ;—that we judge of the health and vitality
of society by the respect paid to moral laws, instead
of judging of the moral laws by the health and
vitality of the society; in other words, that Mr.
Leslie Stephen has endeavoured to explain the more
known by the less known, instead of the less known
by the more known,—that the very cohesion of
society which he makes the true end of the moral
laws, is only measurable by us in terms of those very
moral laws which are treated by Mr. Stephen as the
mere means to that much less intelligible end.

I have now given concisely the drift of Mr. Leslie
Stephen's theory of Ethics, and have insisted on one
principal objection to it.   The doctrine that morality
consists in being and doing whåt tends to the health
and vitality of the social organism, implies two
things,—(1), that we can judge better what tends
towards the health and vitality of the social organism
than we can what tends to morality,—which seems
to me the contrary of the truth ; (2), that when the
two ends appear on the surface of things to be in
conflict,—as, for instance, the Socratic morality with
the health and vitality of Greek society,—the high-
minded man would either regard the innovating and
reforming morality as intrinsically condemned by
the fact of its tending to dissolve the existing social
bond ; or if he did not, he must ground his defence
of the innovating morality on a prophetic certainty
(which no ordinary mortal could well feel) that out
of the ruins of the Society about to be dissolved,
there would arise a much healthier and stronger
Society than that which which the morality he was

advocating tended to undermine. In short, I contend, that in regarding the health and vitality of Society as the test of moral virtue, Mr. Leslie Stephen derives the better known from the less known, and further renders developments of morality which threaten, as developments of morality have so often threatened, the cohesion of an existing society, from any moral point of view almost unintelligible and suicidal.

I must now say a word or two in relation to the replies which Mr. Leslie Stephen gives to what I have termed the fundamental questions of Ethics, namely,—Is there such a thing as volition, and if so, what is it? Is there such a thing as moral obligation? Is there any power by which a bad man can become good, or any reason which you can expect him to recognise why he should become good?

I have already stated that, in my sense of the words, though not, I believe, in his own, Mr. Leslie Stephen gives a negative reply to the first two questions, and a very modified affirmative to the third. Let me take them in order. Mr. Stephen has nowhere explained distinctly what he means by "volition," but he has indirectly suggested what he means by it in several places. Thus, he says (p. 51), in stating that the law of "least resistance" really governs human action, "The various desires operate in such a way that the volition discharges itself along that line in which the balance of pleasure over pain is a maximum" (p. 51). That appears to make volition a mere equivalent for the resultant of all the desires acting upon us,—in other words, to deny that it is anything but a name for that resultant, for where is the scientific necessity for supposing a separate faculty like "volition" at all, if you only mean by it the man himself under the influence of a simple or complex state of desire?   And everything which Mr. Leslie Stephen says on the subject of the words "volition" and "voluntary" appears to me to express this view,—that they are in reality words of supererogation in his system of thought, which he would do much better to dispense with altogether. Thus—"Anticipation and volition spring from the same root" (p. 55), which the context explains to be the root of desire.   Again, he says (p. 159) that if a man is hungry, there is usually a volition to eat whenever there is opportunity, but that if there be some fear which prevents him from eating, as, for example, the fear of poison, "for a volition, we then have only a velleity,"—from which I plainly enough gather that a volition is merely a desire which takes effect.   So, again, Mr. Stephen complains (p. 286) of the language about a man being a slave to his passions, saying that, in using such language, "we declare a man incapable of choice just because he chooses so strongly."   Again, Mr. Stephen tells us (p. 271) precisely what he means by the word "voluntary":—"A man is meritorious so far as he acts in a way which the average man will only act under from the stimulus of some extrinsic motive. The act, therefore, must spring from his character; it must be the fruit of some motive which we regard as excellent; and if it did not arise from a motive— *or in other words, were not voluntary,*—it would not, properly speaking, be his conduct at all." The words I have italicised appear to me to come nearer to an explicit definition of volition as the desire which causes action than any other passage in the book, but throughout it I understand Mr. Stephen to be making the same assertion that volition means nothing in the world except executive desire,—the net desire which takes effect.   So, when he analyses what he calls "an act of free-will" (p. 53), he brings out this result: "I decide by the simple process of feeling one course to be the easiest."   Well, if all this does not amount to saying that volition is not a state of mind distinct from desire at all,—that it has, indeed, no right to a separate name, because, though that name, of course discriminates the effective desire from the non-effective, that discrimination would be much better effected by a word character-ising the resultant desire, and not by a new term,—I am wholly incapable of appreciating what Mr. Stephen's true drift is.   But I believe that he would not question my inference in this case; nay, he might probably maintain that it is a great misfortune for philosophy that words like "volition" and "will" should have been introduced to darken its horizon, and divert the mind from what he certainly holds to be the true view, that the whole of the active forces of the human character are emotions or desires, either single or in combination.   All I can say to this view is that it disposes of ethics as the science of moral obligation altogether.   If the struggle of the man against a wrong action only means the struggle of some of his emotions against others of his emotions, it may, indeed, be a most important matter for him what emotions he has, and which of them are stimulated from outside; but the emotions once granted, and the stimulus once applied to them, he has no more to do with the matter.   This so-called "will" is merely an expression for the resulting emotion which encounters least resistance and in that case to talk of any resistance to it is to talk nonsense. Mr. Stephen still retains, of course, an ideal of char-acter, still retains the right to exhort us all so to

mould any human character over which we may
have influence, that the line of least resistance for it
may be the line of progress for society ; but he gives
up the notion that any man can, or ever does, resist
the resultant of all the emotional influences acting
upon him, and that, in any intelligible sense, therefore, he can be said to be under an obligation to do
that which, as a matter of fact, he does not, and
therefore in Mr. Stephen's view cannot, do.

It is a very curious thing that Mr. Stephen, who
appears to be a thorough-going defender of the
experience philosophy, grounds this thorough-going
denial of true volition—which is, of course, the
absolute condition of moral obligation—on what I
should myself describe as an *intuition a priori* that no
other view is even possible ; and though he would
not so describe his own meaning, he certainly expresses
it in exactly the same kind of language as an intui-
tionist would use to describe an *intuition a priori.*
Take, for instance, the following :—

"The universe is a continuous system ; no abrupt
changes suddenly. take place. We could not suppose
them to take place without supposing that identical
processes might suddenly become different, which is like
supposing that a straight line may be produced in two
different directions. Hence, every agent is a continuation
of some preceding process. He has not suddenly sprung
into existence from nowhere in particular; the man has
grown out of the child. We might (though the language
would be somewhat strained) call the child in this sense
the ' cause ' of the man. But for the child, the man
would not exist. But there is not a child *plus* a man, in
which case there might be a coercion of the man by the
child. The child and man form a continuous whole,
with properties slowly varying according to its character

and the external circumstances. A man, again, has of course qualities which he has inherited ; but this is not to be understood as if there were a man *plus* inherited qualities, which, therefore, somehow, diminish his responsibility. The whole man is inherited, if we may use such a phrase " (p. 289).

And again :—

" When we know from one phenomenon that another exists, it is simply that we can (for some reason) identify the two as parts of a whole of mutually dependent parts. From an eye we infer an ear or a leg ; it is not because the eye has a power to make ears and legs out of formless matter, or because, besides eyes and ears and and legs and every part of the organism, there is some additional coercive force which holds them together, but simply that each part carries with it a reference to the rest.   The difficulty is dispelled so far as it can be dispelled when we have got rid of the troublesome conception of necessity, as a name for something more than the certainty of the observer.   When we firmly grasp and push to its legitimate consequences the truth that probability, chance, necessity, determination, and so forth, are simply names of our own states of mind, or, in other words, have only a subjective validity ; that a thing either exists or does not exist, and that no fresh quality is predicated when we say that it exists necessarily ; and that all dependence of one thing upon another implies a mutual relation, and not an abolition of one of the things,—we have got as far as we can towards removing the perplexity now under consideration " (p. 293-4).

If I rightly apprehend these passages, Mr. Leslie Stephen means by them that any one who introduces volition into human nature as a real power of resisting the resultant of all the desires by which man is actuated,—in other words, who conceives man as capable of making what Dr. Ward has called an anti-impulsive effort,—is guilty of offending against the laws of thought,—is guilty of the same absurdity as a man who supposes that a straight line can be produced in two different directions. But then, is not Mr. Stephen bound to explain how it comes about that men ever do make such a supposition? No one ever does make the supposition that a straight line can be produced in more directions than one, after he has been made to understand the statement. But numbers of men do believe firmly that they themselves might have been very different from what they are, and this, too, without any change at all, either of external circumstances or of the internal conditions of choice; and surely, therefore, Mr. Stephen is bound to explain how so amazing a contradiction of what he evidently regards as a law of thought, is not only possible, but amongst the commonest of all assumptions made both by thinking and by unthinking men. I can understand very well how it may happen that the mere teaching of experience is sometimes mistaken for an *a priori* intuition; but I confess I can hardly understand how the teaching of experience, if it be, as Mr. Stephen holds it to be, so constant that even thinkers like himself describe it just as the school opposed to him describe an *a priori* intuition, can produce so little effect on the imagination alike of ordinary and of carefully-educated men, that they persist in founding their whole moral practice on assumptions which this alleged stream of experience is declared to prove not merely false, but inconceivable.

With regard to the third question discussed in Mr. Leslie Stephen's book,—the question whether there be any power by which bad men can become good men, and any reason which we can bring home to the bad man himself why he should use this power, if he has it, Mr. Stephen, as I have already indicated, replies with a very modified affirmative. We may succeed, he thinks, in convincing a selfish man that it is his interest to conform himself to something like the average standard of the men with whom he must pass his life ; but it is impossible to convince an average man that he will be the happier for exceeding that standard, and impossible for this very excellent reason,—that it is not by any means generally true. It is a much happier thing, says Mr. Stephen, for a man whose dispositions are already virtuous to live a reasonably virtuous life, than to live below his own standard ; but even then, if his own standard required a very great sacrifice— like the sacrifice of life itself—it might well be that he would judge more wisely for his own ultimate happiness by acting below his standard for once, and thinking about this dereliction of duty as little as might be, or even trying to persuade himself that he was justified in making it. Such is Mr. Stephen's view. But I cannot really make out why, on his conception of ethical obligation,—which involves no "categorical imperative," no absolute moral law which your conscience cannot evade,—the virtuous man should not be justified in declining to cement the social tie or to stimulate social vitality by the sacrifice of himself. Mr. Leslie Stephen admits that to the question, 'Why should I do what tends to the welfare of society ?' there is no adequate reply, except this,—'I care more for the welfare of society than for my own welfare.' And that of course need not be a true reply. But he does not even say that a man *ought* to care more for the welfare of society than his own welfare ; indeed, he does not like the word "ought." He only says as much as this,— that the disposition to take delight in others' welfare does, as a matter of fact, grow up in every mind of the type which men praise, and that a man who does sacrifice himself for the welfare of society would certainly belong to the type which men praise. That may be quite true, and the man who declines to sacrifice more than a certain quantity of his own happiness for the welfare of society may well admit it to be true. And yet he might go on to say that though he admits it to be true, he does not see that he "ought" to belong to the type which men agree to praise, unless he prefers to do so, and that he is only prepared to pay a limited and not an unlimited price for the privilege of belonging to that type.

This being so, I cannot admit Mr. Leslie Stephen to have laid down a Science of Ethics at all. In the first place, ethical principles are both clearer and higher than the principle that we ought to contribute to the health and cohesion of society. In the next place, a system which does not recognise the will of man as anything distinct from his desires, cannot be regarded as an ethical system. Lastly, a system which admits virtually that the idea "ought," exists only for the virtuous, and only so far as they are virtuous, ignores the most distinguishing and characteristic of all the features of the moral life. Mr. Leslie Stephen has written, not on the Science of Ethics, but a very thoughtful and, in many respects, a very candid book to prove that Science, and what most men mean by Ethics, are incompatible ideas.

MR. LESLIE STEPHEN ON JOHNSON

1878

MR. LESLIE STEPHEN's interesting and graphic account of Johnson, in Mr. John Morley's new series of *English Men of Letters*,[1] will make that great man's figure familiar to many who would not otherwise recognise its singular interest for the present day. Most men of letters, like most men of science, have gained their reputation by their power of entering into and understanding that which was outside of them and different from them. Johnson gained his reputation by his unrivalled power of concentrating his own forces, of defending himself against the aggression of outer influences,—and striking a light in the process. Of course Johnson was a man of very strong general understanding. Had he not been so, he could not have commanded the respect he did, for those who do not in a considerable degree understand others, will never be themselves understood. Still, admitting freely that it both takes a man of some character as well as insight, to understand distinctly what is beyond his own sphere, and a man of some insight as well as

[1] Macmillan and Co.

character, to teach others to understand distinctly what is within himself, it is clear that Johnson's genius lay in the latter, not in the former direction, —in maintaining himself against the encroachments of the world, and in interpreting himself to that world, not in enlarging materially the world's sympathies and horizons, except so far as he taught them to include himself. The best things he did of any kind were all expressions of himself. His poems, —"London" and "The Vanity of Human Wishes,"— many parts even of his biographies, like his *Life of Savage*,—almost all his moral essays of any value, and above everything, his brilliant conversation, were all shadows or reflections of that large and dictatorial, but in the main, benign character which he has stamped for us on all he did. Of his companions and contemporaries, all but himself won their fame by entering into something different from themselves, —Burke by his political sagacity, Garrick by imitating men and manners, Goldsmith by reflecting them, Reynolds by painting them, Boswell by devoting his whole soul to the faithful portraiture of Johnson. But Johnson became great by concentrating his power in himself, though in no selfish fashion, for he concentrated it even more vigorously in his un-selfish tastes,—for example, in the home which he so generously and eccentrically made for so many un-attractive dependents,—than in the mere self-assertion of his impressions and his convictions. What made Johnson loom so large in the world was this moral concentrativeness, this incapacity for ceasing to be himself, and becoming something different in defer-ence to either authority or influence. His character was one the surface of which was safe against rust, or any other moral encroachment by things without.

And it is his capacity for not only making this visible, but for making it visible by a sort of electric shock which announces his genius for repelling any threatening influence, that constitutes the essence of his humour. Some of his finest sayings are concessions *in form* to his opponent, while in reality they reassert with far greater strength his original position. They are, in fact, fortifications of his personal paradox, instead of modifications of it,—the fortification being all the more telling because it took the form of an apparent concession. Thus when he said of the poet Gray, "He was dull in company, dull in his closet, dull everywhere,—he was dull in a new way, and that made people think him great," his concession of novelty to Gray was, in fact, an aggravation of his attack upon him. And still more effective was his attack on Gray's friend, Mason. When Boswell said that there were good passages in Mason's *Elfrida*, Johnson replied that "there were now and then some good imitations of Milton's bad manner." Or take his saying of Sheridan, "Why, Sir, Sherry is dull, naturally dull; but it must have taken him a great deal of pains to become what we now see him. Such an excess of stupidity, Sir, is not in nature." Of course you are not prepared to find that Sheridan's improvements on "nature" were all in the direction of the dulness of which Johnson had been accusing him. Johnson's humour, indeed, generally consists in using the forms of speech appropriate to giving way, just as he puts the crown on his self-assertion, as in the celebrated case of his attack on Scotch scenery, in answer to the Scotchman's praise of the "noble, wild prospects" to be found in Scotland:— "I believe, Sir, you have a great many. Norway, too, has noble, wild prospects, and Lapland is remarkable for prodigious noble, wild prospects.   But, Sir, let me tell you, the noblest prospect which a Scotchman ever sees, is the high-road that leads him to England."

But this curious power of Johnson's of strengthening himself in his position the moment it was threatened, was the secret of a great deal that was morally grand in him, as well as of a great deal of his humour.   His great saying to Boswell, on which Carlyle lays so much stress, that he should clear his mind of cant, and not affect a depression about public affairs which he did not really feel, was, in fact, a protest against the demands which conventionalism makes on men's sincerity.   Distinctly aware, as he was, that the state of public affairs seldom or never made him really unhappy, he resented the habit of speaking as if it did, as an act of treachery to his own self-respect.   So nothing irritated him like a sentimental eulogy on "a state of nature," because it demanded from him an admission that one of the strongest and soundest of his own instincts was utterly untrustworthy.   When somebody had told him with admiration of the soliloquy of an officer who lived in the wilds of America,—"Here am I free and unrestrained, amidst the rude magnificence of nature, with the Indian woman by my side, and this gun, with which I can procure food when I want it! What more can be desired for human happiness?"— Johnson, well aware that what he, and indeed what every sane man, valued most was partly the product of intellectual labour and civilisation, retorted, "Do not allow yourself, Sir, to be imposed upon by such gross absurdity.   It is sad stuff.   It is brutish.   If a bull could speak, he might as well exclaim, 'Here am I, with this cow and this grass; what being can enjoy greater felicity ? ' " Nor would Johnson ever allow himself to be betrayed into pretending to approve what he hated, simply because such approval would have fitted in with other prejudices and tastes that were very deep in him. High Tory as he was, when any one defended slavery he would burst out into vehement attacks. On one occasion, says Mr. Stephen, he gave as a toast to some "very grave men" at Oxford, "Here's to the next insurrection of negroes in the West Indies"; and he was accustomed to ask, "How is it that we always have the loudest yelps for liberty amongst the drivers of negroes ? " Indeed, the hearty old man would have been a most valuable ally during the American Civil War of seventeen years back, when English society got quite sentimental about slave-drivers who were yelping their loudest for liberty to drive slaves.

But no matter what the subject was, nor what was to be the logical or analogical consequence of his confession of his own belief,—whether he were to be called cold-hearted for confessing (perhaps mistakenly) that he should not eat one bit of plum pudding the less if an acquaintance of his were found guilty of a crime and condemned to die,—or were to be branded as grossly inconsistent for admiring such a "bottomless Whig" as Burke,—or were to be taxed with ridiculing Garrick one day as a mere trick-playing monkey, and defending him vigorously the next when attacked by some one else,—Johnson was always determined to be himself, and always was himself. He was himself in collecting round him so strange a household of companions, who would have been miserable but for his generosity, and were to some extent miserable, and the causes of misery, in spite of his generosity, and in remaining true to them in spite of their taunts and complaints against him. He was himself, in spurning the patronage of Chesterfield when he found out its utter insincerity; himself, in his strange acts of occasional penance; in his loudly and even scornfully avowed value for his dinner,—and for a good dinner; himself, in his strange and tender acts of humanity to the lower animals; himself, in his knock-down blows to his conversational companions; himself, in his curious superstitions, and in his not less curious scepticisms. For a long time he disbelieved, as Mr. Stephen notes, the earthquake which destroyed Lisbon, though he believed in the Cock Lane Ghost. But whatever he did or declined to do, whatever he believed or rejected, he was always the first to avow it, and to assert himself as not only not ashamed, but eager to avow it, even though it were an act which he thought a blot on his own past life. It was this indomitable self-respect and dignity, in the highest sense, which gave not only much of the freshness and force to his conversation, but the grandeur to his life. His devotion to his wife and to his wife's memory,—she was said by those who knew her to have been an affected woman, who painted herself, and took on her all the airs and graces of an elderly beauty, though she was fifteen years older than he was,—his courage in carrying home a half-dying woman of bad character whom he found in the streets, and did his best to cure and to reform,—his incessant, though rough benevolence to his poor dependents, and indeed almost all the traits of his remarkable character, bespeak a man who was never ashamed of himself when he thought himself right, and was never ashamed to be publicly ashamed of himself, when he thought himself wrong. It was this quality, almost as much as his great wit and strength of conversation, which made him the literary dictator of his time,—and it is in this quality that our own day needs his example most.   A day in which men are almost ashamed to be odd, and quite ashamed to be inconsistent, in which a singular life, even if the result of intelligent and intelligible purpose, is almost regarded as a sign of insanity, and in which society imposes its conventional assumptions and insincerities on almost every one of us, is certainly a day when it will do more than usual good to revive the memory of that dangerous and yet tender literary bear who stood out amongst the men even of his day as one who, whatever else he was, was always true to himself, and that too almost at the most trying time of all, even when he had not been faithful to himself,—a man who was more afraid of his conscience than of all the world's opinion—and who towers above our own generation, just because he had the courage to be what so few of us are,—proudly independent of the opinion in the midst of which he lived.

XVIII

JOHN STUART MILL'S AUTOBIOGRAPHY [1]

1873

THAT this curious volume delineates, on the whole, a man marked by the most earnest devotion to human good, and the widest intellectual sympathies, no one who reads it with any discernment can doubt. But it is both a very melancholy book to read, and one full of moral paradoxes. It is very sad, in the first instance, to read the story of the over-tutored boy, constantly incurring his father's displeasure for not being able to do what by no possibility could he have done, and apparently without any one to love. Mr. James Mill, vivacious talker, and in a narrow way powerful thinker as he was, was evidently as an educator, on his son's own showing, a hard master, anxious to reap what he had not sown, and to gather what he had not strawed, or as that son himself puts it, expecting "effects without causes." Not that the father did not teach the child with all his might, and teach in many respects well; but then he taught the boy far too much, and expected him to learn besides a great deal that he neither taught him nor

[1] *Autobiography by John Stuart Mill.* London : Longmans.

showed him where to find.   The child began Greek at three years old, read a good deal of Plato at seven, and was writing what he flattered himself was "something serious," a history of the Roman Government,—not a popular history, but a constitutional history of Rome,—by the time he was nine years old.   He began logic at twelve, went through a "complete course of political economy" at thirteen, including the most intricate points of the theory of currency.   He was a constant writer for the *Westminster Review* at eighteen, was editing Bentham's *Theory of Evidence* and writing habitual criticisms of the Parliamentary debates at nineteen.   At twenty he fell into a profound melancholy, on discovering that the only objects of life for which he lived,—the objects of social and political reformers,—would, if suddenly and completely granted, give him no happiness whatever.   Such a childhood and youth, lived apparently without a single strong affection,— for his relation to his father was one of deep respect and fear, rather than love, and he tells us frankly, in describing the melancholy to which I have alluded, that if he had loved any one well enough to confide in him, the melancholy would not have been,— resulting at the age of eighteen in the production of what Mr. Mill himself says might, with as little extravagance as would ever be involved in the application of such a phrase to a human being, be called "a mere reasoning machine,"—are not pleasant subjects of contemplation, even though it be true, as Mr. Mill asserts, that the over-supply of study and undersupply of love, did not prevent his childhood from being a happy one.   Nor are the other personal incidents of the autobiography of a different cast. Nothing is more remarkable than the fewness, limited character, and apparently, so far as close intercourse was concerned, temporary duration, of most of Mr. Mill's friendships.   The one close and intimate friendship of his life, which made up to him for the insufficiency of all others, that with the married lady who, after the death of her husband, became his wife, was one which for a long time subjected him to slanders, the pain of which his sensitive nature evidently felt very keenly.   And yet he must have been aware that though in his own conduct he had kept free from all stain, his example was an exceedingly dangerous and mischievous one for others, who might be tempted by his moral authority to follow in a track in which they would not have had the strength to tread.   Add to this that his married life was very brief, only seven years and a half, being unexpectedly cut short, and that his passionate reverence for his wife's memory and genius—in his own words, "a religion"—was one which, as he must have been perfectly sensible, he could not possibly make to appear otherwise than extravagant, not to say an hallucination, in the eyes of the rest of mankind, and yet that he was possessed by an irresistible yearning to attempt to embody it in all the tender and enthusiastic hyperbole of which it is so pathetic to find a man who gained his fame by his "dry-light" a master, and it is impossible not to feel that the human incidents in Mr. Mill's career are very sad.   True, his short service in Parliament, when he was already advanced in years, was one to bring him much intellectual consideration and a certain amount of popularity.   But even that terminated in a defeat, and was hardly successful enough to repay him for the loss of literary productiveness which those three years of practical drudgery imposed.

In spite of the evident satisfaction and pride with which Mr. Mill saw that his school of philosophy had gained rapid ground since the publication of his *Logic*, and that his large and liberal view of the science of political economy had made still more rapid way amongst all classes, the record of his life which he leaves behind him is not even in its own tone, and still less in the effect produced on the reader, a bright and happy one. It is "sicklied o'er with the pale cast of thought,"—and of thought that has to do duty for much, both of feeling and of action, which usually goes to constitute the full life of a large mind.

And besides the sense of sadness which the human incident of the autobiography produces, the intellectual and moral story itself is full of paradox which weighs upon the heart as well as the mind. Mr. Mill was brought up by his father to believe that Christianity was false, and that even as regards natural religion there was no ground for faith. How far he retained the latter opinion,—he evidently did retain the former,—it is understood that some future work will tell us. But in the meantime, he is most anxious to point out that religion, in what he thinks the best sense, is possible even to one who does not believe in God. That best sense is the sense in which religion stands for an ideal conception of a Perfect Being to which those who have such a conception "habitually refer as the guide of their conscience," an ideal, he says, "far nearer to perfection than the objective Deity of those who think themselves obliged to find absolute goodness in the author of a world so crowded with suffering and so deformed by injustice as ours." Unfortunately, however, this "ideal conception of a perfect Being" is not a *power*

on which human nature can lean.   It is merely its
own best thought of itself; so that it dwindles when
the mind and heart contract, and vanishes just when
there is most need of help.   This Mr. Mill himself
felt at one period of his life.   At the age of twenty he
underwent a crisis which apparently corresponded
in his own opinion to the state of mind that leads to
"a Wesleyan's conversion."   I wish we could extract
in full his eloquent and impressive description of this
rather thin moral crisis.   Here is his description of
the first stage :—

"From the winter of 1821, when first I read Bentham,
and especially from the commencement of the *Westminster
Review*, I had what might truly be called an object in life ;
to be a reformer of the world.   My conception of my
own happiness was entirely identified with this object.
The personal sympathies I wished for were those of fellow-
labourers in this enterprise.   I endeavoured to pick up
as many flowers as I could by the way ; but as a serious
and permanent personal satisfaction to rest upon, my
whole reliance was placed on this ; and I was accustomed
to felicitate myself on the certainty of a happy life which
I enjoyed, through placing my happiness in something
durable and distant, in which some progress might be
always making, while it could never be exhausted by
complete attainment.   This did very well for several
years, during which the general improvement going on
in the world and the idea of myself as engaged with others
in struggling to promote it, seemed enough to fill up an
interesting and animated existence.   But the time came
when I awakened from this as from a dream.   It was in
the autumn of 1826.   I was in a dull state of nerves,
such as everybody is occasionally liable to ; unsusceptible
to enjoyment or pleasurable excitement ; one of those
moods when what is pleasure at other times, becomes
insipid or indifferent ; the state, I should think, in which

converts to Methodism usually are, when smitten by their first 'conviction of sin.'   In this frame of mind it occurred to me to put the question directly to myself: 'Suppose that all your objects in life were realised ; that all the changes in institutions and opinions which you are looking forward to could be completely effected at this very instant ; would this be a great joy and happiness to you ?' And an irrepressible self-consciousness distinctly answered, 'No !'   At this my heart sank within me : the whole foundation on which my life was constructed fell down. All my happiness was to have been found in the continual pursuit of this end.   The end had ceased to charm, and how could there ever again be any interest in the means ? I seemed to have nothing left to live for.   At first I hoped that the cloud would pass away of itself ; but it did not.   A night's sleep, the sovereign remedy for the smaller vexations of life, had no effect on it.   I awoke to a renewed consciousness of the woful fact.   I carried it with me into all companies, into all occupations.   Hardly anything had power to cause me even a few minutes' oblivion of it.   For some months the cloud seemed to grow thicker and thicker.   The lines in Coleridge's 'Dejection'—I was not then acquainted with them— exactly describe my case :—

> 'A grief without a pang, void, dark and drear,
> A drowsy, stifled, unimpassioned grief,
> Which finds no natural outlet or relief
> In word, or sigh, or tear.'

In vain I sought relief from my favourite books ; those memorials of past nobleness and greatness from which I had always hitherto drawn strength and animation.   I read them now without feeling, or with the accustomed feeling *minus* all its charm ; and I became persuaded, that my love of mankind, and of excellence for its own sake, had worn itself out.   I sought no comfort by speaking to others of what I felt.   If I had loved any one sufficiently to make confiding my griefs a necessity, I should not have been in the condition I was."

It is clear that Mr. Mill felt the deep craving for a more permanent and durable source of spiritual life than any which the most beneficent activity spent in patching up human institutions and laboriously recasting the structure of human society, could secure him,—that he himself had a suspicion that, to use the language of a book he had been taught to make light of, his soul was thirsting for God, and groping after an eternal presence, in which he lived and moved and had his being.   What is strange and almost burlesque, if it were not so melancholy, is the mode in which this moral crisis culminates.   A few tears shed over Marmontel's *Mémoires*, and the fit passed away :—

" Two lines of Coleridge, in whom alone of all writers I have found a true description of what I felt, were often in my thoughts, not at this time (for I had never read them), but in a later period of the same mental malady :—
    ' Work without hope draws nectar in a sieve,
      And hope without an object cannot live.'

In all probability my case was by no means so peculiar as I fancied it, and I doubt not that many others have passed through a similar state ; but the idiosyncrasies of my education had given to the general phenomenon a special character, which made it seem the natural effect of causes that it was hardly possible for time to remove. I frequently asked myself, if I could, or if I was bound to go on living, when life must be passed in this manner. I generally answered to myself, that I did not think I could possibly bear it beyond a year.   When, however, not more· than half that duration of time had elapsed, a small ray of light broke in upon my gloom.   I was reading, accidentally, Marmontel's *Mémoires*, and came to the passage which relates his father's death, the distressed position of the family, and the sudden inspiration by which he, then a mere boy, felt and made them feel that he would be everything to them—would supply the place of all that they had lost. A vivid conception of the scene and its feelings came over me, and I was moved to tears. From this moment my burden grew lighter. The oppression of the thought that all feeling was dead within me, was gone. I was no longer hopeless ; I was not a stock or a stone. I had still, it seemed, some of the material out of which all worth of character, and all capacity for happiness, are made. Relieved from my ever present sense of irremediable wretchedness, I gradually found that the ordinary incidents of life could again give me some pleasure ; that I could again find enjoyment, not intense, but sufficient for cheerfulness, in sunshine and sky, in books, in conversation, in public affairs ; and that there was, once more excitement, though of a moderate kind, in exerting myself for my opinions, and for the public good. Thus the cloud gradually drew off, and I again enjoyed life : and though I had several relapses, some of which lasted many months, I never again was as miserable as I had been."

And the only permanent fruit which this experience left behind it seems to have been curiously slight. It produced a threefold moral result,—first, a grave alarm at the dangerously undermining capacities of his own power of moral analysis, which promised to unravel all those artificial moral webs of painful and pleasurable associations with injurious and useful actions, respectively, which his father had so laboriously woven for him during his childhood and youth ; and further, two notable practical conclusions,—one, that in order to attain happiness (which he "never wavered" in regarding as "the test of all rules of conduct and the end of life"), the best strategy is a kind of flank march,—to aim at something else, at some ideal end, not consciously as a means to happiness, but as an end in itself,—so, he held, may you have a better chance of securing happiness by the way, than you can by any direct pursuit of it,—and the other, that it is most desirable to cultivate the feelings, the passive susceptibilities, as well as the reasoning and active powers, if the utilitarian life is to be made enjoyable. Surely a profound sense of the inadequacy of ordinary human success to the cravings of the human spirit was never followed by a less radical moral change. That it resulted in a new breadth of sympathy with writers like Coleridge and Wordsworth, whose fundamental modes of thought and faith Mr. Mill entirely rejected, but for whose modes of sentiment, after this period of his life, he somehow managed, not very intelligibly, to make room, is very true ; and it is also true that this lent a new largeness of tone to his writings, and gave him a real superiority in all matters of taste to that of the utilitarian clique to which he had belonged, —results which enormously widened the scope of his influence, and changed him from the mere expositor of a single school of psychology into the thoughtful critic of many different schools. But as far as I can judge, all this new breadth was gained at the cost of a certain haze which, from this time forth, spread itself over his grasp of the first principles which he still professed to hold. He did not cease to be a utilitarian, but he ceased to distinguish between the duty of promoting your own happiness and of promoting anybody else's, and never could make it clear where he found his moral obligation to sacrifice the former to the latter. He still maintained that actions, and not sentiments, are the true subjects of ethical discrimination ; but he discovered that there was a significance which he had never before suspected even in sentiments and emotions of which he continued to maintain that the origin was artificial and arbitrary. He did not cease to declaim against the prejudices engendered by the intuitional theory of philosophy, but he made it one of his peculiar distinctions as an Experience-philosopher, that he recommended the fostering of new prepossessions, only distinguished from the prejudices he strove to dissipate by being, in his opinion, harmless, though quite as little based as those in ultimate or objective truth. He maintained as strongly as ever that the character of man is formed by circumstances, but he discovered that the will can act upon circumstances, and so modify its own future capability of willing; and though it is in his opinion circumstances which enable or induce the will thus to act upon circumstances, he thought and taught that this makes all the difference between fatalism and the doctrine of cause and effect as applied to character. After his influx of new light, he remained as strong a democrat as ever, but he ceased to believe in the self-interest principle as universally efficient to produce good government when applied to multitudes, and indeed qualified his democratic theory by an intellectual aristocracy of feeling which to our minds is the essence of exclusiveness. " A person of high intellect," he writes " should never go into unintellectual society, unless he can enter it as an apostle; yet he is the only person with high objects, who can ever enter it at all." You can hardly have exclusiveness more extreme than that, or a doctrine more strangely out of moral sympathy with the would-be universalism of the Benthamite theory. In fact, as it seems to me, Mr. Mill's unquestionable breadth of philosophic treatment was gained at the cost of a certain ambiguity which fell over the root-principles of his philosophy,—an ambiguity by which he won for it a more catholic repute than it deserved. The result of the moral crisis through which Mr. Mill passed at the age of 20 may be described briefly, in my opinion, as this,—that it gave him *tastes* far in advance of his philosophy, foretastes in fact of a true philosophy; and that this moral flavour of something truer and wider, served him in place of the substance of anything truer and wider, during the rest of his life.

The part of the *Autobiography* which I like least, though it is, on the whole, that on which I am most at one with Mr. Mill, is the section in which he reviews his short, but thoughtful Parliamentary career. The tone of this portion of the book is too self-important, too minutely egotistic, for the dry and abstract style in which it is told. It adds little to our knowledge of the Parliamentary struggles in which he was engaged, and nothing to our knowledge of any of the actors in them except himself. The best part of the *Autobiography*, except the remarkable and masterly sketch of his father, Mr. James Mill, is the account of the growth of his own philosophic creed in relation to Logic and Political Economy, but this is of course a part only intelligible to the students of his more abstract works.

On the whole, the book will be found, I think, even by Mr. Mill's most strenuous disciples, a dreary one. It shows that in spite of all Mr. Mill's genuine and generous compassion for human misery and his keen desire to alleviate it, his relation to concrete humanity was of a very confined and reserved kind, —one brightened by few personal ties, and those few not, except in about two cases, really hearty ones. The multitude was to him an object of compassion and of genuine beneficence, but he had no pleasure in men, no delight in actual intercourse with this strange, various, homely world of motley faults and virtues. His nature was composed of a few very fine threads, but wanted a certain strength of basis, and the general effect, though one of high and even enthusiastic disinterestedness, is meagre and pallid. His tastes were refined, but there was a want of homeliness about his hopes. He was too strenuously didactic to be in sympathy with man, and too incessantly analytic to throw his burden upon God. There was something overstrained in all that was noblest in him, this excess seeming to be by way of compensation, as it were, for the number of regions of life in which he found little or nothing where other men find so much. He was strangely deficient in humour, which, perhaps, we ought not to regret, for had he had it, his best work would in all probability have been greatly hampered by such a gift. Unique in intellectual ardour and moral disinterestedness, of tender heart and fastidious tastes, though narrow in his range of practical sympathies, his name will long be famous as that of the most wide-minded and generous of political economists, the most disinterested of utilitarian moralists, and the most accomplished and impartial of empirical philosophers. But as a man, there was in him a certain poverty of nature, in spite of the nobleness in him,—a monotonous joylessness, in spite of the hectic sanguineness of his theoretic creed,—a want of genial trust, which spurred on into an almost artificial zeal his ardour for philosophic reconstruction ; and these are qualities which will probably put a well-marked limit on the future propagation of an influence such as few writers on such subjects have ever before attained within the period of their own lifetime.

XIX

JOHN STUART MILL'S PHILOSOPHY
AS TESTED IN HIS LIFE

1873

In the previous essay attention was drawn to a
remarkable passage in Mr. J. S. Mill's "Autobiography" describing a moral crisis through which he
passed at the age of twenty. I return to it now to
notice the curious bearing which that passage has on
Mr. Mill's philosophy, a bearing of which he seems to
have been himself only obscurely conscious. It will
be remembered that the melancholy into which he
fell was caused, as far as he knew, by suddenly
becoming aware that, if all the chief aims which he
had in life,—his aims as a social and political
reformer,—were in an instant completely effected,
instead of deriving a great happiness from the knowledge, he would have derived none, nay, apparently,
would have been conscious of a great blank, from
the sudden failure of all the moral claims on his
energies. This induced him to consider more carefully the view of life in which he had been educated,
and though he "never wavered in the conviction
that happiness is the test of all rules of conduct and
the end of life," he was led by his new experience to

modify his general conception of life in two directions. First, he made up his mind that though happiness is the only end of life, it must not be *directly* aimed at, if it is to be successfully secured. Next, he discovered that no manipulation of mere outward circumstances without a special culture of the feelings, can so educate the character as to make a man what he should be. Let me take the first point first. Happiness, Mr. Mill said, is the true measure of human good, and the one thing that makes life worth having;—but, nevertheless, he had now discovered that there is this peculiarity about it, that it cannot be obtained by driving directly at it; you must aim at something else, and then you may get happiness in the rebound. "Those only are happy (I thought), who have their minds fixed on some object other than their own happiness; on the happiness of others, on the improvement of mankind, even on some art or pursuit, followed not as a means, but as itself an ideal end. The enjoyments of life (such was now my theory) are sufficient to make it a pleasant thing, when they are taken *en passant*, without being made a principal object. *Once make them so, and they are immediately felt to be insufficient.* They will not bear a scrutinising examination. Ask yourself whether you are happy, and you cease to be so. *The only chance, is to treat not happiness, but some end external to it, as the purpose of life.* Let your self-consciousness, your scrutiny, your self-interrogation, exhaust themselves on that; and if otherwise fortunately circumstanced, you will inhale happiness with the air you breathe, without dwelling on it or thinking about it, without either forestalling it in imagination or putting it to flight by fatal questioning. This theory now became the basis of my philosophy of life. And

I still hold to it as the best theory for all those who have but a moderate degree of sensibility and of capacity for enjoyment, that is, for the great majority of mankind."

Now surely it is a very curious comment on the utilitarian principle, to discover that the one absolute end, according to the utilitarian theory, of human existence, won't bear being made the direct and acknowledged end, but can only be successfully obtained, if at all, as the reward of aiming at something else which is not the true end of human life, but utterly subordinate to it. Is not this a paradox which should suggest to utilitarians the deepest possible suspicion of the truth of the fundamental idea of their philosophy? That the true end of life should be always in the position of the old gentleman's macaroons, which he hid about amongst his papers and books, because he said he enjoyed them so much more when he came upon them unawares, than he did if he went to the cupboard avowedly for them, is surely a very odd compliment to the true end of life. The old gentleman in question did not regard the macaroons as the true end of life; and as a rule, unquestionably what we do regard as the true end of life will bear contemplating and working for as such, while only the secondary and incidental ends are the better for being taken in by side glimpses, in the way which Mr. Mill seems to regard as the best mode of mastering the main end. We hear, no doubt, sometimes of ambitious men who lose the prize of their ambition by aiming directly at power, while others who are not ambitious, and who aim directly at the public good, gain power by the very indifference to power which they show. Of course that is so, but the reason is very plain. It is obvious that it is so because the desire of power itself is universally held to be inferior to the desire of the public good as the ulterior end of power, and because, therefore, the man who has the inferior desire paramount, is distrusted by society whose help is needful for the possession of power, while he who has the superior desire paramount is trusted and aided to obtain it. But in the case of happiness, there is no such reason for the failure of the direct aim. According to the utilitarian, the final aim is happiness, and any other ideal aim is good only so far as it results in happiness. Why, then, should it be necessary to put the cart before the horse, the means before the end ? In the other case, the public good is held to be a better end than the possession of power, to which power should only be a means, and therefore the man who visibly pursues the means with more eagerness than the end, is not likely to succeed even in getting the means. But in the belief of utilitarians, all ideal ends, even including 'good' itself, are only names for the various ways to happiness. It seems, then, to be perfectly inexplicable why it should be advisable to hoodwink yourself as to the end, and aim only at the means for the purpose of attaining the end. Take another case where the pursuit of the end defeats itself. The love of being loved, the love of social admiration and popularity, is, as we all know, apt to defeat itself. The man who aims at being popular and admired is not nearly so likely to be popular and admired as the man who thinks little or nothing about it, but aims simply at his own individual ideal. Here, again, the failure of the direct aim appears to be due to its real and perceived inferiority to those aims which usually secure it. The man who directly aims at getting admiration and esteem will hardly deserve them, for he cannot deserve them without cherishing plenty of aims which would be very likely to risk or forfeit other persons' admiration and esteem.   The man who lives for the good opinions of others cannot be deserving of those good opinions, for he cannot contribute much to teach others, by the independence of his own life, to what those good opinions ought to be given.   In this case also, then, the ill-success of the direct pursuit of admiration is simply due to the fact that that pursuit is a lower aim than any consistent with the attainment of the admiration pursued. But if happiness be the true standard and end of life, why should it fall into the hands only of those who do not directly seek it?   Surely, if it is not safe to pursue it directly, it can only be because it is not the proper end and aim of life,—because while it may be the natural reward of the pursuit of better ends, it is not itself the chief end.   Nothing could well be more improbable than that the one standard and best fruit of human action should be carefully wrapped up in the folds of inferior ends, so that you may come upon it by accident, if you are to taste it properly at all. The very fact that pleasures are so much more enjoyable when they are *not* made the ultimate aims of life, seems to us to be something very like proof that they are not the ultimate aims of life, but only the incidental refreshments which help us to attain them.

Again, it seems to be deducible from Mr. Mill's second result of the moral crisis through which he had passed, that the great principle of "the association of ideas" from which his father and he derived so much, was no more equal to what was expected from it, than the utilitarian theory had been.   He had learned to believe implicitly in the hard-worked doctrine of "the association of ideas," and especially to believe as one application of that doctrine, that "all mental and moral feelings and qualities, whether of a good or of a bad kind, were the results of associations; that we love one thing and hate another, take pleasure in one sort of action or contemplation, and pain in another sort, through the clinging of pleasurable or painful ideas to those things from the effect of education or of experience." All our loves and hatreds, therefore, are, to a very great extent, of an arbitrary kind, dependent on habits of association. "There must always be something artificial and casual in associations thus produced. The pains and pleasures thus forcibly associated with things are not connected with them by any natural tie, and it is therefore, I thought, essential to the durability of these associations, that they should have become so intense and inveterate as to be practically indissoluble before the habitual exercise of the power of analysis had commenced." As it was not so with Mr. Mill himself,—as he found on experiment that he could dissolve again the tie between the personal pleasure he had learnt to associate with the happiness of others and the perception of that happiness, and that he was liable to find himself none the happier for seeing other men suddenly made more prosperous, he at first saw no hope for his own future. The principle of "the association of ideas" had left him at the commencement of his voyage "with a well-equipped ship and a rudder, but no sail," "without any real desire for the ends which I had been so carefully fitted out to work for, no delight in virtue or the general good, but also just as little in anything else." And what was his remedy for this? Why, the cultivation of

the same class of artificial emotions which had thus
left him stranded, only in a direction a little more
inward than before ;—to try and take delight in that
in which he found it so difficult to take delight, by
the help of his imagination,—to try and create anew
more subtle ties of association between the happiness
of others and his own. He thought he knew that
all such feelings were purely artificial, liable to
be dissolved at the touch of analysis into their separate elements,—namely, a pleasure of his own, felt
simultaneously with a perception of another's happiness,—the selfish pleasure being, however, not
connected with the perception of external happiness
by any real tie, except indeed the almost accidental
one of contiguity in time. And yet he encouraged
himself and others to try and form more and more
of these artificial emotions by the use of more subtle
means, and he praises the poet Wordsworth especially
for helping him in this delicate attempt,—for having
developed a happy knack of connecting a personal
pleasure of fancy or imagination with a vivid vision
of the common joys of ordinary human beings.
Indeed this culture of the feelings,—this deliberate
attempt to associate, as Wordsworth's poetry succeeds
in doing, personal enjoyments of the imagination
with the picture of even common-place persons'
common-place happiness,—became a part, he tells us,
of his new philosophy. Instead of only studying as
in time past how to make external circumstances
contribute to the happiness-producing qualities of
human character, he proposed for the future to teach
men that they might so form their internal circumstances as to get various subtle and artificial enjoyments out of associations between their own visionary
faculty and the common ways of vulgar men. It was

true, of course, that this association of ideas was as purely artificial as any one of those associations which had lost their power for him so early. There could be no real connection (except of time and habit) between the thrill of imaginative pleasure in his own intellect, and the perception of the common-place sources of human enjoyment which accompanied it ; but none the less—rather, indeed, the more heartily —would he strive to rivet the artificial link between the two, if it promised, from the very fact of its intellectual character, to survive in minds in which powers of analysis had done so much to dissolve the ordinary rivets of the associative faculty.

I confess I can hardly imagine a more remarkable admission than all this, that the principle of the association of ideas was as insufficient for the explanation of Mr. Mill's real state of mind on this second point, as the utilitarian principle had been for the explanation of his state of mind on the first point. Is it not clear that Mr. Mill's spirit of philanthropic reform was very far indeed from that artificial compound of pleasant associations with a particular kind of effort, which, for example, will sometimes make any study closely associated with childish memories of marmalade or treacle, delightful not only to the child, but to the man ? If that kind of accidental association had been the origin of Mr. Mill's feeling, why should it have grieved him to think that the complete success of his efforts would not make him happy ? According to the associative theory, it was the effort itself which was delightful,—as riding is delightful for the sake of the motion and the air,— not any end which it might attain. The rider does not lose his pleasure in riding, because the place he reaches in his ride is uninteresting to him ; nor the

child his pleasure in the study associated with marmalade or other such delights, because he finds the
ultimate outcome of that study flat and profitless.
Mr. Mill's melancholy itself proves that his reforming
zeal was not due to the artificial compound of associations to which he attributed it.   Analysis does not
weaken the pleasure of memories associated with the
fragrance of violets and primroses and the spring
woods ; and analysis would not have weakened Mr.
Mill's delight in philanthropic labours, if his delight
had ever been due to the mere strength of pleasant
early associations.   The very fact that he lost his
pleasure in the means, directly he fancied that he
felt no delight in the end, shows that it was the presumed nobility of his desire or purpose which had
animated him, and not the mere thrill of pleasant
associations.   Nothing could show more clearly than
this how false is that analysis of his father's school
which makes a desire to consist in "the idea of a
pleasure," instead of a pleasure in the satisfaction
of a desire,—which makes the pleasure generate
the desire, instead of the desire generating the
pleasure.   And then, again, how could the remedy
he discovered for his melancholy have been a
real remedy, if the "associative" theory had been
adequate ? Wordsworth taught him to cultivate
a new class of meditative exercises, by the help of
which he might find personal delight in realising to
himself the common pleasures of the common lot.
But if that remedy were due merely to the forging
of a new link of association between the pleasures of
his own imagination and the lot of the multitude, it
would not have been a remedy at all, for it would
have associated the pains quite as much as the
pleasures of the multitude with this new imaginative

joy.   In point of fact, Wordsworth's poems on the sufferings of common hearts are as fine or finer than those on the joys, and inspire as much meditative rapture in the reader.   The obvious explanation of the moral crisis is that Mill, in the ardour of his study of the means, had lost his full grasp of the meaning of the end in view,—had forgotten, in his various abstract prescriptions for the diminution of social miseries, the comprehensive human detail involved in all popular joys and miseries.   Wordsworth's homely raptures restored to him the fulness of that meaning, helped him to see what common human joys and sufferings were, and so flooded once more the failing well-springs of his sympathy.   But this they could never have done, without the real existence of that sympathy in him.   Wordsworth's poems did not make for him a new feeling, but only appealed to an old one, well-nigh choked up by the fragments of a dreary and false philosophy.   In short, the chief use of Mr. Mill's curious "moral crisis" is to show that, tried by the standard of his own experience, his utilitarianism would not hold water; and again, that the great magic-wand to which such extraordinary transformation scenes are due in the dissolving views of his own and his father's psychology,—the vaunted principle of 'the association of Ideas,'—is quite innocent of nine-tenths of the wonders to which it is supposed to give rise.   Nothing is stranger than that Mr. Mill did not see how ill his own philosophy explains the most unique and intense of his own moral experiences. But it may help others to discover what he never discovered himself,—that his father's psychology was, to a true psychology of human nature, much what the science of the manufacture of artificial flowers is to the science of the growth of blade and leaf and blossom.

XX

J. S. MILL'S ESSAYS ON RELIGION [1]

1874

IT is a little hard on Mr. John Stuart Mill that the school which once treated him as an oracle, now turns round on him, because he has in many respects transgressed its very narrow limits, and speaks of him as little better than a crack-brained fanatic. As far as his wordly repute is concerned, he would have done much better to abide in those tents of Kedar in which he was brought up. The wider and wider flights which he indulged in round the centre of his hereditary philosophy,—a philosophy never really deserted, though he circled so far beyond its customary boundaries that his brethren in the craft almost looked upon him as a renegade and an adventurer,—never had the effect of convincing any fresh class of minds that he was of their kith and kin, though these excursions had the effect of exciting suspicion, jealousy, and contempt amongst his colleagues of the empirical school. And the result is that he has to some extent fallen between the two stools. The Millites of fifteen years ago know him no more. The believers in an

[1] *Nature, the Utility of Religion, and Theism.* By John Stuart Mill. London : Longmans.

Ethics that are something more than utility in disguise, and in a Religion which is something beyond a naked induction from the facts of human life, are disposed to claim him rather as an instance of a mind too great for the philosophy on which he was nourished, than as one great enough to throw off the trammels of its origin and grasp at the higher truth beyond.   And no doubt this is the natural reward of Mr. Mill's candour, and of that expansion of his intellectual apprehensions which his candour betrayed. His step-daughter tells us, in the preface to these essays, that "whatever discrepancies may seem to remain after a really careful comparison between different passages" cannot properly be held to be really fundamental, since he himself was intending to publish the first essay,—that on "Nature,"—in the year 1873, after he had already completed the last of the three, and that which is most religious in tone, namely, that on "Theism."   But in truth, by far the most striking discrepancy in view in these essays is not one between anything in the first essay and the third, but one between a passage in the second essay and the third,—*i.e.*, between the essay on the "Utility of Religion" and that on "Theism."   In the former of these, Mr. Mill expressly declares that an ideal religion,—*i.e.*, a religion without any personal *object*, which consists solely in the cultivation of a particular class of ideal admirations and hopes in relation to humanity, is not only capable of fulfilling "every important function of religion, but would fulfil them better than any form whatever of supernaturalism.   It is not only entitled to be called a religion, it is a better religion than any of those which are ordinarily called by that title."   It is true that even in the course of the same essay, he makes a great exception to this

assertion. He admits that to give up the hope of
reunion in another world with those who have gone
before us in this, is a loss "neither to be denied nor
extenuated. In many cases, it is beyond the reach
of comparison or estimate." But there Mr. Mill is
speaking of a loss to the human heart, more than of
one to the religious affections properly so called. In
the final essay on "Theism," he goes far beyond this,
and deals a blow at the relative influence of mere
religious idealisms of all kinds, as compared with that
of religious supernaturalism properly so called. "It
cannot be questioned," he says, "that the undoubting
belief of the real existence of a Being who realises
our own best ideas of perfection, and of our being in
the hands of that Being as the ruler of the universe,
gives an increase of power to these feelings [aspira-
tions towards goodness] beyond what they can receive
from reference to a merely ideal conception." That
seems to me in direct contradiction of the assertion
that the idealisation of human life is not only a religion,
but a better religion than any which supernaturalism
is capable of affording us. In fact, it is evident that
this progress of his mind from religious idealism towards religious realism, no less than its progress from
something like pure indifference to Christianity to a
genuine enthusiasm for Christ, shows Mr. Mill to have
been unconsciously working his way out of the philosophical system in which he was *cast*, and so earning
for himself the agreeable reputation of presenting to
the world fruit "sour and cankered with a worm at
its wasted core." For my own part, Mr. Mill's progress from a narrow and barren set of word-bound
notions into a true religion of what he himself calls
"hope,"—though it was nothing more,—seems to
show that he had a nature far richer than his intellect

and even an intellect capable of discerning in what direction the growth of his life was breaking down the barrier of his preconceived thoughts.

Still, though these essays contain ample evidence of a growing mind, it would be impossible to say that the great subjects treated in them are treated with the fulness and care exhibited in Mr. Mill's earlier works. They are rather outlines than dissertations, outlines which require filling up to produce their full effect on the reader. There are writers, as there are artists, with whom the rough sketch is even more than the finished work,—whose first designs are more fruitful of impression and suggestion than the elaborately executed picture. But Mr. Mill was never one of that class. Execution and elaboration were his forte ; he exerted half his influence through the fidelity of his detail, and essays like these, which are mere rough outlines, do not produce the characteristic effect of painstaking exhaustiveness which we find in his *Logic*, or his *Examination of Sir William Hamilton*. Consider, for instance, how exceedingly faint and imperfect is his exposition here of the most remarkable and characteristic idea of this work. That idea I take to be that the existence of pain, and evil, and even of contrivance and design, in the Universe, is in itself ample evidence that the Creator of it, if there be a Creator, is either greatly limited in power, or morally imperfect, or both. This is the idea running through all the essays. To Mr. Mill, the Creator, if there be one, must be the Demiurgus of the Gnostics, hampered by the obstructions of some intractable material, not the Omnipotent being of Christian theology. Here are fair specimens of his mode of supporting his view :—

"If there are any marks at all of special design in creation, one of the things most evidently designed is that a large proportion of all animals should pass their existence in tormenting and devouring other animals. They have been lavishly fitted out with the instruments necessary for that purpose ; their strongest instincts impel them to it, and many of them seem to have been constructed incapable of supporting themselves by any other food. If a tenth part of the pains which have been expended in finding benevolent adaptations in all nature had been employed in collecting evidence to blacken the character of the Creator, what scope for comment would not have been found in the entire existence of the lower animals, divided, with scarcely an exception, into devourers and devoured, and a prey to a thousand ills from which they are denied the faculties necessary for protecting themselves ! If we are not obliged to believe the animal creation to be the work of a demon, it is because we need not suppose it to have been made by a Being of infinite power. . . . It is not too much to say that every indication of Design in the Kosmos is so much evidence against the Omnipotence of the Designer. For what is meant by Design ? Contrivance : the adaptation of means to an end. But the necessity for contrivance—the need of employing means—is a consequence of the limitation of power. Who would have recourse to means, if to attain his end his mere word was sufficient ? The very idea of means implies that the means have an efficacy which the direct action of the being who employs them has not. Otherwise they are not means, but an incumbrance. A man does not use machinery to move his arms. If he did, it could only be when paralysis had deprived him of the power of moving them by volition. But if the employment of contrivance is in itself a sign of limited power, how much more so is the careful and skilful choice of contrivances ? Can any wisdom be shown in the selection of means, when the means have no efficacy but what is given them by the will of him who employs them, and when his will could have bestowed the same efficacy on any other means? Wisdom and contrivance are shown in overcoming difficulties, and there is no room for them in a Being for whom no difficulties exist. The evidences, therefore, of Natural Theology distinctly imply that the author of the Kosmos worked under limitations ; that he was obliged to adapt himself to conditions independent of his will, and to attain his ends by such arrangements as those conditions admitted of."

Now, in these and many other passages, Mr. Mill has assumed that Omnipotence is a perfectly intelligible conception to finite minds, the absence of which, or else the absence of perfect goodness, it is perfectly possible for us to prove, by merely producing evidence of pain or evil, and reasoning that if God were both perfectly good in the human sense, and could have removed such pain or evil, he must have done so ;— therefore, either he is not omnipotent, or he is not perfectly good. But this seems to me to be mere groping in the dark. No doubt, goodness must mean, in an infinite being, the same *quality* which it means in a finite one, or it can mean nothing at all to us. But it does not in the least follow that because it must mean the same quality, it must involve, to an omniscient Creator, the same actions. When we, who never have any but the most strictly conditioned and minute power, come to lay down the laws regulating the exercise of his power by a being of infinite power, we are wholly out of our depth. Is, for instance, Omnipotence, or infinitude of power, better shown by the production of an infinitude of grades, and scales, and modes of moral being, or by the production of only one,—the perfect mode ? Is it more an evidence of Omnipotence to exhibit a world of power and joy growing within the very heart of

weakness and suffering, or to limit itself to the creation
of beings in whom there are no paradoxes?   Are a
number of true gaps,—of really dark lines,—in the
moral spectrum of existence, greater proofs of power
than the discovery that within these dark lines themselves there are a host of previously unsuspected
bright lines, the light of which is only the brighter
and tenderer by the contrast with the darkness?
The truth is, that we no sooner come to try the idea
of Omnipotence, than we see how utterly impossible
it is for such a creature as man to say what is, and
what is not, consistent with Omnipotence.   Mr. Mill
lays it down very peremptorily that an Omnipotent
Being who permits the existence of a moral imperfection or a sensitive pain, cannot be a perfect Being.
But what if the very idea of the maximum of moral
being, positively includes, as it well may, the existence
of relations between moral perfection and moral pro-
gression (which last implies, of course, moral imperfection)?   What if a universe consisting exclusively of
perfect beings would be a smaller and poorer moral
universe than one consisting both of perfect and of
imperfect beings, with a real relation between the
two?   What if the world of pain, as treated by God,
includes secrets of moral glory and beauty, of which
a world without pain would be incapable?   Mr. Mill
would apparently reply,—"That only means that
God is not Omnipotent.   If he were, he could do as
much without pain, which is in itself an evil, as with
it.   And if he cannot, he works under conditions
which exclude Omnipotence."   Such I understand,
for instance, to be the drift of the following
passage :—

" It is usual to dispose of arguments of this description
by the easy answer, that we do not know what wise reasons

the Omniscient may have had for leaving undone things which he had the power to do. It is not perceived that this plea itself implies a limit to Omnipotence. When a thing is obviously good and obviously in accordance with what all the evidences of creation imply to have been the Creator's design, and we say we do not know what good reason he may have had for not doing it, we mean that we do not know to what other, still better object—to what object still more completely in the line of his purposes—he may have seen fit to postpone it. But the necessity of postponing one thing to another belongs only to limited power. Omnipotence could have made the objects compatible. Omnipotence does not need to weigh one consideration against another. If the Creator, like a human ruler, had to adapt himself to a set of conditions which he did not make, it is as unphilosophical as presumptuous in us to call him to account for any imperfections in his work ; to complain that he left anything in it contrary to what, if the indications of design prove anything, he must have intended. He must at least know more than we know, and we cannot judge what greater good would have had to be sacrificed, or what greater evil incurred, if he had decided to remove this particular blot. Not so if he be omnipotent. If he be that, he must himself have willed that the two desirable objects should be incompatible ; he must himself have willed that the obstacle to his supposed design should be insuperable. It cannot therefore *be* his design. It will not do to say that it was, but that he had other designs which interfered with it ; for no one purpose imposes necessary limitations on another in the case of a Being not restricted by conditions of possibility."

But this kind of reasoning seems to me purely verbal. Even Mr. Mill can hardly include in his idea of Omnipotence the power to make a thing both *be* and *not be* at the same time. All we *can* mean by Omnipotence is the power to do anything not self-contradictory. Now the power *both* to create the joy appropriate to the heart of pain,—what Mr Arnold calls "the secret of Jesus,"—*and* to keep all pain itself out of existence, is a power to reconcile contradictions.   Mr. Mill might have said, perhaps, that in a strict sense, Omnipotence would imply the power to prevent any association between joy and pain, to keep all the highest joys pure and independent of self-abnegation or sorrow of any kind.   Possibly. But as we really cannot conceive Omnipotence, and yet can compare together two different degrees of power, is it not the more instructive for us to compare the power which brings a divine joy out of pain and self-surrender, with the power which keeps joy quite aloof from pain ; and if we do so, will not the former exercise of power seem much the greater of the two ?   The truth is, Mr. Mill evidently never gave himself the trouble to compare relative degrees of power, or he would have seen at once that a universe containing absolute perfection in an infinite variety of relations with imperfection is a universe which would at once impress us as one of larger scope and power, than one containing only the former. And this is really all man can do towards judging of Omnipotence.   We are utterly unable to conceive the absolute attribute.   But we are able to say whether a power that has created, and is always creating, all shades and degrees and varieties of progressive life, as well as perfect life, is greater or less than one which produces and sustains perfection only. It seems to me perfectly obvious that though moral goodness in man and in God must be of the same kind, it is childish to say that *actions* which are wicked in man, in whom they imply one kind of motive, must be evil in God, who sees the whole scope of what he is doing, and in whom they may imply a totally different kind of motive. You might much more reasonably identify capital punishment with murder, than identify, as Mr. Mill does, the infliction of death by the imposition of natural laws, with murder. Yet this confusion between the moral evil involved in the rash actions of ignorant and finite beings, and the same when proceeding from utterly different motives in an omniscient Being, pervades the whole of Mr. Mill's essay on "Nature."

Such is a characteristic specimen of the feebleness of thought and execution visible in these Essays. It will be replied, no doubt, that even if Mr. Mill were hazy in conceiving, or rather, in his disinclination to test his own power of conceiving, what is meant by Divine Omnipotence, he was not bound to attempt to apprehend an idea which is purely abstract to man, and one over the positive contents of which, as I have always admitted, man can have no command. If we cannot approximate to the meaning of Omnipotence, what business has such a notion in Religion at all, whether Natural or Revealed? To this I can only reply that the idealising faculty, of which even Mr. Mill thinks so highly as the foundation of a religion which is purely aspiration, blends itself so inevitably with the conviction that there is some *real* Power in communication with man, and one infinitely superior to him in knowledge, goodness, might, and life . generally, that it becomes an effort, and an exceedingly unnatural effort, to disentangle the two lines of thought, and maintain that while our ideal faculty leads us to *imagine* One infinite in knowledge, goodness, and power, and our actual experience to *believe in* One infinitely above ourselves in all these qualities, the two modes of thought have no right to coalesce and blend into an actual faith in a God infinite in wisdom, power, and goodness. That such an effort of discrimination is conceivable enough, no one can deny. But I must say I think Mr. Mill has signally failed in his attempt to prove that if God were both perfect morally and also omnipotent, the state of the world could not be what it is. Were the fragment of the universe we see all, his case might be better ; for it will be found that his implicit assumption throughout is, that the world of which we are cognisant is, morally speaking, the whole, instead of (probably) an infinitely small part. Now, it is quite beyond us to affirm that infinite goodness and power must at once annihilate moral evil and misery in all portions of the universe, when we know, as a matter of fact, that the highest pinnacles of goodness and power of which we have any personal knowledge are reached in the struggle with moral evil and misery, and that the absolute exclusion of such evil and misery would have involved the absolute exclusion also of the brightest summits of divine love. On the whole, Mr. Mill's chief endeavour,—his attempt to prove that God, if he exists,—which, as I understand him (though his language wavers), Mr. Mill thought more probable than not,—is either a being of considerable, but very limited power, or not a good being, appears to collapse utterly. But Mr. Mill was precluded by his philosophy from taking note at all of the attestation of God's goodness by the human conscience, and on this side also his essays seem to me deplorably defective for the purpose to which he intended them to contribute.

AMIEL AND CLOUGH

1886

MRS. HUMPHRY WARD, in the interesting introduction which she has prefixed to her beautiful
translation of *Amiel's Journal* indicates, though not
as distinctly as I should like, the close analogy
between Amiel's dread of practical life and Clough's
dread of practical life. And there certainly was a
close analogy, as well as a wide difference, between
their views. Amiel, it is clear, never did anything
at all equal to his powers, through a jealous regard
for his own intellectual independence. He could not
bear to commit himself to any practical course
which would mortgage, as it were, his intellectual
freedom. "The life of thought alone," he wrote,
"seems to me to have enough elasticity and
immensity, to be free enough from the irreparable;
practical life makes me afraid." And yet he knew
that a certain amount of practical life was essential
even to a true intellectual life, only he was anxious
to reduce that practical life to a minimum, in order
that the intellectual life might remain as free as
possible. Clough, too, had the greatest distrust of
the practical ties into which he felt that the tender-

ness of his nature would bring him. The whole drift of his *Amours de Voyage* was to show that fidelity to the intellectual vision is inconsistent with the class of connections into which the sentiments of a tender heart bring men ; and not only inconsistent with them, but so superior to them, that sooner or later the intellect would assert its independence and break through the dreams to which, under the influence of feeling, men submit themselves. The difference between the two men's views was in substance this,—Amiel rather condemned himself for his fastidious assertion of intellectual freedom, and held that had his character been stronger, he would have embarked more boldly on practical life, and would have made a better use of his talents in consequence ; Clough, on the contrary, rather condemned himself for the weakness which allowed him to drift into the closer human ties. He speaks of them as more or less unreal, as more or less illusions, out of which he must some day recover, and return to the assertion of his old intellectual freedom. Amiel reproached himself for not trusting his instincts more, and for living the self-conscious life so much ; Clough reproached himself for letting his instincts dispose of him so much, and for not resisting the illusions into which his instincts betrayed him. It is very curious to compare the different modes in which the Genevan student of Hegelian philosophy and the English student of Greek thought, writing at very nearly the same time, express the ˙same profound terror of embarrassing themselves by all sorts of ties with the narrownesses and imperfections of the human lot. In Amiel's case, however, in spite of the moral self-reproach with which he viewed his intellectual fastidiousness, it was undoubtedly in great measure

the contagion of Hegelian Pantheism which made
him fancy that he could identify himself with the
universal soul of things ; and, on the the other hand,
it was the timidity of an excessive moral sensitiveness
which made it intolerable to him to enter into the
very heart of practical life, with the fear before his
eyes that he might create for himself a lifelong
regret by taking an irreparable false step. This, he
seems to say, was the reason why he never married,
just as it was in part the reason why Clough, in the
Amours de Voyage, makes his hero reproach himself
for his desire to marry. Amiel felt that to enter
into a relation of which he had the highest ideal, and
then to find it far below his ideal, would entail on
him a shame and a remorse which he would simply
be unable to endure. And at the very close of his
life, he writes, with much less than his usual feeling
of self-reproach, a sort of defence of his own detachment from the world. He declares that to have
done anything voluntarily which should bring upon
him an inner shame, would have been unendurable
to him. "I think," he says, "I fear shame worse
than death. Tacitus said, 'Omnia serviliter pro
dominatione.' My tendency is just the contrary.
Even when it is voluntary, dependence is a burden
to me.' I should blush to find myself determined
by interest, submitting to constraint, or becoming the
slave of any will whatever. To me, vanity is slavery,
self-love degrading, and utilitarianism meanness. I
detest the ambition which makes you the liege man
of something or some one. I desire simply to be
my own master. If I had health, I should be the
freest man I know. Although perhaps a little hardness of heart would be desirable to make me still
more independent. . . . I only desire what I am

able for ; and in this way I run my head against no
wall, I cease even to be conscious of the boundaries
which enslave me. I take care to wish for rather
less than is in my power, that I may not even be
reminded of the obstacles in my way. Renunciation
is the safeguard of dignity. Let us strip ourselves,
if we would not be stripped." There you have the
moral secret of Amiel's pride, without the self-blame
with which he usually accompanied it. His pride
was due partly to a moral dread of incurring
responsibilities he could not bear,—"responsibility,"
as he said, "is my invisible nightmare,"—and partly
to the dread of appearing ridiculous and contemptible
to himself if he should find himself unequal to them.
That reminds one of the spirit which Cardinal Newman, as a young man,—before he entered on his
great Tractarian mission,—rebuked in himself :—

> "Time was, I shrank from what was right
>   From fear of what was wrong ;
> I would not brave the sacred fight
>   Because the foe was strong.
>
> But now I cast that finer sense
>   And sorer shame aside ;
> Such dread of sin was indolence,
>   Such aim at Heaven was pride."

Amiel's feeling is absolutely described in these lines,
though the keen censure cast upon it by Dr. Newman
was probably not reflected,—at least in the latter
part of his career,—in Amiel's own conscience. But,
as I have already hinted, there was doubtless another
and a more intellectual strand in the feeling,—the
deep impression that by binding himself in a number
of complex relations to only half-known or utterly
unknown human beings,—to persons who might

disappoint him bitterly, and to children unborn who might turn out anything but the beings to whom he could sustain the close tie of fatherhood,—he should fritter away the power of reverie in which he took such delight. Under the spell of some of the more ambitious German philosophies, he fancied that he could identify himself with the soul of things; and this dreaming power he valued, as it seems to me, much beyond its real worth, if indeed that worth were real at all :—

"My privilege is to be the spectator of my own life-drama, to be fully conscious of the tragi-comedy of my own destiny, and, more than that, to be in the secret of the tragi-comic itself—that is to say, to be unable to take my illusions seriously, to see myself, so to speak, from the theatre on the stage, or to be like a man looking from beyond the tomb into existence. I feel myself forced to feign a particular interest in my individual part, while all the time I am living in the confidence of the poet who is playing with all these agents which seem so important, and knows all that they are ignorant of. It is a strange position, and one which becomes painful as soon as grief obliges me to betake myself once more to my own little *rôle*, binding me closely to it, and warning me that I am going too far in imagining myself, because of my conversations with the poet, dispensed from taking up again my modest part of valet in the piece.—Shakespeare must have experienced this feeling often, and Hamlet, I think, must express it somewhere. It is a *Doppelgängerei*, quite German in character, and which explains the disgust with reality, and the repugnance to public life, so common among the thinkers of Germany. There is, as it were, a degradation, a Gnostic fall in thus folding one's wings and going back again into the vulgar shell of one's own individuality. Without grief, which is the string of this venturesome kite, man would soar too quickly and too high, and the chosen souls would be lost for the race, like balloons which, save for gravitation, would never return from the empyrean."

This passage gives the intellectual facet of the moral feeling at the root of Amiel's "finer sense" and "sorer shame,"—the moral feeling which made him shrink back from all sorts of practical responsibility, lest he should undertake what was beyond him, or lose his complete detachment from the narrowness of life. The two feelings together—the love of reverie in the larger sense, and the dread of responsibility,—sealed up his life almost hermetically within his own bosom, and made him a stranger to the world. He longed to free himself from the narrow shell of his own individuality, and consequently dreaded accepting duties and obligations which would have made that individuality more definite and more oppressive. And yet Amiel felt himself tied down to this narrower life by one string which he could not ignore. When he felt the touch of grief,— which, as Mrs. Browning says, is something more than love, since "grief, indeed, is love, and grief beside,"—then he was aware that he was hemmed within the conditions of a distinct individual lot, that he was seeking something which he could not obtain, while yet he could not suppress, or even wish to suppress, his desire to obtain it. Grief brought home to him the strict limits of his individuality as nothing else brought them home. He could deny himself the more intimate ties of life, but he could not deny himself grief for the severance of such ties as he had. He could not soar above his own individual nature when his heart was bleeding. Then he felt that it was not for him to look at his own life with an impartial imagination, as he would look at any other person's, or as Shakespeare might have looked at one of the characters he created ; for then he felt that throb of anguish which he could not evade by any soaring on imaginative wings, however lofty and free the flight. His intellect was held captive by his griefs,—otherwise, as he said, he might have almost lost his individuality in the ecstasy of reverie.

Clough's attitude of mind towards these practical ties, of which he, too, dreaded the constraining power, was very different. He evidently regarded the intellectual life as the true life, and the life of ordinary man as more or less a condescension to conditions within which his nature could never suffer itself to be long confined. He looked on at the actual experience of his sensitive and tender nature with a little amusement and a good deal of contempt. This is how he makes his hero lecture himself, for instance, when he finds himself gradually falling in love :—

"Yes, I am going, I feel it,—I feel and cannot recall it,—
  Fusing with this thing and that, entering into all sorts
    of relations,
  Tying I know not what ties, which, whatever they are,
    I know one thing,
  Will and must, woe is me, be one day painfully broken—
  Broken with painful remorses, with shrinkings of soul
    and relentings,
  Foolish delays, more foolish evasions, most foolish
    renewals.
  But I have made the step, have quitted the ship of
    Ulysses ;
  Quitted the sea and the shore, passed into the magical
    island ;

Yet on my lips is the *moly*, medicinal, offered of Hermes.
I have come into the precinct, the labyrinth closes
    around me,
Path into path rounding slyly ; I pace slowly on, and
    the fancy
Struggling awhile to sustain the long sequences, weary,
    bewildered,
Fain must collapse in despair ; I yield, I am lost, and
    know nothing ;
Yet in my bosom unbroken remaineth the clue ; I shall
    use it.
Lo, with the rope of my loins, I descend through the
    fissure, I sink, yet
Truly secure in the strength of invisible arms up above
    me,
Still, wheresoever I swing, wherever to shore, or to
    shelf, or
Floor of cavern untrodden, shell-sprinkled, enchanting,
    I know I
Yet shall one time feel the strong cord tighten about
    me,—
Feel it relentless upbear me from spots I would rest in,
    and though the
Rope swing wildly, I faint, crags wound me, from crag
    unto crag re-
Bounding, or, wide in the void, I die ten deaths, ere the
    end, I
Yet shall plant firm foot on the broad lofty spaces I
    quit, shall
Feel underneath me again the great massy strengths of
    abstraction,
Look yet abroad from the height, o'er the sea whose salt
    wave I have tasted."

Evidently, to Clough's mind, "the great massy
strengths of abstraction" were the levels on which
only he could tread firmly, while all the experiences

he was destined to undergo in the region of feeling were a sort of illusion, a sort of dream. To Amiel, grief was the cord which kept him from soaring into aimless reverie. To Clough, thought was the rope which kept him from sinking into the enchantments of a world of illusions. He trusted his thoughts, not his feelings. Clough's feelings charmed him away from the life of thought, and thought brought him home again to the real and solid. Amiel's thoughts charmed him away from the life of feeling, and his feelings brought him home again to the real and solid.

Was either of them right? I should say not. Thought undoubtedly does correct, and correct with most salutary inexorability, the illusions of feeling. And, again, feeling does correct, and correct with equally salutary inexorability, the day-dreams of thought. The man who habitually distrusts his feelings is just as certain to live in a world of illusion as the man who habitually distrusts his thoughts. But undoubtedly Amiel, who allowed the illusion of imaginative reverie and intellectual freedom to govern his career much more absolutely than Clough ever allowed his faith in "the massy strengths of abstract- tion" to govern his career, made the greater mistake of the two. Had Amiel not been so sedulous to ward off the pressure of responsibilities to which he did not feel fully equal, he might doubtless have made mistakes, and entered into relations which he would have found painful to him and a shock to his ideal. But the truth is that those relations which are not all that we desire them to be in human life, which are not ideal relations, are of the very essence of the discipline of the will and of the affections, and no man ever yet escaped them, without escaping one

of the most useful experiences of life. Amiel, like
Clough, was far too much afraid of hampering the
free play of his intellect. No man ever yet did a
great work for the world, without hampering the
free play of his intellect. And yet it is no paradox
to say that no man ever yet had the highest command
of his intellect who had not times without number
hampered its free play, in order that he might enter
the more deeply into the deeper relations of the
human heart.

XXII

MR. ARNOLD'S SUBLIMATED BIBLE

1874

MR. MATTHEW ARNOLD returns, in the October number of the *Contemporary Review*, to his curiously hopeless task of convincing people that the Bible can be read, understood, enjoyed, and turned to the most fruitful moral account, without according any credit to the supernatural experience and beliefs of its writers ;— that all that is most characteristic and noblest in the Bible can be appropriated without even once assuming that its solemnly reiterated, century-long belief in a divine Love and Care, was due to anything but the imaginative mould of poetic thought.   That this hopeless task is undertaken by Mr. Arnold in the interests of the Bible, and with no other view, I heartily believe. He thinks the only scientific substratum in the meaning of the word 'God' which needs to be assumed in reading the Bible, is "the Eternal not-ourselves which makes for righteousness," and that everything which imputes to God affections, and rule, and purpose, is of the nature of poetry, to be paralleled, we suppose, rather in Wordsworth's poetical language about Nature than in the thoughts which children entertain about their father's and mother's care.   This extraordinary view,—which seems to me nearer pure illusion and extravagance than I ever before found in connection with the fine, critical judgment of a man as calm and clear in insight as Mr. Arnold,—he presses with the greatest earnestness through a great part of the book on 'Literature and Dogma,' and now again through the answer he makes to the various criticisms upon it.   Well, if the personifying language about God is mere poetry, it seems quite impossible to say where the poetry of the Bible ends and its serious meaning begins.   Mr. Arnold thinks that all which concerns the law of righteousness and the secret of the sweetness of self-surrender, is serious meaning.   But how is any one to feel the least security of that, who takes Mr. Arnold's view about the poetical vagueness and uncertainty of the language ascribing care and love and judgment to God? Open the Bible anywhere where it speaks of righteousness in connection with God,—and that is almost everywhere,—and see whether there is any more exactness or realism, any less poetic vagueness in speaking of the former than of the latter.   "The Lord hath made known his salvation; his righteousness hath he openly showed in the sight of the heathen.   He hath remembered his mercy and his truth towards the House of Israel; all the ends of the earth have seen the salvation of God."   Now, that is an average passage, chosen almost at random, and not peculiar in any way in its mention of "God" or of "righteousness."   Is it in any degree easier to ascribe a vague, poetical sense to the words in this passage which express activity, will, love, mercy, than to the word "righteousness" itself? If one were painfully to paraphrase the passage, so as to get rid of all personification in it, one might construe it

as asserting that a specific stream of tendency had resulted in man's knowledge of his proper wholeness and
integrity, and had further resulted in a clear conviction
on the part of foreign races that tendencies "making
for righteousness" are in the ascendant on earth;
nay, that a certain similarity between the existing
drift of things and that of former days, even suggests
an analogy between the recurrences of specific results
after specific historical causes, and that which in the
life of a man we should call *memory* of his former acts
of mercy and fidelity; and further, that the whole
Earth had come to know in what human wholeness
and integrity consist. Now, is not such a paraphrase
far more monstrous and alien to the Bible, in a literary sense, far less in keeping with the whole tenor of
its thought, than one which should keep the literal
meaning of all the personal words, but which should
sublimate the meaning of 'righteousness' into a mere
disposition to accommodate oneself to the supreme
volition, no matter what that might be?

I maintain that if Mr. Arnold will treat the most
characteristic thoughts and words of the Bible as
vague, poetical metaphors, he cannot by any possibility be allowed to assign a strict and uniform interpretation to the one word on which his whole
construction of the Bible rests. I am not arguing
that "righteousness" has no specific meaning in the
Bible. I believe it has. In the Fifteenth Psalm, for
instance, the righteous man is described as one who
speaketh the truth in his heart, backbiteth not with
his tongue, nor doeth evil to his neighbour; in whose
eyes a vile person is contemned, but who honoureth
them that fear the Lord; who sweareth to his own
hurt and changeth not; who is not an usurer, and
who takes no reward to injure the innocent. No

description can be more definite, so far as it goes, and there are plenty of passages where similar descriptions of what is meant by righteousness are given. But descriptions of God's love and care and judgment quite as definite are given quite as repeatedly. "The Lord is merciful and gracious, slow to anger, and plenteous in mercy. He will not always chide, neither will he keep his anger for ever. He hath not dealt with us after our sins, nor rewarded us according to our iniquities; for as the heaven is high above the earth, so great is his mercy towards them that fear him." Now how is it conceivable that language of this kind should be treated as poetical metaphor, if the language describing human righteousness is to be treated as exact definition? Mr. Arnold must choose between two alternatives. He must evaporate the whole; must make the prophecies and teachings of the Bible a mere series of imaginative lyrics, in which no one can say, with any certainty, what is fancy and what is fact; or he must take the personal language about God as straightforwardly as he takes the moral language about man. It is not criticism at all, it is playing fast-and-loose with language in the most ridiculous manner, to regard the long series of passionate appeals to God by his faithfulness and his mercy and his truth as mere efforts of poetry, while all the words describing the moral conceptions of man are interpreted with scientific strictness. If Mr. Arnold compares the personifying language of the Bible about God, with the personifying language of Wordsworth about Nature, I can only ask where it appears that Wordsworth seriously inculcates prayer to Nature, or treats distrust in the promises of Nature as a sin, or addresses her in the matter-of-fact, down-right, eager mood of real expectation and confidence so common in the Psalms, "Thy word is a lamp unto my feet and a lantern to my path. I have sworn and I will perform it, that I will keep thy righteous judgments. I am afflicted very much. Quicken me, O Lord, according unto thy word." Could 'Nature' be addressed in that way? The truth is, that one has a real difficulty in believing, what is, nevertheless, evident, that Mr. Arnold is serious on this head. He seems to me to have taken up a purely childish position in relation to it. Of course, a rational man may hold that the Bible represents nothing but the imaginative side of man, more or less mixed with other purely human apprehensions. But it seems to me very nearly impossible for a rational man to assert that the authors of the Bible used the personal language about God in any less serious and profoundly convinced sense than that in which they spoke of the secrets of man's moral experience. The teaching as to the human and as to the divine character may stand together or fall together. But it is not serious criticism, it is playing on human credulity, to maintain that the prophets are less convinced of God's care and love and mercy and judgment, in relation to man, than they are of the best mode of attaining inward peace. Sublimate the Bible, if you will. But at least let Mr. Arnold be a reasonable critic, and sublimate all its serious teaching together. He cannot pick and choose, and say that this is poetry, because he does not think its drift can be 'verified'; and that that, on the other hand, is prose, because he has persuaded himself that he has 'verified' it.

And so, again, in relation to Mr. Arnold's view as to "the secret of Jesus,"—dying that we may live, —giving up the eager human longing, that we may

have the higher and purer life which consists in renouncing your own will for something better.   No
one can write more eloquently of this than Mr. Arnold.
No one can, so far, interpret more truly and delicately
the teaching of our Lord and of St. Paul.   But it is
not criticism, it is not sense, to separate their language
on this subject from their language as to the springs
of the new life which they gain by dying to this.
Nothing can be more explicit than the language held.
It is not the sweetness of mere renunciation, it is the
sweetness of the life in Him who demands the renunciation, which Christ and St. Paul preach.   If you
are to suppose that they are only talking poetry on
the latter head, why not on the former also?   The
secret of the sweetness of renunciation is set forth in
such words as these :—" I have glorified thee on the
earth: I have finished the work which thou gavest me
to do.   And now, O Father! glorify me with thine own
self, with the glory which I had with thee before the
world was."   " In all these things we are more than
conquerors, through Him who loved us.   For I am
persuaded, that neither death, nor life, nor angels, nor
principalities, nor powers, nor things present, nor
things to come, Nor height, nor depth, nor any other
creature, shall be able to separate us from the love
of God, which is in Christ Jesus our Lord."   Now,
is it conceivable that any critic can read this language
and think of the personification of God in it as
poetical metaphor, and not serious in every sense in
which the secret of self-renunciation is regarded as
serious ?   Why, the gain of the self-renunciation is the
gain of God's love ; and without God's love, where
would be the gain ?   St. Paul even goes so far as to say,
perhaps with some exaggeration, that without this
hope of a life in God after death, he should be of all

men the most miserable. And what sane critic could substitute for the personal language in such passages as these, Mr. Arnold's equivalent for God, " the Eternal not-ourselves that makes for righteousness,"—I do not mean, of course, for the clumsiness of the literary effect, *that* Mr. Arnold would grant at once,—but even with any hope of saving the sense ? How could an impersonal tendency glorify Christ with the glory that he had with it before the world was ? How could an impersonal tendency be so dear to St. Paul as to make him more than a conqueror, and wrap him in the ecstasy of a perfect union ? These are questions which do not bear even asking. Mr. Arnold seems to be merely imposing on us. It is open to him to maintain that the Bible is a dream, but it is not open to him to maintain that it never seriously expresses faith in the personal life and love and goodness of God, in the very same sense in which it attaches the most intense moral significance to the righteousness of man.

XXIII

MATTHEW ARNOLD AS CRITIC

1888

THE volume of *Essays in Criticism* which had been collected by Matthew Arnold from various periodicals before his death, and which has just been published by Messrs. Macmillau with a few admirable words of preface,—I suppose by Lord Coleridge,—is a worthy memorial of the great critic we have lost. For sureness as well as confidence of literary judgment, I doubt whether Matthew Arnold had his equal. Some very good critics are sure without having sufficient confidence to speak out plainly their sure judgments when those judgments are likely to be unpopular. Others,—not usually good,—are confident without being sure. But it is very rarely that we meet with a critic so nearly infallible as Matthew Arnold on any question of the finer taste, who has the confidence to express a judgment that is not welcome to the public at large with the calm authority of Matthew Arnold. I cannot give a better instance of what I mean than the authority with which he declines to regard the sentiment expressed in Burns's singularly popular poem, "A man's a man for a' that," as expressing the core of

Burns's most serious conviction. "The accent of high seriousness born of absolute sincerity," he decides, is not there. "Surely, if our sense is quick, we must perceive that we have not in these passages" [one of which is chosen from "A man's a man for a' that"] "a voice from the very inmost soul of the genuine Burns ; he is not speaking to us from those depths ; he is more or less preaching. And the compensation for admiring these passages the less, for missing the perfect poetic accent in them, will be that we shall admire more the poetry where that accent is found." This is admirably said, and the general judgment on Burns is as sound as it is incisive :—"His genuine criticism of life, when the sheer poet in him speaks, is ironic ; it is not—

> 'Thou Power Supreme, whose mighty scheme
>   These woes of mine fulfil,
> Here firm I rest ; they must be best,
>   Because they are Thy will :'

it is far rather 'Whistle owre the lave o't.' Yet we may say of. him, as we say of Chaucer, that of life and the world as they come before him, his view is large, free, shrewd, benignant,—truly poetic therefore,"—but still that Burns has not "the accent of the poetic virtues of the highest masters." Matthew Arnold sees with admiration "the spring," the "bounding swiftness" in Burns's manner. He reckons Burns a far greater force than Chaucer, though "the world of Chaucer is fairer, richer, more significant than that of Burns ; but when the largeness and freedom of Burns gets full sweep, as in 'Tam O'Shanter,' or still more in that puissant and splendid production, 'The Jolly Beggars,' his world may be what it will, his genius triumphs over it." No bolder and yet surer piece of criticism was probably

ever written than that which virtually puts not only
"Tam O'Shanter," but "The Jolly Beggars," above
"The Cotter's Saturday Night" and "A man's a man
for a' that,"—and yet the criticism is sound.   In the
two latter pieces, Burns was expressing what he *wished*
to feel, but on the whole did not succeed in feeling,
though it would have been better for him if he had
succeeded.   But in the two former he gave his genius
full swing, and succeeded in impressing on them a
perfectly superb effect of force and reality.   Of "The
Jolly Beggars" Matthew Arnold justly remarks, that in
spite of its hideousness, squalor, and even bestiality,
"it has a breadth, truth, and power which make the
famous scene in Auerbach's Cellar, of Goethe's *Faust*,
seem artifical and tame beside it, and which are only
matched by Shakespeare and Aristophanes."

Bolder and surer criticism than that it would be
hard to find, and we shall not easily find it again,
now that Mr. Arnold has left us.   But when I speak
of Mr. Arnold's criticism as "sure," I should limit
this judgment to his criticism of that sort of poetry
which aims at giving us reality, for occasionally,
in dealing with Shelley, who certainly managed to
create an unearthly sphere of his own and to fill it
with music, Arnold's judgment is not so sure.   And
one might gather as much from the theoretic part of
his critical essays.   His chief conception of the
sphere of true poetry is what he calls the higher
criticism of life, and on all poetry which can properly
be called the criticism of life, whether it be criticism
of the life of a flower or a bird, or criticism of the
higher life of man, his judgment is most sure.   But
poets like Shelley cannot be tested by any standard
of this kind.   They create a world of their own, and
it will be the few rather than the many who enjoy

such a world and can live in it. And for appreciation of that kind of poetry, Matthew Arnold's judgment, fine as it was, was not light and flexible enough. He loved clear outlines and unambiguous drift. He did not understand either the fine witchery of Shelley, or his air spirits and earth spirits, his power of wailing like a banshee, or of singing a song of triumph over the evanescence of his shadowy conceptions. That was not criticism of life, and Matthew Arnold's vivacity of sympathy hardly extended to worlds of which it was so difficult to judge whether or not they really call up a corresponding world of emotion that has a beauty and unity of its own, though it is not ordinary human emotion, and does not answer to the ordinary exciting causes of human joy or grief. Of course, there will necessarily be something hazardous in the criticism of poets who are, like Shelley, essentially poets of the unreal, who, when their spell is most powerful, make shadows take the place of things, and fill the ear with the vibrations of a new æolian harp constructed out of the sensitive nerves of a unique nature. Sure as Mr. Arnold's criticism is when he is dealing with Milton, or Gray, or Burns, or Wordsworth, or Keats, or Byron, he is thrown out when he touches Shelley, more perhaps by the want of a standard by which to judge him, than by want of sympathy, but probably to some extent by both causes. Indeed, this defect is connected with one of Arnold's merits as a critic. He always asked himself so pointedly what it was that a poet meant to convey, and whether he had really succeeded in conveying it, that his method almost debarred him from answering the very difficult question whether Shelley's evanescent lights and shadows and essences and potencies of melody, did or did not constitute a genuine new creation at all. The very qualities which made him a most sure critic of poets who, to use his own phrase, attempted the highest criticism of life, made him an uncertain critic of poets who attempted something altogether different,—the composition of a fantasia of which the only test was its delightfulness to the ear that heard it. Matthew Arnold's mind was essentially positive. He knew what was false and true to life, and hardly ever failed to point out where the truth was, where the falsetto note came in. But his confidence in this positive ear of his was a disqualification for criticising those unique efforts to supply both the world to be criticised and the standard of criticism, in which once and again strange spirits like Shelley's have attained success.

Matthew Arnold as a critic has rendered us all his debtors not only by the substance of his criticisms, but by their style. He has celebrated duly the grand style of Milton, and he has done something to give to his own literary judgments that air of sincerity, confidence, and clear authority which give to true criticisms almost all their charm and half their finality. Here is Matthew Arnold's fine criticism on Milton's style :—

" Virgil, whom Milton loved and honoured, has at the end of the *Æneid* a noble passage, where Juno, seeing the defeat of Turnus and the Italians imminent, the victory of the Trojan invaders assured, entreats Jupiter that Italy may nevertheless survive and be herself still, may retain her own mind. manners, and language, and not adopt those of the conqueror.

'Sit Latium, sint Albani per secula reges !'

Jupiter grants the prayer; he promises perpetuity and the future to Italy—Italy reinforced by whatever virtue the Trojan race has, but Italy, not Troy. This we may take as a sort of parable suiting ourselves. All the Anglo-Saxon contagion, all the flood of Anglo-Saxon commonness, beats vainly against the great style but cannot shake it, and has to accept its triumph. But it triumphs in Milton, in one of our own race, tongue, faith, and morals. Milton has made the great style no longer an exotic here; he has made it an inmate amongst us, a leaven, and a power. Nevertheless he, and his hearers on both sides of the Atlantic, are English, and will remain English—

'Sermonem Ausonii patrium moresque tenebunt.'

The English race overspreads the world, and at the same time the ideal of an excellence the most high and the most rare abides a possession with it for ever."

Has Matthew Arnold not almost rendered Milton's poetic style into prose,—prose far better than Milton's prose, which was turgid and violent,—prose which is at once stately and lucid, sonorous and simple, graceful and vigorous?

XXIV

M. RENAN

1883

THERE is hardly so curious a study among the many curious autobiographical studies to be found in English literature, as that which M. Renan has recently given to the world in the *Revue des Deux Mondes*, under the title of " Memories of Infancy and Youth." It is much franker, if I remember Gibbon's autobiography accurately, than that of Gibbon, though it has a somewhat similar ring of calm self-complacency. Of course, there is nothing in M. Renan of Gibbon's old-fashioned pomp. Renan is, as he says, a man of his age, and the culture of his age ridicules the pomp of manner which the culture of Gibbon's age admired, though, by the way, there is a little of the same stiltedness in the records remaining from Renan's youth. The letter to his Director, in which he avowed his doubts and his inability to return to Saint Sulpice, has the air of a somewhat pompous young man. In it he magnificently reproaches God for having brought him into such straits, and takes credit to himself for the generous confidence which, in spite of this ill-treatment, he still placed,—though he did not continue to place it very long,—in God's providence and government.   There is a note of grandiosity in this : —" In fact, Monsieur, when I contemplate the inextricable thfead in which God has entangled me during the sleep of my reason and my liberty, at a time when I was following docilely the path which he traced before me, desolating thoughts spring up in my soul. . . . I have never doubted that a wise and good Providence guides the universe, guides me to conduct me to my goal.   Nevertheless, it is not without effort that I have been able to give a formal contradiction to apparent facts.   I often tell myself that common good-sense is hardly capable of appreciating the government of Providence, whether it be of humanity, or of the universe, or of the individual. The isolated consideration of facts would never lead one into optimism.   It needs some courage to make this generous admission to God, in spite of experience. I hope never to hesitate on this point, and whatever may be the evils which Providence still reserves for me, I shall always believe that he leads me to my greatest possible good, by way of the least possible evil."   However, this generous admission was not persevered in for any very long time.   M. Renan had hardly emancipated himself from the rule of the Seminary, when he withdrew his confidence from Providence.   With his belief in verbal inspiration, the whole of his theological creed collapsed at once. For him, everything appears to have depended on his power of retaining his belief that the Book of Judith was not a physical impossibility; that the second part of Isaiah was written by the same prophet who wrote the first part; that the Fourth Gospel is never in the smallest contradiction with the first three, nor any of these last with each other.

So soon as this belief went, all belief went ; and this though, so far as I know, the Roman Catholic Church has never yet defined the meaning it attaches to the word "inspiration," or the amount of those finite and human misconceptions the traces of which may be permitted to remain embodied amidst the evidences of an overruling divinity. Doubtless, the Protestant Church has usually inclined to a much greater liberality in this matter than the great majority of Roman Catholic divines. Still, there seems to be very little excuse in the actual decisions of the Roman Church for M. Renan's eagerness—I may almost call it—to stake everything on the question of the verbal infallibility of Scripture. He repeats again and again in these recollections of his youth that to detect Scripture in a single minute error was enough for him. "Let us assume that amidst the thousand skirmishes in which criticism and the apology of the orthodox faith have engaged, there have been some in which, by accident and contrary to appearances, the orthodox side is right ; it is impossible that it is right a thousand times in its wager, and it is enough that it should be wrong in but a single instance for the thesis of inspiration to be annihilated." Of course if the Roman Church had ever committed itself absolutely to the rigid accuracy of every number and every human phrase in Scripture, clear evidence of a single error would be enough to extinguish belief in the infallibility of that Church. But the Roman theologians utterly deny that this is so, and at all events, M. Renan knew perfectly well that in other Christian communions there is ample liberty of criticism of the human documents in which revelation is embodied, and ample freedom to combine this liberty of criticism with a profound belief in the reality of that revelation. But in truth, if we may trust his account of himself, that opinion which he describes as being formed "by a sort of impersonal concretion outside oneself, of which one is in some manner nothing but the spectator," was at work almost immediately after his exit from the Catholic Church, forming itself into the most polished concrete of absolute sceptical impenetrability to supernatural influence imaginable by man. Supernatural influence has, indeed, no existence for M. Renan, except as a dream of the past, which stimulates more than anything else the play of his good-humoured irony and his genial contempt. It is true that he speaks of his first impressions of life after giving up Christianity as very desolate impressions,—impressions of a world from which all that was great had vanished away; but even this portion of his reminiscences does not convey to us any very deep feeling of reality. One gathers rather that it was the giving-way of the ecclesiastical framework of life that M. Renan missed, much more than his faith itself. "Like an enchanted circle," he says, "Catholicism embraces the whole life with so much force that, when one is deprived of it, everything seems *fade* and sad. I felt terribly like an exile (*dépaysé*). The universe produced on me the effect of a dry, cold desert. From the moment that Christianity ceased to be the truth, the rest appeared to me frivolous, and hardly worth taking an interest in. The collapse of my life upon itself left me with a feeling of vacuity, like that which follows a fever or a disappointed love. The struggle which had entirely occupied me had been so intense that I now found everything narrow and contemptible. The world

seemed to me mediocre and poor in virtue.   What I
saw appeared to me a fall, a decadence ; I regarded
myself as lost in an ant-hill of pigmies."   That has
more in it of the dejection which attends the loss of
the sense of a mighty organisation behind one, than
the loss of a mighty companionship within one.
And, indeed, there is no evidence at all in these
reminiscences that M. Renan ever did lose this
conviction, or, indeed, that he ever held it as more
than a creed vouched for by the highest dogmatic
authority.   It is true, he says in one place, " The
idea that in abandoning the Church, I should
remain faithful to Jesus, got full control of me ; and
if I had been capable of a belief in apparitions, I
should certainly have seen Jesus saying to me,
'Abandon me, in order to be my disciple.'"   But, as
a matter of fact, whatever, as M. Renan so quaintly
says, he might or might not have seen, if he had
been "capable of" a particular belief,—which I take
the liberty of remarking that he no more knows,
than any of us know what we might see, if we
thought something different from what we do think,
—there is nothing approaching to the attitude of
discipleship towards Christ visible either in this or
any other of his writings known to the world.   On
the contrary, what one feels is that from the moment
when he abandoned Christianity, M. Renan took
Christ under his historical patronage, and made a
sort of vow to himself to be a generous sceptic,
courteous and benignant to his old Roman-Catholic
masters, full of gracious sentiment to his former
Lord, and constant to maintain the fascinating
character of the childish faith which he had
deliberately renounced.   Unlike Gibbon, M. Renan
would mingle suavity with all his scepticism, thereby,

as he well knew, making it all the more effective. The scorn which is really kindly and appreciative, tells much more effectively than the scorn which is purely contemptuous. When you can afford frankly to praise,—as you praise a child,—there is no danger of your returning to adore. M. Renan certainly misled himself, if he supposed, as he tells us, that the papers, even of his earliest sceptical period, were in any sense Christian. No doubt, they expressed "a lively liking [*goût*] for the Evangelical ideal, and for the character of the Founder of Christianity," just as they also expressed a lively liking for the fathers of Saint Sulpice. So Wordsworth had undoubtedly a lively liking for the little girl at Goodrich Castle, who spoke of her dead brother and sister as still belonging to the little family of which she herself was the joy, and as lying under the grass to listen while she sat and sang to them. But the whole spirit of M. Renan's reminiscences, as well as of his better known writings, belies the notion that he ever carried a Christianity of any sort out of his Roman Catholicism. From the time he left the Roman Church, he lived apparently under a sort of honourable understanding with himself, that he would be tender and gentle and generous in his recognition of the better aspects of the religion he had thrown off. But every trace of obedience to it, of reverence for it, of inward piety towards it, disappeared finally from the moment when he escaped into the shade,—as he reminds himself that chrysalises do when they are about to assume the form of a butterfly,—when he cast off his *soutane*, and took the dress of a layman.

Nothing is so disagreeable in these reminiscences as Renan's account of the change which his scepticism

gradually made in his estimate of moral conduct.
It is not, indeed, always easy to say when M. Renan
is talking seriously, and when he is talking in a tone
of deliberate badinage. He has a large fund of mild
humour, and does not scruple to avail himself of it
to mystify his readers. When, for instance, he tells
us of his publisher's first visit to him, and of that
imposing stamped agreement which M. Lévy brought
with him, the very sight of which prevented M.
Renan from making the few suggestions which were
in his mind to obtrude, lest so beautiful a sheet of
paper should be lost, he is no more serious than
when he tells us how he had to renounce travelling
by omnibus, because the conductors had ceased to
regard him as a passenger of whom any account
need be taken. Possibly he is not quite serious
when he explains how pleasant it is in the East to
go accompanied by an armed man whom one
positively forbids to use his arms, or how much he
should like to have the power of life and death over
every one, in order not to use it; or how he should
delight to keep slaves, solely in order to pet them
and make them adore him. But if he is not serious
when he tells us that after being emancipated from
Christianity, he continued to live a strictly moral life
only because no man should allow himself more than
one breach of social *convenances* at the same time,
and that, therefore, and therefore only, he can boast
of having been loved only by four women, his mother,
his sister, his wife, and his daughter; or again, when
he says that he soon discovered the vanity of the
virtue of chastity, "as of all others," and recognised
especially that Nature does not in any way "attach any
importance to man being chaste"; when he assures
us that there is "something ridiculous in being

virtuous, when one is not obliged to be so by any professional obligation"; that "the priest, recognising it as his object in life to be chaste, just as the soldier recognises it as his to be brave, is almost the only one who can, without ridicule, hold to the principles concerning which morality and fashion indulge themselves in such strange combats"; if M. Renan is not serious, I say, in all this part of his autobiography, I can only express my opinion that the net result is very nearly as bad as if he is. To write in this fashion, with the wish to mystify the world, and make every one believe that morality, like religion, is mere matter for badinage, is at least as bad as holding specifically that unprofessional virtue is rather ridiculous than otherwise. M. Renan says that a good deal of his gentleness is probably due to a bottom of indifference,—and, on the whole, I agree with him. Complacency with himself, a sentiment of kindliness to the world at large, a deeply-rooted horror of the selfishness of exclusive friendships, a vague feeling of gratitude to some one, "without exactly knowing to whom I ought to be grateful,"—this last naturally enough, as M. Renan is deeply convinced that there is no appreciable trace of the action of any Will in the world superior to that of man,—such is the stock of moral virtues of which M. Renan has made salvage, after the wreck of his faith. In fine, they do not leave me with any very deep respect for this smooth, humorous, learned, industrious, imaginative man, who has slipped so easily along the "charming promenade" of his extremely sentimental existence.

PROFESSOR TYNDALL ON PHYSICAL AND MORAL NECESSITY

1877

PROFESSOR TYNDALL is a great populariser, and I cannot doubt that his attempt at the Midland Institute on Monday to reason from the principle that the quantity of physical energy in the world is a fixed amount, and that none is ever either lost or gained, to the principle of moral necessity, namely, that every man is merely what his circumstances and his wishes make him, his wishes being as truly circumstances dependent on the hereditary and other conditions of his organisation as any other of the determining forces around him,—may have a great effect on the ripening intelligence of the country, if only from the influence naturally attaching to his name. But though he puts his case with his usual force and vivacity, he adds nothing whatever to the substance of what has been stated and re-stated hundreds of times by his predecessors in the same field. Indeed, the force with which he states the case conduces, as all force of statement naturally must, to a clear indication of the points at which his view entirely fails to meet the facts; and the natural candour of a genuinely scientific man renders the exposition of these glaring deficiencies of his view more striking still. I hope, therefore, that those who do not merely accept Professor Tyndall's authority as conclusive, but who go over the same ground without his obvious bias towards the physical explanation of our moral nature, will soon find themselves pulled up by difficulties far more striking than any which are involved in the view of life which Professor Tyndall was endeavouring to refute. These difficulties accordingly I shall attempt to point out, and I shall succeed best probably in doing this by humbly following in Professor Tyndall's footsteps, only pushing to their legitimate consequences all the principles of his address.

Professor Tyndall teaches us, then, first, that as a given stock of heat is generated by a given amount of motion, and that the same amount of motion may be produced by the loss of that stated amount of heat, so also the force we employ in muscular exertion is the force due to a given amount of fuel supplied to the body. The oxidation of food within the body leads to the development of an exactly equivalent amount of heat, some of it within the body, some of it outside it. "We place food in our stomachs as so much combustible matter. It is first dissolved by purely chemical processes, and the nutritive fluid is poured into the blood. Then it comes into contact with atmospheric oxygen, admitted by the lungs. It unites with oxygen, as wood or coal might unite with it in a furnace. The matter-products of the union, if I may use the term, are the same in both cases,—namely, carbonic acid and water. The force-products are also the same, heat within the body, or heat and work outside the body. Thus far, every action of the body belongs to the domain either of physics or of chemistry." Further, Professor Tyndall shows us how the action of the nerves consists in liberating a vast amount of stored force which is latent in the muscles, just as the power of steam is latent in the steam-engine till some one opens a valve which sets the steam to work, or as the electric force is stored in a galvanic battery till some one completes the circuit which sets the battery to work. It is not that the nervous energy directly produces the muscular energy, but that it liberates muscular energy which had been previously stored up. Then Professor Tyndall quotes from Lange the following illustration of this liberation of pent-up force :—

" A merchant sits complacently in his easy chair, not knowing whether smoking, sleeping, newspaper-reading, or the digestion of food occupies the largest portion of his personality. A servant enters the room with a telegram bearing the words ' Antwerp, etc.—Jones and Co. have failed.'—' Tell James to harness the horses.' The servant flies. Up starts the merchant, wide awake, makes a dozen paces through the room, descends to the counting-house, dictates letters and forwards despatches. He jumps into his carriage, the horses snort, and their driver is immediately at the Bank, on the Bourse, and among his commercial friends. Before an hour has elapsed he is again at home, when he throws himself once more into his easy chair, with a deep-drawn sigh, ' Thank God, I am protected against the worst ! And now for further reflection.' This complex mass of action, emotional, intellectual, and mechanical, is evolved by the impact upon the retina of the infinitesimal waves of light coming from a few pencil-marks on a bit of paper. We have, as Lange says, terror, hope, sensation, calculation, possible ruin, and victory compressed into a moment. What caused the merchant to spring out of his chair ? The contraction of his muscles. What made his muscles contract ? An impulse of the nerves, which lifted the proper latch, and liberated the muscular power. Whence this impulse ? From the centre of the nervous system. But how did it originate there ? This is the critical question."

And Professor Tyndall warns us not to assume that it was a soul or intelligence within the body which, stimulated by an act of knowledge and a consequent emotion of apprehension, set all this chain of nervous antecedents and muscular consequents in motion, lest we try to explain the little known by the less known, or indeed, by the absolutely unknown. On the contrary, he assures us that the only scientific procedure is to refer this impulse originating in the centre of the nervous system to other changes in nerve-tissue which have preceded it, seeing that all our scientific knowledge teaches us to refer physical effects to physical causes. "Who or what is it," says Professor Tyndall, "that sends and receives these messages through the bodily organism ? You picture the muscles as hearkening to the commands sent through the motor-nerves, and you picture the sensor-nerves as the vehicles of incoming intelligence ; are you not bound to supplement this mechanism by the assumption of an entity which uses it ? In other words, are you not forced by your own exposition into the hypothesis of a free human soul ? That hypothesis is offered as an explanation or simplification of a series of phenomena more or less obscure. But adequate reflection shows that, instead of introducing light into our minds, it increases our darkness. You do not in this case explain the unknown in terms of the known, which, as stated above, is the method of science, but you explain the unknown in terms of the more unknown." "The warrant of science extends only to the statement that the terror, hope, sensation, and calculation of Lange's merchant are psychical phenomena, produced by or associated with the molecular motion set up by the waves of light in a previously prepared brain." On these principles, then, it is obvious that heat and motion, and nervous action and muscular tissue, and the mode in which touching a valve liberates steam, are all phenomena which are knowable in a sense in which the subject that knows them is not knowable. It is scientific to be quite certain that "a bowler who imparts a velocity of thirty feet to an 8-lb. ball consumes in the act one-tenth of a grain of carbon." But it is thoroughly unscientific to be certain that there is "some one" who has this knowledge and who acts on it. It is scientific to be sure of the laws of motion. It is thoroughly unscientific to be sure of the existence of the person who is thus sure. The self which is the assumed centre of all knowledge, is a mere centre of darkness, and while various true propositions can be stated, the assertion that I or any one can *know* them to be true is a false and unscientific one, which confounds the relation between phenomena with an unknowable personality that has no relation to them. But then, if there be no true nominative to the verb "to know," does not that throw doubts at least as great on the object of knowledge? If I seem to myself to have observed and mastered the laws of heat and motion, and am yet going quite astray in assuming that there is any self to master those laws, how am I to be certain that the heat or motion which is the thing I appear to know, has any existence either? Deny all reality, as Professor Tyndall teaches us to do, to the nominative of the sentence, "I know heat and motion," and can any one be sure that the accusatives have any reality either? They exist to me only as they exist in my consciousness. But if the very pronoun 'my' is an illusion, how can I be sure that the illusion does not affect all that that little word qualifies? Expunge the delusive notion that there is really an 'I,'—there is no need to use the word 'soul' at all,—to perceive, to receive sensations, and to transmit commands, and why should not that which is as closely coupled to this 'I' in the very act of perception as one end of a stick is to the other end by the stick itself, be rejected with it? Professor Tyndall is untrue to his own principles. If it is thoroughly unscientific to assume an entity who perceives and feels and wills, it is clearly unscientific to assume that there is anything perceived, or felt, or willed. The fictitious character of the whole act of knowledge must surely follow from the fictitious character of the central assumption which gives that act a meaning. If there is no reason to suppose that there is a person to apprehend the external world, there can be no reason to suppose that there is an external world to apprehend, for it is only through the act of apprehension that any one even supposes himself to reach it.

Again, Professor Tyndall teaches us that because we cannot produce physical energy, but can only release or direct it, therefore the supposed human will can play no real part in human affairs,—meaning, as I understand him, that it always takes other physical energy to determine how any special stock of physical energy shall be released or expended, so

that it as much depends on the set of the currents
in the previously existing physical energy, which
valve shall be opened and which kept shut, as
it depends on the previous accumulations of such
energy how much energy shall emerge when the
particular valve is opened. Professor Tyndall,
following Mill, and other such teachers, warns us
that though we can determine our actions according
to our wishes, we cannot determine our wishes,
these being determined for us by the laws of physical
organisation, of hereditary transmission, of social
circumstance, and other conditions of our previous
life. But assuming this teaching to be true, whither
does it lead us? Why, of course, to the doctrine of
pure materialism, that physical energy is the primal
fount from which all mental phenomena ultimately
proceed,—and proceed by an immutable process of
evolution. If not only is the stock of physical
energy in the universe a fixed stock, but if also the
distribution of that stock is absolutely dependent on
the character and amount of it, then it is clear there
is nowhere for wishes and other such mental phenomena to come out of, except the one stock of physical
energy which is the primary assumption with which
Professor Tyndall starts, and it cannot, in his belief,
be wholly uncreated and self-caused. Wishes,
motives, volitions, aspirations, and the rest, must
either be unexplained phenomena somehow due to
this primary stock of physical energy, or must be
uncaused, which is clearly not Professor Tyndall's
view, since he defines science as the effort to explain
the unknown by what is better known. If, then,
he believes, as we understand him, that physical
energy contains within itself the laws and causes of
its own distribution, mind is a mere unexplained

phenomenon of physics. If that be not true, if 'the whole stock of physical energy in existence' does not regulate its own laws of distribution, then there must be something else which does regulate it, and human will might well be defined as that which, though not able to create physical energy, is able to liberate and direct it in this direction or that, to concentrate it on one purpose or on another, within certain limits, as it will. Evidently, then, Professor Tyndall either teaches us pure materialism, or leaves us free to believe that though the stock of physical energy in the world is always the same, incapable of increase or decrease, the way in which it is to be applied, whether by one channel to one purpose, or by another channel to another purpose, is left more or less at our disposal. Yet, as I understand him, he forbids us to believe either of these alternatives. He wishes us to regard physical energy as containing in itself the precise laws of its own distribution, in one place, and yet forbids us in another to refer consciousness and its states to these laws. He says, almost in the same breath, "molecular motion produces consciousness," and then again, "physical science offers no justification for the notion that states of consciousness can be generated by molecular motion." Which does he wish us to believe? If the first, then we know what he means, and that it is pure materialism. If the second, he leaves plenty of room for the influence of freewill, in spite of that absolute limitation of the stock of physical energy in the world which he teaches. But it is hardly reasonable to take credit for *both* assumptions,—that molecular motion is the ultimate cause of everything —and that mental states are not caused by it, any more than it is caused by them.

Still more difficult is it to follow out Professor Tyndall's teaching as to moral necessity, when at length he has somehow skipped the gulf between physics and morals, and come to assume moral necessity as the truth. He says, very justly, that if the doctrine of Necessity does away with moral responsibility, it yet leaves in all their strength the motives for discouraging actions injurious to society, and encouraging those which are beneficial to society. That is quite true. But Professor Tyndall appears to admit that though we should encourage what we find useful and discourage what is injurious by every means in our power, *approbation* and *disapprobation* are unmeaning, except on that hypothesis of moral freedom which he has rejected. We may visit what is injurious with disagreeable results in order to prevent others doing it, but it is childish to talk of being morally offended with what was as inevitable as the fall of an apple when its stalk breaks. This being granted, then, being shut off from the dispensing of approbation and disapprobation, we shall be unfortunately also shut off from using by far the most powerful of the moral hindrances to wrong and crime. As the German thinker said of God that if He did not exist, it would be necessary to invent Him, so we might fairly say of moral approbation and disapprobation. If they did not exist, we should be obliged to invent them. Mere bestowal of pleasure or pain would be of little use without that approbation and disapprobation which make the pleasure and pain really effective, and give them their stimulating or deterrent power. It is not shutting up a man in prison, but shutting him up because his action is treated by society as morally disgraceful, which is the formidable thing. Professor

Tyndall in giving this up, gives up the very sting of the penalty, and deprives it of more than half its deterrent effect.   And as for the preacher,—why, to suppose that the preacher could preach against iniquity with good effect, as Professor Tyndall says, after he had ceased to believe that there was such a thing at all as iniquity in any sense except that in which deformity and iniquity are the same, Professor Tyndall is the most sanguine of men if he thinks so. Indeed the punishment of persons who are believed to have been incapable of doing anything but what they did, would soon become as impossible as it has already become impossible to punish criminal lunatics. Follow Professor Tyndall's principles out to their proper limits, and all punishment, properly so-called, would cease.

One word more.   Why does Professor Tyndall say so airily that he has no objection to talk " poetically " of a soul, though he has a strong objection to believe in one really ?   " If you are content to make your soul a poetic rendering of a phenomenon which refuses the yoke of ordinary mechanical laws, I, for one, would not object to this exercise of ideality." But surely he *ought* to object to it, if it is false and misleading.   We mean by the 'self' a real thing, altogether distinguishable from any organisation ; and if it is not that, the use of the word 'self,' or ' I,' or 'soul,' is not a harmless exercise of "ideality," but a falsehood, and a very dangerous one.   I do not understand this liberty granted by Professor Tyndall to tell " poetically " all sorts of fibs which he objects to as matter of serious belief.   The belief in the free self is either a most dangerous fiction or the greatest of truths, and Professor Tyndall's willingness to deal with it in a poetic and ideal way, without insisting on the strict truth about it, as it seems to him, is not, I think, quite so catholic a feature of his character, or so creditable to him as he evidently supposes it to be.   Let us tell the truth about ourselves, even if that truth be only that there is no truth to tell.

THE APPROACH OF DOGMATIC ATHEISM

1874

PROFESSOR HUXLEY has said something lately about
the drum ecclesiastic, but it seems that there is
another kind of drum whose low reverberations are
beginning to be heard, nay, whose vibrations send
very perceptible tremors down the sensitive nerves
of our modern society, and which is far from unlikely
to take the place of the ancient drum ecclesiastic, both
in relation to the power of which it may become the
signal, and the terror which its notes may carry with
them.   About three years ago, when Professor Huxley
intimated, in a very telling speech at the London
School Board, that there were enemies of the human
race whom it might become quite necessary for wise
men to disqualify at least for the function of education,—I do not profess to quote his words, but only
the impression they produced at the time on almost
all who heard them,—I remarked on the tendency of
the modern representatives of physical science, while
denying all absolute certainty, to draw the most im-
periously dogmatic conclusions from the most ostentatiously hypothetic premisses. That tendency has
certainly persevered, and rather more than persevered,

among scientific Englishmen in the intervening period ; and now, in Professor Clifford, one of the most able and eloquent of the school, scientific thought in relation to religion and morality appears to be undergoing a transformation from its chrysalis condition of Agnosticism, in which it fed so heartily and throve so fast on the vague hopes it killed, and to be taking to itself ephemeral wings with which it proposes to soar high above the humility of its previous condition, and, indeed, to flutter up into those empty spaces from which science, we are now told, has all but succeeded in expelling the empty dreams of a presiding Mind in the universe, and of a life after death. Automatism, which was a wild hypothesis yesterday, and is still so difficult to state without self-contradiction that Professor Clifford's own language is constantly at cross-purposes with his theory, is, if one may trust his paper, published in the December *Fortnightly,* to become the creed of all reasonable men to-morrow ; the faith in Providence is soon to be recognised as "immoral"; and we are to expect before long evidence that "no intelligence or volition has been concerned in events happening within the range of the solar system, except that of animals living on the planets,"—nay, evidence "of the same kind and of the same cogency" as that which forbids us to assume the existence between the Earth and Venus of a planet as large as either of them. These calm anticipations, moreover, are recorded in a lecture which is as much distinguished by confident but utterly unreasoned assertions, and wild but dogmatic surmises, as it is by the eloquent audacity of its negative teaching, and by the scorn with which it compares the region of faith to that "good man's croft" of the Scotch superstition, which is left untilled for the Brownie to live in, in the hope that "if you grant him this grace, he will do a great deal of your household work for you in the night while you sleep." Let us just look at this body of "truth," as Professor Clifford regards it, and enumerate the theses which he either holds to be established now, or to form part of those sagacious divinations of scientific prescience, the verification of which we may expect in the immediate future.

1. "All the evidence that we have goes to show that the physical world gets along entirely by itself, according to practically universal rules. That is to say, the laws which hold good in the physical world hold good everywhere in it,—they hold good with practical universality, and there is no reason to suppose anything else but those laws in order to account for any physical fact." In other words, men and animals are physical automatons, with more or less of a consciousness annexed, the states of that consciousness, however, not forming necessary links, or any links at all, in the chain of physical events. "There is no reason why we should not regard the human body as merely an exceedingly complicated machine, which is wound up by putting food into the mouth." This I understand Professor Clifford to regard as *practically* certain.

2. "If anybody says that the will influences matter, the statement is not untrue, but it is nonsense."

3. "The only thing which influences matter is the position of surrounding matter or the motion of surrounding matter." (These two latter propositions are quite certain, I gather, in Professor Clifford's view, the contradictory of them being simply unintelligible. He reiterates his statement thus :—"The

assertion that another man's volition, a feeling in his consciousness which I cannot perceive, is part of the train of physical facts which I may perceive,—this is neither true nor untrue, but nonsense : it is a combination of words whose corresponding ideas will not go together.")

4. "The human race, as a whole, has made itself during the process of ages. The action of the whole race at any time determines what the character of the race shall be in the future."

5. "The doctrine of a destiny or providence outside of us, overruling human efforts and guiding history to a foregone conclusion," is "immoral,' "if it is right to call any doctrine immoral,"—the reason for the strong epithet thus applied to this doctrine being that the authority of this doctrine has so often been used to "paralyse the efforts of those who were climbing honestly up the hill-side towards the light and the right," and has so often also "nerved the sacrilegious arm of the fanatic or the adventurer who was conspiring against society." (How loose and rhetorical, by the way, is the moral language of the Professor ! What is the sin of conspiring against society ? If there were two or three scientific men united with Professor Clifford in his propaganda, would not that be as near to a "conspiracy against society" as ordinary men, who hold religion to be the chief bond of society, could conceive ?) I do not know with how much intellectual confidence the Professor regards this purely moral thesis, but it will be admitted that it is very dogmatically expressed.

6. The following, however, is a probable hypothesis only :—"The reality which underlies matter, the reality which we perceive as matter, is that same stuff which, being compounded together in a particu-

lar, way produces mind."   " The actual reality which underlies what we call matter is not the same thing as the mind, is not the same thing as our perception, but it is made up of the same stuff."   It is not " of the *same* substance as mind (homo-ousion), but it is of *like* substance,—it is made of similar stuff differently compacted together (homoiousion)."

7. If this last proposition be true, as seems probable to Professor Clifford, then, as " mind is the reality or substance of that which appears to us as brain-action, the supposition of mind without brain " is " a contradiction in terms."

8. On the same supposition, there can be no mind in the universe except where there are animals with animal brains.   And of this opinion we may expect to be one day as certain as we are now that there is no planet between the Earth and Venus as large as either of them.

Such are the main theses of this remarkable essay, of which the first five, if I understand Professor Clifford rightly, are moral certainties of the highest conceivable validity, while the last three are as yet but divinations of science, but divinations of high scientific probability.   As Professor Clifford says that not one man in a million has a right to any opinion on the subjects on which his own opinion is so very confidently expressed,—and I certainly do not suppose that I am one of thirty-two men in the United Kingdom alone qualified to have a view on the subject,—it may be desirable to say why I cannot regard Professor Clifford's authority on the subject, in spite of his obviously great ability, as worth very much, and why therefore I need not accept his warning of the temerity of entering the lists against one of the thirty-two.   In his very clever, though, as usual, arrogant introductory observations, Professor Clifford admirably calls science "organised common-sense." Now there is not one of the eight propositions I have treated as the leading dogmatic principles of his lecture which seems to me to deserve that character; and those seven of the eight which alone I clearly understand, might, I think, be more nearly described as disorganising but fortunately very uncommon nonsense.   With regard, first, to the first thesis :— If the physical world gets along by itself, without any interference from the mental world,—if the human body is an automaton wound up by putting food into the mouth,—why, I should like to know, is Professor Clifford so impressed with the mischief worked by the doctrine of Providence, and why does he describe it as "nerving the sacrilegious arm of the fanatic"?   In his view, no belief ever nerves any arm at all.   "The food which is put into the mouth," and which winds up the automaton, at once nerves the arm and results in the belief ; but on his theory, belief nerves no arm, and it is not so much untrue as "nonsense,"—words without a meaning,—to say that it does nerve any arm.   I am perfectly aware that popular language, like our language about sunrise for instance, often involves a fundamental blunder, and that not the less men go on using the blunder, on the tacit understanding that it shall be interpreted to stand for its own correction.   And of course, Professor Clifford would say that what *he* means by condemning a belief for nerving the sacrilegious arm of the fanatic, is that the condition of nerve and brain which at one and the same time produces the belief and also "nerves the sacrilegious arm of the fanatic," is a degenerate or diseased condition. But substitute the one phrase for the other, and you

destroy its whole meaning. If the belief is not even
a link in the chain, if no belief is capable of being a
link in the chain of causes leading to bad actions, if
the mischief altogether arises in the nervous structure,
in the unhealthy organism, or the inadequate, or
else the too violent winding-up of the automaton,—
then why blame the belief, instead of the antecedent
of the belief? Talk no more of sacrilegious beliefs,
but only of the evil cellular tissues, the disgraceful
foods, and the infamous air, leading to such beliefs.
On the theory of Professor Clifford, the physical
structure of the automaton is a whole in itself, with
the movement of which consciousness never interferes, though it varies with it. You might reform
the belief by reforming the brain, but you could not
reform the brain by reforming the belief. Again,
to go to the next thesis, what assumption can be
more bewilderingly arbitrary than the assumption
that "volition cannot influence matter"? I had
always thought that the tendency of the new physical
science was not to say what can or cannot be, but
what is or is not; and that in its language,
"influence" is only a word for invariable ante-
cedence. Now it is quite certain that, be volition
what it may, it invariably precedes all the actions
we call voluntary, and that these actions do influence
matter,—my present volition to write on this paper,
for instance, causing a rearrangement of certain
particles of ink. If the only thing which can
influence matter is "the position of surrounding
matter or the motion of surrounding matter," the
question is of course at an end. But this assumption
appears to be a return into that region of *a priori*
necessity which Professor Clifford's school usually
regards as so sterile, and so much condemns. As a

matter of fact, I know that thoughts are as invariable antecedents of certain classes of actions as any physical conditions could be, and it is the mere omniscience of an *a priori* materialism to declare the former mere conjoint consequents of the same antecedents, instead of causes of the actions. As for the doctrines that the human race has "made itself," that the faith in providence has paralysed honest upward effort,—a doctrine which I have shown to be unintelligible on Professor Clifford's theory,—and the assertion that we may soon have proof that what we call "mind" cannot exist without a "brain," and that it will then be as easy to disprove God as to disprove the existence of a planet between the Earth and Venus of the same size as either of them,—it seems to me that these doctrines are the very extravagances of a riotous imagination. The first of these three statements is, I suppose, only an intellectual inference from the last, since unless the existence of God,—in men's usual understanding of the word,—can be disproved, it certainly is not true that the human race made itself. And as for the second of them, the contradictory is just as true, even for the very reason Professor Clifford gives as the thesis itself. If the appeal to the doctrine of Providence has been used to keep down some honest effort, it has animated and nerved a great deal that Professor Clifford himself would acknowledge,—as, for example, Luther's whole life. If the disbelief in Providential guidance has ever,—which I doubt,— relieved any honest effort of an incubus, it is matter of biographical record that it has quenched a good deal more honest effort in utter despair. A more luxuriant use of unreasoned assumptions than is to be found in Professor Clifford's lecture I do not think it would be possible to discover, even in the most desolate wastes of theological literature.

But what is the most striking point in this lecture is that a thinker who throws the word 'nonsense' so recklessly at the head of his opponents, should treat the whole domain of religious belief as one springing out of pure intellectual hypothesis, and as one for which there is no conceivable excuse apart from theories of body and mind. That religious belief has its source in a totally different region of life, which is no less real than the external world itself to those who have never even heard of any theory of the relation of body to mind, he either disbelieves or wholly ignores. And yet to millions of men who have heard no more about the relation of brain to consciousness, than they have about Berkeley's theory of vision, the love of God has been as true a constituent of their life as the light of the sun. For the consciousness of sin and the dread and remorse caused by it, Professor Clifford has no room in his theory except that he may of course, if he will, admit that our automatons are all of very defective structure, and that by dint of greater care in selecting the reproductive machines, and more scientific caution in winding them up, their works may be improved. Responsibility, he expressly states, cannot exist unless a man's brain is as much the source of his actions as the springs of a machine are of its operations. "The notion that we are not automata destroys responsibility, because, if my actions are not determined by my character [brain], in accordance with the particular circumstances which occur, then I am not responsible for them, and it is not I that do them"; so that a man is responsible only for what he cannot help doing, which means that he is responsible for the twitch of his eyebrows, and the consumptive tendency in his lungs, and the heat or coldness of his inherited passions, and the alertness or dullness of his constitutional intelligence, — but that if it be conceivable that at any point he had a true choice as to what he would or would not do, then he would not be responsible, because it would be only the free, momentary "self," and not the mere sum and issue of all the streams of previous tendency, which made the choice.   Professor Clifford's fallacy is a very old one, which has been repeated thousands of times before, but it is one the plausibility of which the human mind steadily resists,— the laws of all civilised peoples declining every day to punish a man for what there is evidence that he could not help, and taking pity even on the lunatic, who may possibly be responsible for being a lunatic at all, but who, if he be not responsible for that, cannot usually be responsible for the individual crimes which, as a lunatic, he commits.   The doctrine which this clever theorist professes to substitute for the old faith in God and duty, is one which has repeatedly proved too unreal to overcome the "organised common-sense" of the human race, and it is likely enough to prove equally feeble again ; but if ever it does conquer the belief of an intelligent people, we are likely to have such a result as no necessitarianism of the Calvinist or Augustinian type could ever produce.   Suppose for a moment that the Scotch, — a people, as I believe, far more really competent to master and apply abstract ideas than the Germans,—were, in the intimate confidence of their belief in the "conservation of energy," as Mr. Clifford interprets that hypothesis, to take to the automaton doctrine in all its nakedness,—in other

words, to a materialistic Calvinism, without the
sublimity of the belief in an Almighty Will that
forces purity on at least some of us, or the terror of
the belief in an awful torment for those of us who
cannot hate the evil at their heart.   Is it conceivable
that a people really believing that the body is a
machine which goes on, when it is wound up, independently of consciousness, would struggle against
temptations which they would regard as modes of a
mechanical force, the antagonism to which, if it were
possible to resist it, would manifest itself in their
natures as powerfully as the temptation itself ?   Why
should they refuse to wind up the automaton, say
with whiskey, or any other watch-key that might
seem most attractive, if they confidently held that
whatever it was which they might do, they would
do as inevitably as a clock goes right or goes wrong ?
Effort *against the grain* is altogether a superfluity
of worry for one who believes that his interior
mechanism settles for him whether he shall make it
or no.   Of course if he makes it, he could not but
make it.   But if he does not make it, he could not
help not making it, and why not, therefore, drift, if
drifting seem the easier ?   I venture to affirm that
the automato-atheistic theory once earnestly adopted
by a nation of graphic and logical mind, like the
Scotch, would make such a hell upon earth, such a
world of languors where languors were most agreeable,
and of vehement and lawless moral pressures where
the application of such pressures was most in keeping
with the temperament of the individual, as civilised
men would never have seen before.   The happy
device of combining Atheism with a distinct and vivid
confidence in the absolutely mechanical character of
man's bodily life, may be consistent, in a few isolated

instances, as doubtless it is in Professor Clifford's case, with a lofty mind, a strenuous character, and a firm will, but in ninety-nine cases out of a hundred it would lead to the natural or artificial selection and elaboration of those wheels in the corporeal machine which would produce the kind of motion their owners found most pleasurable ;—and then the crash and battle of the various revolving cogs of self-interest would be such as even savage life could not rival. Professor Clifford is great in his own field. In the field he has now chosen he is hurling about wildly loose thoughts over which he has no intellectual control. These are indeed what Mr. Kingsley once called some suggestions of his own, "loose thoughts for loose thinkers."

CLIFFORD'S "LECTURES AND ESSAYS" [1]

1879

THE late Professor Clifford was a meteoric sort of moral phenomenon, who to many, even of those who had some personal knowledge of his extraordinary powers, was more of a bewilderment than a light. He was a man of rare wit and rare powers of fascination, of extraordinary courage and extraordinary agility—both physical and mental, very great kindliness and very great audacity, enthusiastic disinterestedness and almost measureless irreverence. He was a great master of gymnastic, who, when he came out second wrangler at Cambridge, was much prouder of being mentioned in *Bell's Life* as a great athlete, than of being second wrangler. "His nerve at dangerous heights," wrote a friend who was his rival in gymnastic feats, "was extraordinary. I am appalled now to think that he climbed up and sat on the cross-bars of the weather-cock on a church-tower; and when, by way of doing something worse, I went

[1] *Lectures and Essays.* By the late William Kingdon Clifford, F.R.S. Edited by Leslie Stephen and Frederick Pollock. With an Introduction by F. Pollock. London: Macmillan and Co.

up and hung by my toes to the bars, he did the same."   During a journey in France, when the boat had left the quay at Havre, Clifford, arriving late, jumped on board it, "with one of those apparently unpremeditated springs which look so well in the gymnasium."   His flexibility and complete command of his own powers, both of mind and body, were probably as great as any human being ever possessed. And as he seems to have been entirely free from anything like giddiness in his gymnastic feats, so he seems to have been equally free from anything like awe in the equally marvellous gymnastic feats of his mind, treating the infinity and eternity in which his fellow-creatures believed with the same sort of contemptuous familiarity with which he treated the ecclesiastical height he had once reached, only to balance himself by his toes on the weather-vane.   He speaks, indeed, in the least irreverent of his antitheistic papers, of having parted from his faith in God " with such searching trouble as only cradle faiths can cause." [1]   And no doubt he must have felt something which entitled him to use this language, for Clifford was sincerity itself.   Nevertheless, this is almost the only passage I have met with which points to his having gone through any crisis of the kind, while there are a great many in which he treats the faith in God with such utter, such cold contempt, that it is not easy to understand how he could ever have regarded it as being the light of his light and the life of his life, and much less how he could have realised that other men were still so regarding it, while he was launching his satire at them.   In such a passage as the following, for example, he seems to be trying to show that he

[1] *The Influence upon Morality of a Decline in Religious Belief.*   Vol. ii., p. 247.

was as reckless of the awe which the faith in God and eternal life generate, as when hanging with his toes on the church vane, he was reckless of the fears which such a position as his would impart to most men :—"For, after all, such a helper of man outside of humanity, the truth will not allow us to see.   The dim and shadowy outlines of the superhuman deity fade slowly away from before us; and as the mist of his presence floats aside, we perceive with greater and greater clearness the shape of a yet grander and nobler figure,—of Him who made all gods, and shall unmake them.   From the dim dawn of history, and from the inmost depth of every soul, the face of our father Man looks out upon us with the fire of eternal youth in his eyes, and says, 'Before Jehovah was, I am.'"   I transcribe the words of this parody with reluctance, and something almost of shame, but still with the feeling that they are essential to the understanding of the erratic man who wrote them, and who never could have written them if he had not been strangely deficient in those many fine chords of sympathy with his fellow-men which in other sceptics like himself remain vibrating, and securing for them a certain community of sentiment with their fellows, long after the sympathy of conviction necessary originally to agitate them to their full extent, has vanished.   Doubtless, Clifford held all moral conventionality in utter horror.   As he once told an audience,—in face of the great danger which threatens nations that they may crystallise, like the Chinese, into inflexible habits of thought and feeling which would shut them out from progress, "it is not right to be proper."   But still such a parody as I have quoted on what is to so many men the most sacred of human utterances,—one, indeed, embodying the

most solemn passion of conviction, through which
the heart of man has ever passed,—would not have
been, in most men's mouths, so much a violation of
propriety, as a deliberate insult to the heart of
multitudes.   That Professor Clifford did not so
regard it, seems quite evident.   But that only shows
how curiously destitute he was of some of those
chords of sympathetic feeling, without the help of
which it is impossible to judge with any adequacy
the moral world in which you live.   And with all
his wonderful talent for society, and that extreme
kindliness of his nature which so fascinated children,
Professor Clifford certainly showed signs of a curious
nakedness of the finer moral sympathies, a nakedness
diminishing in great degree both the impression of
cruelty which the mordant and contemptuous character of his attacks on religion would otherwise make
upon us, and also, in some degree at least, the
intellectual weight to be attached to his undoubted
genius, when it worked upon subjects of this kind.
It is clear that Professor Clifford must have *enjoyed*
dealing a stunning because a contemptuous blow at
those who acknowledge the deepest of human beliefs.
He does it not only in the passage just quoted, but
in many other passages of his addresses,—that, for instance, in his lecture on " Body and Mind," in which
he coolly estimates the chance of an early and final
disproof of God ; and again, in such a sarcasm as
this, contained in his review of *The Unseen Universe* :—

"Our authors 'assume as absolutely self-evident the
existence of a Deity who is the creator of all things.'
They must both have had enough to do with examinations
to be aware that 'it is evident' means 'I do not know
how to prove.'   The creation, however, was not necessarily
a direct process ; the great likeness of atoms gives them

'the stamp of the manufactured article,' and so they must have been made by intelligent agency ; but this may have been the agency of finite and conditioned beings. As such beings would have bodies made of one or other of the ethers, this form of the argument escapes at least one difficulty of the more common form, which may be stated as follows :—' Because atoms are exactly alike and apparently indestructible, they must at one time have come into existence out of nothing. This can only have been effected by the agency of a conscious mind, not associated with a material organism.' Forasmuch as the momentous character of the issue is apt to blind us to the logic of such arguments as these, it may not be useless to offer for consideration the following parody :—' Because the sea is salt and will put out a fire, there must at one time have been a large fire lighted at the bottom of it; this can only have been effected by the agency of the whale who lives in the middle of Sahara.' "

It would have been fairer to have *quoted* the imbecile argument adduced from some outwardly respectable authority, than to have manufactured it in a form inviting a parody so crushing as this. But I am far from denying that Professor Clifford might have found in the rubbish-heaps of natural theology an argument as silly as the one which he made in order that he might travesty it. I quote his travesty only to illustrate the grim delight with which he appears to have driven his knife up to the quick into the faith of unintelligent believers. These bitter sarcasms,—and these are but specimens of many,—would certainly do more to confirm those who hold that the abler antagonists of Theism indulge a sort of personal anger against the belief in God and all who entertain it, and wish to punish them for clinging to it,—than to kill that belief in

the mind of anybody. Parodies, however witty, on
sacred subjects, borrow half their pungency from
their irreverence, and seldom have much force as
arguments,—more especially when the arguments
which they parody are not derived from any actual
author. Professor Clifford did not, I believe, really
enjoy inflicting pain on any one. But he was totally
unable to enter into the moral atmosphere which
surrounds these subjects in the minds of those
against whom he launched his ridicule. Evidently
he was a very great and a very original mathematician.
As evidently, I should say, he had no large grasp of
the moral and spiritual world, and had never entered
at all•into the minds and hearts from which he did
his best to expel all religion, and even, as I should
say, very nearly all moral faith, endeavouring to
substitute for it the very remarkable assortment of
opinions set forth in the raw and curious theories
hastily invented by an intellectual acrobat.

And what are these opinions ? Professor Clifford
was far too acute and too strong a thinker not to
have got hold of a philosophy of his own which he
proposed to substitute for the faith which he so
utterly scorned. He saw, for instance, that an
Atheistic philosophy which held by the principle of
evolution, must be able to identify the germs of the
higher mental, no less than the germs of the higher
material phenomena, in those initial rudiments or
elements from which he supposed everything to
have been evolved. And this, Professor Clifford
effected—to his own satisfaction. He regarded
consciousness as the inside view of the highest
form of that which we call organised matter when
we look at it from outside. But he held consciousness to be a highly complex form of what he called

" mind-stuff," *i.e.*, a highly-organised tissue of simpler feelings, just as he regarded the human brain as a highly complex form of material tissue. And he thought that there was some simpler element of " mind-stuff " in the simplest forms of matter, just as there is a highly complex kind of mind-stuff in the highest forms of matter ;—and that as elementary cells by aggregation and organisation at last reach the highly-organised form of a nervous system, so the elementary forms of mind-stuff, those simple feelings far below the range of what is called consciousness, which he attributed to inorganic and the lower forms of organic matter, get aggregated and organised, as the matter which is the outside form of them gets aggregated and organised, till at last in the highest forms of organic existence, they appear in those complex " streams of feeling " which we call consciousness. Thus, by the help of " a law of evolution," did Professor Clifford eventually evolve mind out of the supposed " simple feelings " inherent in wood, and even in stone, just as he conceived the brain to be evolved out of the simple elements of inorganic chemistry. He never seems to have considered the difficulty that we are acquainted with very high forms of organised matter,—the gray matter in the brain for instance, the outer skin, the blood, the nails, and the hair,—which either have no high form of mind-stuff belonging to them at all,—certainly no consciousness,—or else have one that is entirely outside the range of that consciousness on which alone he relies for his proof that the higher forms of organised matter *are* the outside forms of that which, from the inside, we call consciousness. If consciousness be the reality, as Professor Clifford held, behind the human organisation,—the " thing in itself," of which the nervous bodily organisation is the mere external vesture,—how is it that parts of that organisation either have no more "mind-stuff" than a tree or grass or stone, or else have it in some region quite outside the range of that which he regards as the "mind-stuff" of the brain. His view, if I understand it rightly, would assign a full consciousness to all the highest organised matter, by virtue of its high organisation,—just as it attributes the lowest forms of "mind-stuff" to the lowest forms of matter. But there are very high forms of organised matter,—perhaps some of the highest,—which can be dealt with as you will, without any reflection of your dealings with them in consciousness at all, at least in that consciousness in which there is the fullest reflection of our dealings with other parts of the same organisation. If Professor Clifford's theory were worth anything, consciousness would develop *pari passu* with the organic development of all forms of matter, and we ought to have as much consciousness behind the action of the motor nerves as behind the action of the sensitive nerves, as much consciousness of the growth of our hair, as of the flush on our cheeks or the music in our ears. Really and truly, consciousness belongs only in the most fitful way even to the very highest parts of our bodily organisation, of which many elements are as little represented in that consciousness or, so far as we know, in "mind-stuff" of any kind, as the trees in the field or the stones in the road. The *wish* to discover "mind-stuff" to evolve into higher forms, wherever he found matter to evolve into higher forms, seems to have caused this very wild leap of Professor Clifford's nimble imagination.

The next great effort of these lectures is to find a

theory of ethics which will dispense with the old morality, as Professor Clifford had already found a theory of mind-stuff which would dispense with the old view of mind. This theory is the theory of the tribal self, or the partly-inherited, partly-acquired sense of what the good of your clan requires, which must often be at war with what your own individual pleasure seems to require,—the conflict representing the first emergence of conscience. From this principle of course it follows, as Professor Clifford is never tired of repeating, that there is no such thing as a self-regarding virtue,—the idea of virtue not arising at all till the notion of what you owe to the group in which you live,—be it family, tribe, or nation,—begins to conflict with the notion of what you would like for yourself alone. "The virtue of purity, for example, attains in this way a fairly exact definition; purity in a man is that course of conduct which makes him to be a good husband and father, in a woman that which makes her to be a good wife and mother, or which helps other people so to prepare and keep themselves. It is easy to see how many false ideas and pernicious precepts are swept away by even so simple a definition as that,"—and how many true ones, too, I should add. Again, of course, under Professor Clifford's hands, praise and blame become, what they must be in this philosophy, *prospective calculations*, intended to affect the future conduct both of the persons praised and blamed and of the rest of the community, but wholly irrelevant otherwise,—the idea of moral desert having, of course, wholly vanished with the moral freedom which is its first condition. The vital defect of the philosophy which makes the tribal self the source of conscience, is clearly that it does not account for the facts. It is not true that the only reason for being sincere with yourself, is that duty to your fellow-men requires it. It is not true that purity means only the conduct which will make you the best domestic character. The tribal self has often lower claims than the individual self; and can only be purified by the revolt of the individual self against the tribal self.

Finally, for religion, Professor Clifford proposes to substitute the cultivation of what he calls "cosmic emotion,"—emotion, that is, roused in us by the consideration of the external and internal laws of the cosmos in which we live. Professor Clifford selects, as the most refreshing and religious of these emotions, as the one most calculated to supply the place of lost faith, the reverence which an evolutionist feels for changes produced by the spontaneous vital movements of society from within, as distinguished from those which are imposed on it by the conditions of the external environment in which it lives. All those variations due to spontaneous variation from within, testify, he says, to the vitality of an organism, and increase its elasticity. But this is too delicate a point for me to explain, except in Professor Clifford's own words. I quote his account of those higher actions which are fitting subjects for "cosmic emotion":—

"Only actions originating in the living part of the organism are to be regarded as actions from within; the dead part is for our purposes a portion of the external world. And so, from the internal point of view, there are rudiments and survivals in the mind which are to be excluded from that *me*, whose free action tends to progress; that *baneful strife which lurketh inborn in us* is the foe of freedom—*this let not a man stir up, but avoid and flee.* The way in which freedom, or action from within, has effected the evolution of organisms, is clearly brought out by the theory of Natural Selection. For the improvement of a breed depends upon the selection of *sports*— that is to say, of modifications due to the overflowing energy of the organism, which happen to be useful to it in its special circumstances. Modifications may take place by direct pressure of external circumstances; the whole organism or any organ may lose in size and strength from failure of the proper food, but such modifications are in the downward, not in the upward, direction. *Indirectly* external circumstances may of course produce upward changes; thus the drying-up of axolotl ponds caused the survival of individuals which had 'sported' in the direction of lungs. But the *immediate* cause of change in the direction of higher organisation is always the internal and quasi-spontaneous action of the organism.

> 'Freedom we call it, for holier
>   Name of the soul there is none;
> Surelier it labours, if slowlier,
>   Than the metres of star or of sun;
> Slowlier than life into breath,
> Surelier than time into death,
>   It moves till its labour be done.'

The highest of organisms is the social organism. To Mr. Herbert Spencer, who has done so much for the whole doctrine of evolution, and for all that is connected with it, we owe the first clear and rational statement of the analogy between the individual and the social organism, which, indeed, is more than an analogy, being in many respects a true identity of process, and structure, and function. Our main business is with one property which the social organism has in common with the individual, namely, this, that it aggregates molecular motions into molar ones. The molecules of a social organism are the individual men, women, and children of which it is composed. By means of it, actions which, as individual, are insignificant, are massed together into the important movements of a society. Co-operation, or *band-work*, is

the life of it.   Thus it is able to ' originate events independently of foreign determining causes,' or to act with
freedom."

I am never quite sure that I understand these great
thoughts.   To me it seems that the spontaneous, not
to say capricious changes, which we call changes of
fashion, most nearly satisfy the conditions here laid
down as proper subjects for cosmic emotion.—I
should admit, however, that the great poets of " cosmic emotion " quoted by Professor Clifford appear to
be Mr. Swinburne and Mr. Walt Whitman, and I
do not suppose that either of them are exactly oracles
of the world of fashion.   The defect of these cosmic
emotions, as substitutes for religious emotions, seems
to be that so far from strengthening us and subduing
us for our duty here, they dissipate us in a world so
vague and so unintelligible, that we are left weaker
than before.   Fancy striving hard to develop in our
society, as a good *per se,* some spontaneous variation
which is not one of conformity to our environment,
but put forth from within, and indulging ourselves
in grand emotions of delight at the *freedom* of these
stirrings in the heart of a people associated in bandwork ?   The only cosmic emotion which appears
appropriate to his genuinely scientific expectations,
is one on which Professor Clifford does not dwell.
He tells us, in the paper on " The Influence upon
Morality of a Decline in Religious Belief," that " we
are all to be swept away in the final ruin of the
earth," and that " the thought of that ending is a sad
thought " ; but he does not recommend it as a fitting
theme for " cosmic emotion," because, I suppose, this
is not an emotion arising in any spontaneous action
of the organism, but rather in reflecting on the

destiny which will be imposed upon us by the hard laws of the environment.   Still, I should have thought it one of the most natural and one of the most distinct of the " cosmic emotions " possible to scientific atheists,—though it is, perhaps, characteristic of a philosophy of materialistic evolution, to bid us think as little as may be of the depressing aspects of that evolution, and do all in our power to rally whatever spontaneous force there may be in us to rebellion against its sway.   Yet without the help of a different creed, there would not be much power left in us to rally.   Professor Clifford says in one place, in his usual witty way, that it is a very bad habit of religious people that they are always trying to climb up " the backstairs of a universe which has no backstairs."   And yet this indulgence in cosmic emotion seems very like pitching ourselves down the backstairs of a universe which has backstairs,—the backstairs of gradual dissolution and decay,—which backstairs, however, we need not descend quite so rapidly, if we only refused to indulge in such cosmic emotions as Mr. Swinburne's and Mr. Walt Whitman's.

XXVIII

MR. COTTER MORISON ON "THE SERVICE OF MAN"

1887

MR. COTTER MORISON has published a very vigorous
book on *The Service of Man* which will make a
sensation, and a sensation of a highly complicated
kind.   Its object is to preach the service of man,
and to abolish the service of God as obsolete.   Mr.
Morison runs down Christianity, but patronises the
Christian saints.   He ridicules theology, but recognises with gratitude the service which the false
hypothesis of a God rendered to humanity after the
fall of the Roman Empire, and even reproves Gibbon
for making light of the consubstantiality of the
divine Son.   He tells more unpleasant stories than
were at all necessary for his purpose, of the dissolute-
ness of the Christian clergy in various periods of the
Church, but he balances them by stories of ascetic
saintliness which are not to his purpose at all, except
so far as it may be part of his purpose to concentrate
a strong light on Positivist candour at the cost
of Positivist teaching.   Indeed, the book, which
contains in its preface a high compliment to Mr.
Bradlaugh for his proclamation of the necessity of

checking the increase of population, is a curious compound of excerpts reminding us of *The Convent Exposed*, with excerpts reminding us of the *Lives of the - Saints* and excerpts reminding us of the *National Reformer*, or some other publication meant to bring all theology into contempt. The result is a book which produces, in Christians at least, a certain creeping sensation like that excited by a vivisector's dissertation on the gratitude which he feels to the dog to which he owes the success of a painful experiment on its vitals, or by one of Robespierre's skilful preparations of the minds of his audience for the proposal of a fresh batch of massacres. Mr. Cotter Morison will probably say that it is not his fault that in attempting to demolish a complex system like Christianity, in which the most various threads of what he holds to be true and false sentiment are inextricably interwoven, he excites the most painfully discordant feelings in those who believe in that which he would like to sweep away. Nor do I deny that this plea is fair enough. Only I think that he might reasonably have spared us a little of the unction with which he has enlarged on the character of the saints, and which, coming where it does, affects us rather as a pressing offer of pork-chops affects a sea-sick person. It was to his purpose, no doubt, to show that he could appreciate what Christianity had done to introduce a nobler element into human society. But his whole book shows that it was *not* to his purpose, —that it was, indeed, absolutely inconsistent with his purpose,—to give credit to any influence whatever for filling human hearts with passionate hatred of their own sins, as distinguished from strong dissatisfaction at the mischiefs those sins might have caused to others and the desire never to be the cause of such mischiefs again. Mr. Morison regards as a grave and grievous waste of power that sense of responsibility for evil-doing of which he encourages us to rid ourselves as soon as we can, though that feeling was at the very core of the passionate self-reproach and contrition in which the heart of the Christian saint expressed itself most vividly. He does not, of course, morally condemn it, for he wishes to rid human society of the idea of moral condemnation altogether. He thinks that the saint was no more responsible for the waste of power in which he delighted, than is the criminal for his lusts and crimes. But as he regards all that side of the saint's character as part of the necessary moral waste in the process of evolution, I think that he might have spared us so many unctuous references to that world of interior passion ; for they add much to the disagreeableness of the complicated emotions excited by his book. I do full justice to the sense of fairness which leads Mr. Cotter Morison to express his high appreciation of the disinterestedness, or, as he and his school prefer to call it, barbarous as the phrase is, the 'altruism,' which the true Christian saint has so gloriously displayed. But since he does not approve, nay, cordially disapproves of the waste, on penitence, of power which he thinks ought all to be directed into the formation of better habits, I do think that he might have suppressed the pages in which he gloats over the spiritual experience of saints. Holding their misapplied meditations and emotions to be instruments as clumsy and inferior for the production of altruism, compared with the true Positivist's teaching, as the savage's clumsy and often abortive method of obtaining fire is inferior to a modern safety-match, he need not, I think, have withdrawn the veil from experiences which he must deem so unedifying.

However, let me come to Mr. Morison's main end, which is to recommend his new religion, "the Service of Man," as well-nigh ripe for superseding the old religion of the service of God as manifested in Christ. His indictment against Christianity is, first, that it is neither true, nor even in modern times so much as believable ; next, that it is not serviceable for the production of virtue in average men and women, though it has produced a very high kind of virtue in those few exceptional characters which reach or approach the saintly type. And on these assertions,—for his acceptance of which he gives a great variety of reasons,—he founds, of course, the inference that the time has come for getting rid of an obsolete creed which is no longer doing its work, and for setting up Positivism in its place. It is impossible to pass over in an article a ·surface of criticism which occupies a volume. I can only indicate the points at which I regard Mr. Cotter Morison's attack as breaking down. With a great deal that he says as to the untenability of the old view of inspiration, I heartily agree. The Roman Church will find some day, I suspect, that the only way in which it can explain the words of the Vatican Council that all the Scriptures have God for their originator, *habent Deum auctorem*, will be tantamount to explaining them away, and making every wise Catholic regret that such words should ever have been used. But the real value of the Bible as the record of a race whose greatest rulers and most trusted guides were taught from above, and who recognised the influence of a higher nature on their own as the primary certainty of their life, is not affected by the recognition that its books are full of human elements, including both good and ill. If we can read the Bible and believe that all who recognised the reality of this personal divine influence as acting upon them and leading them into the way of righteousness, were mistaken enthusiasts misled by the complexity of the human consciousness, we may acquiesce in Mr. Cotter Morison's view; and if not, not. But those who utterly reject that view, have no reason in the world to burden themselves with the defence of all the defective science and defective history, and all the evidence of ordinary human passions, which the Bible, like all other human literatures, contains. If the central fact be true, as I do not doubt for a moment, that the Bible contains in outline the history of a race guided into righteousness by an invisible divine person with whom the communion of all their greatest minds was constant and ardent, and that this communion reached its perfection, its absolute climax, in our Lord's life and death, that is a fact the significance of which no evidence as to the errors and passions to which the human authors of the Bible were subject, can in the least tend to undermine. I am not even anxious to meet Mr. Cotter Morison's contention that Genesis is unscientific; and as for his position that the whole conception of original sin, of a transmitted taint which revealed religion was intended to help us to counteract, is morally false, I can only say that a more demonstrable moral truth is not to be found in the range even of Positivist dogmas. Mr. Cotter Morison's favourite doctrine as to the force of habit itself is not indeed more certain. When he speaks of the Fall as an evident falsehood, he uses the Fall in a sense in which no theologian ever yet understood it. It is childish to suppose that the doctrine of the intellectual degeneration of man,—of which there is no trace in Hebrew literature,—is so much as hinted at in Scripture. But that there is such a thing as sin in human nature, and that the tendency to sin is transmitted from father to son, is as conspicuous a truth to every one who believes in sin at all,—of course, Mr. Cotter Morison does not,—as the truth that physical characteristics are so transmitted. Naturally, if there be no sin, there is no transmission of sinfulness. It needs no Positivist to tell us that. But what in the world *is* the subject of the great literature of human remorse and contrition, if the notion be a pure chimera that sin is something as altogether different in kind from faultiness, as is disobedience from misunderstanding? Again, there is no occasion to meet Mr. Cotter Morison's perfectly true charge against theologians of almost all sects that they have preached about Hell in a way to malign God, and, as I believe, to travesty frightfully the teaching of Christ. None the less is it true that the worst fate which man can conceive, is the fate of those who, when they have the choice between the upward and the downward path in their moral life, choose the latter. Mr. Morison believes that there neither is nor can be any such choice for any man. And he is, of course, therefore logically quite right in regarding Christianity as a gigantic development of misleading error. That is no reason at all why those should be dismayed at his teaching who are a great deal surer that freedom, responsibility, and sin are realities and not dreams, than they are that the sun, the moon, and the earth are realities and not dreams.

Mr. Cotter Morison's proof that even if Christianity were true, it is not believable by the present generation, is open to a similar criticism. Of course, it is not believable by those who have borrowed for the moral and spiritual world the lessons of physical science, and imagine that by doing so they have rendered a service to humanity, instead of having led men off on a most misleading track. But the truth is, that even the devotees of science are beginning to be aware that they must shut their eyes very hard, if they are to deny phenomena utterly inexplicable by any of the physical sciences, if they are to deny, for instance, that "phantasms of the living" do appear at great distances from the living organisations to which they are due, and do convey impressions which turn out to be true impressions and utterly inexplicable by any physical science hitherto known. Mr. Morison refers to this subject with the usual sarcasm that it is the straw at which the supernaturalists catch, in the vain hope of sustaining their dying faith,—being quite unaware, I suppose, that some of the leading men in the Society which has got together this evidence are as sceptical as himself, and as well-disposed to turn the evidence,—as it may be turned,—against the Christian miracles, as to turn it,—as it may be turned,—in their favour. But the truth certainly is that the longer the phenomena of mesmerism and trance and of the less ordinary psychical states are examined, the more certain it becomes, on evidence which no candid mind can reject, that even in this life there is something in man which can occasionally pass far beyond the limits of sense, and that after death there are, in cases relatively rare, but collectively very numerous, phenomena which are not to be explained

at all, unless they can be explained as manifestations
of a still existing personality. As for the plea that
Christianity, even when earnestly believed, produces
its effect only on a few sensitive minds, and not on
any great number of minds, Mr. Morison does not
bring any proof at all beyond the vague charge of
rhetorical preachers. History and experience are
dead against him. Of course, there have always
been multitudes who, while professing to believe
Christianity, paid no attention to its precepts. He
himself admits,—too freely as I think, considering
the very different ideals of Christianity and Positivism,
—that there have always been a fair sprinkling of
men of what even he regards as the most elevated
type, produced by Christianity. But between these
extremes, all who know anything of our Churches
now, or knew anything of them at any time, have
always discerned a very large number of men and
women restrained from sins which they would otherwise have committed, and prompted to good works
which they would otherwise have neglected, by the
constant influence of a religion by which, nevertheless, they were only imperfectly penetrated. Will
Positivists ever produce a result one-tenth part as
satisfactory ?

But the real drift of Mr. Cotter Morison's book
is in his plea for a service of man as distinguished
from the service of God ; and here, too, is its greatest
weakness. His design is to show that in attempting
to train men to be serviceable to each other, there is
room for a religion free from superstition, which
may yet become most potent,—as, indeed, it has, he
thinks, already become potent,—and which will be
involved in none of the difficulties of Christianity,
though it will retain all that, for the purposes of

this life is useful in that great religion. But, as I have said, it is the weakest part of his book. In his attack on Christianity, he often assails vigorously what is not of the essence of Christian teaching, but what has been unfortunately incorporated with it. In his exposition of the "Service of Man" as a religion, he is not vigorous at all. In the first place, by giving up ostentatiously the reality of responsibility, and treating repentance as almost irrelevant, and as most ineffectual exactly where it is most needed, he falls back on training and habit as the only moral forces of the world. "By morality," he says, "is meant right conduct here on earth,—those outward acts and inward sentiments which, by the suppression of the selfish passions, conduce most to the public and the private well-being of the race." Very well, then, wherever those outward acts are absolutely wanting, and those inward sentiments do not exist, there is practically no hope. And that is precisely Mr. Morison's teaching. If we could but stop "the devastating torrent of children for a few years," he says, and organise on right lines the teaching necessary for the new generation, he thinks that all might be hopeful; but in his view there is no hope for degraded adults, and still less for their degraded offspring, unless they can be wholly rescued from their parents' care. And there is a still more serious stumbling-block beyond. What is to be the ideal of man for teachers who do not believe in God's love and mercy? Altruism, they tell us. But what is altruism to mean? Is it not in the highest degree altruistic for men who repudiate repentance and regeneration to extirpate a bad moral stock? If self-reproach is to cease as a waste of power and an utter delusion, must not the corrective system be indefinitely extended, and penalties attached at every step to human misdoings, not, of course, as punitive or retributive, but as supplying motives not to go wrong again? And on altruistic principles, must not a status of evil condition be recognised quite apart from any overt crime, placing all who belong to it under the strictest disability to marry, even if the stock is not to be absolutely exterminated. What a new ideal of moral conduct this implies,— what cultivated mercilessness, what inexorable hardness of heart, what rigidity of moral dogmatism, what indifference to repentance and remorse! The longer Mr. Cotter Morison's ideal for the true "Service of Man" is contemplated, the more evident it will be that, if he is right, Christianity has not only missed the truth, but taught the most deadly falsehood, and that the Christian saint, so far from deserving Mr. Morison's kind patronage, will become to the new teachers who deny responsibility and ridicule repentance, the awful warning from whose example the new generation must be taught to recoil in horror. "Nothing is gained," says Mr. Morison, "by disguising the fact that there is no remedy for a bad heart, and no substitute for a good one." Let that doctrine supersede the belief in God's grace, and we may confidently predict that the Positivists of the future will absolutely reverse Christian morality, and substitute for it a petrifying terror of their own,—a Medusa-head from which average men will start back in horror and dismay.

ARDENT AGNOSTICISM

1888

THE death of Mr. Cotter Morison has deprived the English literary world of one of the most learned and brilliant of that paradoxical group of men who may properly be termed ardent agnostics, men who press their agnosticism with a sort of apostolic unction, and ask us to serve man, as the best men serve God, with a zeal as disinterested and as absorbing as ever missionaries have displayed in the conversion of the heathen. Mr. Cotter Morison has left no work behind him at all adequate to the impression of ability which he produced on the minds of those who could appreciate what he had done. But his studies of St. Bernard, of Gibbon, of Macaulay, and of Madame de Maintenon, have supplied no mean test of his purely literary skill; while his last work, on *The Service of Man* burns with the zeal of a sombre enthusiast who would risk as much to suppress the degraded classes, or at least to prevent them from transmitting their degraded nature to a future generation, as ever an Apostle risked in order to infuse into those classes the spiritual fire of a divine renovation. Mr. Cotter Morison, though he was so thoroughgoing an agnostic that he eagerly desired to sweep what he regarded as the obstacle now presented by Christianity out of the path of human progress, was nothing if not, in his own peculiar sense, religious.   His books are full of what we may call unction. He says of Gibbon that women who could enter into his great book "are better fitted than men to appreciate and to be shocked by his defective side, which is a prevailing want of moral elevation and nobility of sentiment.   His cheek rarely flushes in enthusiasm for a good cause.   The tragedy of human life never seems to touch him ; no glimpse of the infinite ever calms and raises the reader of his pages.   Like nearly all the men of his day, he was of the earth earthy, and it is impossible to get over the fact."   Of Macaulay he says that his "utter inability to comprehend piety of mind, is one of the most singular traits in his character, considering his antecedents," and it is evident that he regards it as one of the most serious blemishes in Macaulay's character.   Of Madame de Maintenon he writes with even sterner reprobation when he is describing what George Eliot called the "other-worldliness." of her religious observances :—" With reference to spiritual affairs, though punctilious about her salvation, she always treats the matter as a sort of prudent investment, a preparation against a rainy day which only the thoughtless could neglect.   All dark travail of soul, anguish, or ecstasy of spirit were hidden from her."   And he marks strongly his dislike of her "utter lack of all spiritual —we will not say fervour, but sensibility."   On the other hand, no one can reproach Mr. Cotter Morison with any want of such sensibility, if that is to be called spiritual sensibility which seems to covet the feelings of a saint without believing in any object for those feelings. "The true Christian saint," he says in *The Service of Man* (p. 196), "though a rare phenomenon, is one of the most wonderful to be witnessed in the moral world; so lofty, so pure, so attractive, that he ravishes men's souls into oblivion of the patent and general fact that he is an exception amongst thousands or millions of professing Christians. The saints have saved the Churches from neglect and disdain." "What needs admitting, or rather proclaiming, by agnostics who would be just, is that the Christian doctrine has a power of cultivating and developing saintliness which has had no equal in any other creed or philosophy. When it gets firm hold of a promising subject, one with a heart and head warm and strong enough to grasp its full import and scope, then it strengthens the will, raises and purifies the affections, and finally achieves a conquest over the baser self in man of which the result is a character none the less beautiful and soul-subduing because it is wholly beyond imitation by the less spiritually endowed. The 'blessed saints' are artists who work with unearthly colours in the liquid and transparent tints of a loftier sky than any accessible or visible to common mortals." Clearly there is no lack of "religious sensibility" here. And the amazing thing is that those saints whom Mr. Cotter Morison so much admired, not only filled their souls with the worship of what he regarded as an empty dream which had no existence in any world, but trained their hearts and minds on a firm belief in what he held to be a moral delusion which could not be too soon exposed and expelled from all reasonable natures, namely, that there are such realities as human responsibility, sin, merit, demerit, and penitence. In a word, Mr. Cotter Morison wanted

to keep the saintly character without its daily bread,
—to keep the "anguish or ecstasy of spirit," which
arises exclusively from the faith in a perfect Being
who condemns or approves us, without the faith to
which it is solely and exclusively due. It was a
very strange state of mind. I can understand the
saint, and I can understand the scoffer at saintly
illusions. But I cannot understand the fervour with
which the man who wants to expose the illusions,
delights in the spiritual delirium which these illusions have produced.

Certainly it is not easy to explain how a man
with so keen an insight into both character and
history as Mr. Cotter Morison's study of Madame de
Maintenon, for instance, betrays, could have admired
passionately the type of character which was produced by the belief in what he held to be mischievous
superstitions, and could have desired to sweep away
those superstitions while retaining the type. Perhaps the best explanation of these ardent agnostics,
of these believers in the ecstasy of a spiritual communion with mere memories and hopes, is to be
found in the fact that they are all more or less
capricious in their individual prejudices, men who, like
Comte, institute impossible devotions which make
nobody devout, and draw up calendars of miscellaneous notables which are to include some of the
saints, and replace the others by persons of very
dubious merit. Mr. Cotter Morison, with all his
learning and all his enthusiasm and unction, frequently showed traces of a singularly capricious and
uncatholic judgment, which accounts in some degree,
perhaps, for his admiration of air-fed idealists. Thus,
in his little study of Macaulay, he expends much
indignant wrath upon him for repeating to himself a

great part of Milton's *Paradise Lost* on board the ship which was taking him to Ireland :—" The complaint is," he wrote, " that Macaulay's writings lack meditation and thoughtfulness. Can it be wondered at, when we see the way in which he passed his leisure hours? One would have supposed that an historian and statesman, sailing for Ireland, in the night on that Irish Sea would have been visited by thoughts too full and bitter and mournful to have left him any taste even for the splendours of Milton's verse. He was about to write on Ireland and the Battle of the Boyne, and had got up his subject with his usual care before starting. Is it not next to incredible that he could have thought of anything else than the pathetic, miserable, humiliating story of the connection between the two islands? And he knew that story better than most men. Yet it did not kindle his mind on such an occasion as this. There was a defect of deep sensibility in Macaulay,—a want of moral draught and earnestness,—which is characteristic of his writing and thinking." Surely there never was a more amazing outburst of indignation than this. It would seem that Mr. Cotter Morison wants men of genius always to reflect the reflections which are specially appropriate to the particular situation in which they find themselves ; to be in a mood appropriate to Ireland as they approach Ireland, and a mood for historical survey as they prepare thenselves for the writing of history. A more capricious assumption of pedantic appropriateness between the mind and its anticipated interests could hardly be conceived. Shakespeare might have taught a man of much less capacity than Mr. Cotter Morison that some of the most reflective characters are disposed to joke when they are on the very edge of the

most solemn experience, and to rise lightly, as it were,
with wings into the air, on the eve of approaching
calamity.   It is the mark of a doctrinaire to demand,
on pain of censure, the mood conventionally appropriate for the occasion from such men as Macaulay.
And the same remark may be made concerning Mr.
Cotter Morison's still stranger criticism on Macaulay's
Lays of Ancient Rome,—all the more remarkable
that it is preceded by a very fine and true apprecia·
tion of the literary value of the ballads themselves,
—namely, that it was not " worthy of a serious
scholar to spend his time in producing mere fancy
pictures which could have no value beyond a certain
prettiness, ' in the prolongation from age to age of
romantic historical descriptions instead of sifted
truth.' "   " Could we imagine," he asks, " Grote or
Mommsen or Ranke or Freeman engaged in such a
way without a certain sense of degradation ? "   To
which I should certainly answer, not merely with an
emphatic yes, but further, that if these historians had
the capacity to produce such ballads as Macaulay's
Lays, they would rise indefinitely in our esteem by
producing them, instead of falling lower in it, as Mr.
Morison thought they should, because they did not
employ their time in " sifting " truth, instead.   Criticisms like this seem to betray the wilfulness and
caprice which have entered as an alloy into the characteristics of most of the curious group of men who
have been what I have called ardent agnostics.   They
are men who indulge themselves in arbitrary intellectual caprices of their own,—in killing the root of
what is great, while insisting on keeping the greatness ; in lamenting the absence of some petty habit
of thought by which they lay great store, and attributing to it a kind of value of which it is wholly

destitute. Mr. Cotter Morison strangely combined the eloquence and fervour of Christian sentiment with the scornful fastidiousness and critical pedantry of a systematic thinker who sternly rejected all that did not fit into his system. " Agnostics," he boasts, "when smitten by the sharp arrows of fate, by disease, poverty, bereavement, do not complicate their misery by anxious misgivings and fearful wonder why they are thus treated by the God of their salvation. The pitiless, brazen Heavens overarch them and believers alike ; they bear their trials or their hearts break, according to their strength. But one pang is spared them,—the mystery of God's wrath, that he should visit them so sorely." Yes, that pang is spared them, and the strength which it gives is spared them also. The Christian knows that whether it is retribution for his sins, or purging for purification, or stimulus intended to give him higher spiritual strength, the pang which comes from above is full of power. But the ardent agnostics of our own day want to throw all the ardour of faith into the propagation of an agnostic service of humanity, and that is an impossible combination which only a capricious intellect could imagine. You cannot combine Gibbon's cold intellect with a saint's passion for communion with " the infinite." You cannot advocate the service of a limited posterity of mortal beings with the passion which is due to the regeneration of a world of immortal beings ; and though here and there, as in such eloquent critics as Mr. Cotter Morison, the paradox may seem to be achieved, we may be quite sure that either the agnostics of the future will cease to be ardent, or that the ardours of the future will cease to be agnostic.

XXX

ASTRONOMY AND THEOLOGY

1888

IN his recent apology for what he is pleased to call the Positivist "faith," Mr. Frederic Harrison has re-stated with his usual eloquence the position which we have so often seen taken before, that the Christian faith could not possibly have been first originated in an age that had had a heliocentric astronomy. "To the old theology, the Earth was the grand centre and sum of the Universe, and the other heavenly bodies were adjuncts and auxiliaries to it. With a geocentric astronomy as the root-idea of science, the anthropomorphic Creator, the celestial resurrection, and the Divine Atonement, were natural and homogenous ideas. No one can conceive the Scheme of Salvation growing up with anything but a geocentric system of thought. With a geocentric science and an anthropomorphic philosophy, all this was natural enough. But with a science where this planet shrinks into an unconsidered atom with a transcendental philosophy to which the anthropomorphic is the contemptible, the Augustinian Theology goes overboard." And the Head-Master of Clifton College, speaking as a Christian clergyman, to some extent echoes, and to some extent goes beyond, Mr. Harrison:—"Our whole attitude towards theology," he says, "has been profoundly altered by the conviction that we have attained, though perhaps scarcely formulated, of the unity of nature. It is seen in many ways. (The remotest ages of the past are now linked with ours in one continuous physical and biological history, and the most distant stars reveal a kinship to our own sun and earth. Our theology has, therefore, to be a theology not of this planet alone, or of this age alone, but a theology of the universe and of all time. The earth cannot be for us any longer the one stage on which the divine drama is played. It is this thought more than anything else which has unconsciously but irresistibly antiquated for us so much of theological speculation.) The most marked and direct effect on theology of this conception of the unity of nature, has, of course, come from the alteration it has made in the position of man. Man was formerly regarded as unique, as separate from nature. The earth was a platform on which Adam and his posterity were working out their eternal destiny in the sight of all creation. But man is now seen to be a part of nature, instead of separate from it. The unity of nature has embraced even ourselves. And the effect of this tremendous reversal of ideas must be felt in our theology."[1] In some respects, then, Mr. Wilson, the Christian clergyman, presents the supposed revolution in our thoughts as even more tremendous than Mr. Harrison had declared it to be. If, indeed, in the ordinary meaning of the words, man had been found to be "a part of nature,"—in the sense

---

[1] *Some Contributions to the Religious Thought of Our Time.* By the Rev. James M. Wilson, M.A., Head-Master of Clifton College. Macmillan and Co. (See pp. 253-254.)

of a mere outcome of the energies germinating in nature,—the obvious inference would be far more fatal to our ethics, and therefore to our theology, than any heliocentric astronomy possibly could be ; for then free-will and responsibility would be dreams, and God's laws nothing but more or less potent inducements which must take their chance of producing an effect upon us amongst the crowd of other inducements, without finding in us any free power on which to make a claim. That implies a revolution of a more astounding kind than any that only leads man to think of his own planet as a sort of petty ant-hill among the mighty suns and planets of an infinite universe. But Mr. Wilson also seems to hold that the mere extinction of the geocentric astronomy has vitally affected the whole world of theological conviction, and that if the Jews had but known that there are hundreds of thousands of other suns in the universe, and, for anything we know, millions of other planets inhabited by races of all possible varieties of physical, mental, and moral stature, there could have been no theology exactly of the type of that which we have inherited from them.

While heartily admitting that if man be nothing but a link in the chain of natural causes, Christian theology must be utterly revolutionised,—a point on which I do not now propose to dwell,—I venture to differ very respectfully from Mr. Wilson in thinking, with him and Mr. Frederic Harrison, that heliocentric astronomy has in any vital respect altered at all the validity of the theological conceptions of the Jewish and Christian revelations. Nay, I would go further, and say that if our astronomy could have been known to the Jews, it would have decidedly reinforced instead of undermining, the general teaching of their

inspired books. Indeed, so far as the Jewish prophets made use of such astronomy as they had, they
used it altogether in the sense in which the modern
agnostics use their heliocentric astronomy,—to impress upon man his utter insignificance in creation.
When Isaiah wants to make his countrymen feel that
princes are mere dust, what does he say? God, he
says, "brought princes to nothing; he maketh the
judges of the earth as vanity. Yea, they have not
been planted; yea, they have not been sown; yea,
their stock hath not taken root in the earth: moreover, he bloweth upon them and they wither, and
the whirlwind taketh them away as stubble. To
whom, then, will ye liken me that I should be equal?
saith the Holy One. Lift up your eyes on high;
and see who hath created these, that bringeth out
their host by number; he calleth them all by name;
by the greatness of his might, and for that he is
strong in power, not one faileth." When the author
of the Book of Job, in urging what another prophet
calls "the Lord's controversy," wants to convince Job
of his nothingness, what is his most impressive
illustration?—"Canst thou bind the sweet influences
of the Pleiades"—[or, as the Revised Version puts
it, "Canst thou bind the cluster of the Pleiades?"]
—"or loose the bands of Orion? Canst thou lead
forth the signs of the Zodiac in their season, or canst
thou guide the Bear with her train? Knowest thou
the ordinances of the heavens? Canst thou establish
the dominion thereof in the earth?"—language
surely, if ever language could be used, which suggests
that to control the heavenly bodies implies a force
of far mightier scope and magnitude than any which
is needed only for our little planet. Or take the
prophet Amos :—"Ye that turn judgment to worm-

wood, and cast down righteousness to the earth, seek
him that maketh the Pleiades and Orion, and turneth
the shadow of death into the morning, that maketh
the day dark with night,"—a passage which seems
a sort of anticipation of Wordsworth's apostrophe to
Duty :—

> " Thou canst preserve the stars from wrong,
>   And the most ancient heavens through thee are fresh
>   and strong."

The prophets of Judæa certainly used astronomy,
so far as they used it at all, entirely in the modern
sense, to lower the pride of man, and to convince him,
as Isaiah says, that " My thoughts are not your
thoughts, neither are your ways my ways, saith the
Lord ; *for as the heavens are higher than the earth*, so
are my ways higher than your ways, and my thoughts
than your thoughts."   Clearly the higher the heavens
had been known to be from the earth, the more
effective, not the less effective for its purpose, would
have been such language as this.   I do not, of course,
imagine for a moment that the Jewish prophets had
any inkling of modern astronomy ; but this I do
assert, that if they had known it in all its physical
magnificence, they could hardly have used astronomi-
cal images with surer effect for the very purpose for
which they did use them,—namely, to make man
feel his own utter insignificance in the presence of
him who, to cite the striking and almost scientific
language of Isaiah, had " weighed the mountains in
scales, and the hills in a balance."

But I go much further, and deny entirely that if
the physics and astronomy of a later age had been
familiar to the generation which saw the rise of
Christianity, it would have made any such difference

in the character of its theology as Mr. Frederic
Harrison maintains. He thinks, as we have seen,
that it would have been impossible to believe in an
Incarnation and an Atonement, for the benefit of our
petty human race, if it had been known that our
world is one of the mere atoms of the physical
universe, and that for anything we know, there may
be countless multitudes of worlds far more important
and far more advanced in the story of evolution than
this little earth. This assertion is the purest and,
as I believe, the most groundless of assumptions.
Where can you find the mind of the Christian theologian of that early day better set forth than in the
Epistle to the Hebrews, whoever may be the writer.
And what position does he take up ? He begins by
stating that the Son of God is the " heir of all things,
through whom also he made the worlds " (the revisers
of our version think that " the ages " may perhaps
be the true meaning, instead of " the worlds," though
they adhere to the old translation) ; " who being the
effulgence of his glory, and the express image of his
person, and upholding all things by the word of his
power, when he had made purification of sins, sat
down on the right hand of the Majesty on high ;
having become so much better than the angels, as he
hath inherited a more excellent name than they."
And then he goes on to argue at length that whereas
the higher spiritual orders of being whom the Jews
called angels, and who were God's ministers, though
not bound by earthly conditions, all rank beneath the
Son of God, this Son of God nevertheless manifested
himself in this petty world of ours to purify us from
sin, and obtain for us the blessedness which sin for-
feits. Of course, I do not dream of attributing to
any writer of the first century speculations like

Professor Whewell's on "The Plurality of Worlds."
But I do say that such writers had gathered, probably
from the time of the Babylonian exile, a very steadfast belief in a vast hierarchy of beings in power far
superior to man, and that their belief in this hierarchy
of superior beings in no degree affected their conviction that the redemption of man from sin is a work
worthy of the divine Incarnation, and of that divine
suffering to which the Incarnation led and in which
it was fulfilled. Why should that conviction have
been altered, if it had been supposed that this
hierarchy of angels, instead of · being placed vaguely
in the heavens, were the fixed inhabitants of any of
those shining worlds of which the prophets had
spoken as showing forth the wonderful power of
God ? How could any illustration of the utter insignificance of man have carried the belief in that insignificance further than it was carried by teachers who
declared that " all flesh is grass, and all the goodliness
thereof is as the flower of the field ; the grass
withereth, the flower fadeth, because the breath of
the Lord bloweth upon it ; surely the people is grass ;
the grass withereth, the flower fadeth, but the word
of our God shall stand for ever." It seems to me
that had the Hebrew teachers of the first or any
previous century been told that there are in creation
myriads of planets infinitely greater than our world,
and possibly inhabited by beings as much more exalted than man as their dwelling-places are greater,
they would not have been staggered in the very least.
They would have said that if in such worlds what
corresponds to human sin had taken place,—which
would, of course, be matter of pure conjecture,—they
had no doubt that the mercy of God would equally
have provided something corresponding to human re-

demption ; but that, at all events, we cannot ground
any but the most worthless objection to what we do
know, on conjectures as to what we do not know.
We do know what God is, and what sin is, and what 
redemption is, and we must act on what we do know.
To disbelieve in a revealed spiritual power of which
we stand in the greatest need, only because physical
astronomers have suggested that there may be countless other races needing the same aid that we need,
or even needing it more, but of the answer to whose
need we can know nothing because we know nothing
about the real existence of it, would be as frivolous
as to shut our eyes to the actual light we have and
ignore its existence, only because we may conjecture
with some plausibility that countless other beings in
other worlds need light as much or more than we
do, while we have no absolute assurance that, if they
do need it, they have it in the same rich abundance.
If the ants in an ant-hill were capable of duty and
sin in the sense in which we are capable of it, why
should not they, too, yearn for and obtain redemption ?   And to show that we are ants in a moral and
spiritual ant-hill relatively to the infinite universe
around us, far from showing that we can afford to
ignore the mercy of God, only because we are such
poor creatures, would only show that we are all the
more bound to accept with gratitude that which prevents us from being poorer than we need be,—poorer
especially in that highest of all blessings which re-
conciles us to the spirit of God.

THE MAGNANIMITY OF UNBELIEF

1877

IN the papers which Mr. Frederic Harrison has contributed to the *Nineteenth Century* on " The Soul and Future Life," and in his reply to the many criticisms which those papers drew down upon him, there is visible precisely the same state of mind which is so curiously illustrated in Harriet Martineau's *Autobiography*,—the state of mind, we mean, which Miss Cobbe, in her striking contribution to a recent *Theological Review*, happily terms one of "magnanimous atheism."   Any one who has seen a shrunken and withered apple apparently revive under the exhausted receiver of an air-pump, may perhaps have some notion, derived from that analogy, of the reason of this swelling of the heart in a sort of triumphant relief at the imaginary evanescence of the religious influences under the pressure of which it had lived.   The apple swells out because the atmospheric pressure on the outside is removed, and the confined air in it consequently expands till it seems as sound and plump as it was while all its juices were rich and full.   And so, we take it, the elation of mind which Harriet Martineau so vividly describes, the gratulation wherewith she looked up to the midnight stars, and thought within herself that the creeds of her youth were a system of illusions which she and Mr. Atkinson had contrived to throw off, was due to the cessation of the pressure of that sense of constant obligation and claim under which she had formerly been living, and its exchange for the conviction that instead of trying to interpret painfully the demands of another and higher spirit upon her own, all she had to do was to give free vent to her own aspirations, and follow the impulses of her own thought. "When,"wrote Miss Martineau,[1] " in the evenings of that spring, I went out (as I always do when in health) to meet the midnight on my terrace, or in bad weather in the porch, and saw and felt what I always do see and feel there at that hour, what did it matter whether people who were nothing to me had smiled or frowned when I passed them in the village in the morning ? When I experienced the still new joy of feeling myself to be a portion of the universe, resting on the security of its everlasting laws, certain that its Cause was wholly out of the sphere of human attributes, and that the special destination of my race is infinitely nobler than the highest prepared under a scheme of divine moral government, how could it matter to me that the adherents of a decaying mythology (the Christian following the heathen as the heathen followed the barbaric-fetish) were fiercely clinging to their Man-God, their scheme of salvation, their reward and punishment, their essential pay-system, as ordered by their mythology ? . . . To the emancipated, it is a small matter that those who remain imprisoned arc shocked at the daring which goes forth into the

[1] *Autobiography*, vol. ii. p. 355.

sunshine and under the stars to study and enjoy, without leave asked, or the fear of penalty." In precisely the same tone, Mr. Frederic Harrison expounds his 'religion of humanity,' and throws off all the beliefs of the theologians, as constructed out of "dithyrambic hypotheses and evasive tropes." There is in all the Positivists, a note of scornful triumph as they clear their souls of what they call the superstitions of ages, and exhort us to be content with worshipping the providence which the race of man exercises over individual men, and with anticipating the 'posthumous activities' which are to be the somewhat worthless, but the only conceivable, equivalents for immortal growth. In all the soliloquies and all the homilies to which the Positivists give utterance, you can see the same sense of relief, in fact the air which Miss Cobbe so well describes as the air of magnanimity,—as if they were doing something rather grand, and rising in their own estimation, as they cast to the winds the old faiths. Yet Miss Martineau, as Miss Cobbe reminds us, was almost dismayed when she thought of the pain which her new belief in personal annihilation would carry to the heart of some friends of hers who were widows, and who lived in the hope not only of a future life in God, but of a future reunion with the objects of their warmest earthly love, and whom she feared it might even deprive of reason to have this hope taken away from them. Yet with all this dismay, she speaks of her new disbelief as a potent remedy for human ills which it would be selfish in her to keep to herself. "My comrade and I both care for our kind, and we could not see them suffering as we had suffered, without imparting to them our consolation and our joy. Having found, as my friend said, a spring in the desert, should we see the multitude wandering in desolation and not show them our refreshment?" Whereupon Miss Cobbe remarks, "Would it not have been a more appropriate simile to say, 'Having found that the promised land was a mirage, we hastened back joyfully to bring the interesting tidings to our friends in the wilderness, some of whom we expected would go mad when they received our intelligence, to which, from their great respect for us, we knew they would attach the utmost importance. By some strange fortuity, however, they did not quite believe our report, and went on their way as before, under the pillar of cloud'?" Yet it is evident that while, on the one hand, the Positivists are conscious that they are trying to remove a faith in which the human spirit profoundly rests, they do really feel, on the other hand, as if those who can share their point of view were throwing off a weight of care, and growing freer and nobler and more dignified beings in so doing,—as if in fact, to use Miss Martineau's phrase, going "to meet the midnight" were an infinitely freer and less humiliating act of mind than going to meet God. They move more easily when they imagine themselves merely under the midnight than they could under the eye of Divine righteousness, and they become higher beings in their own estimation, just as the apple blooms out again under the exhausted receiver. Mr. Harrison, indeed, expressly finds fault with the Christian order of thought for thinking so poorly of man as he is. He speaks of the view of their own lives taken by men who hold that much of what they have done will result in 'posthumous activities' of a very unsatisfactory kind, and a great proportion of their past in posthumous activities that are simply morally indifferent, being neither bad nor good, as they were mere pessimists, and adds, " Pessimism as to the essential dignity of man, and the steady development of his race, is one of the surest marks of the enervating influence of this dream of a celestial glory." In other words, to Mr. Harrison, as certainly to Miss Martineau, all humiliation is pessimism,—even though it touches in no way the essential dignity of man, but rather only the unsuccessful attempts of the individual ego to reach that essential dignity of man. As the belief in God vanishes, the satisfaction with ourselves as we are, grows, and we begin to be quite sure that the vast majority of all our "posthumous activities" will go to increase the store of testimony accumulating to all future ages of "the essential dignity of man."

I am far from blaming the Positivists for this result of their scepticism. It seems to me to be in most cases a certain result of it ;—of course not in all cases, because the vanishing of the belief in God does not in the least extinguish Him ; and to those few who are real enough to see the truth about *themselves*, in spite of the intellectual bewilderment in which they may live as to the Author of their being, the consciousness of the poverty of their motives, and of the vein of selfishness in even their best actions, of the half-and-halfness of their aspirations, of the mixture of self-love in their affections, and of the dull edge of their virtue, must be as keen as if they fully recognised the Presence which really shows them all this about themselves. But there are very few of us who are thus realists. Inevitably, in the cultivated at least, the failure to recognise anything higher than man above us must make man himself, —even as he is,—seem a more satisfactory being

than he can ever seem to those who compare him
constantly with Christ. As certainly as the failure
to recognise the attraction of the sun led our forefathers into all sorts of exaggerations of the stability
of the earth, the failure to recognise the divine love
and righteousness, will lead those who miss them to
exaggerate the worth and value of human love and
righteousness. It is the weight of our debt and
obligation which makes us see what poor creatures,
except through the divine help, we really are. Remove the sense of these higher obligations, and we
grow inevitably in our own estimation, just as the
withered apple revives when the air ceases to press
upon it. Indeed, the real issue between the Positivist
and the Christian might fairly well be summed-up in
the one question whether humility be a morbid and
misleading quality, or the very truth and core of all
real self-knowledge. If the former, the Positivists
are right; if the latter, the Christians. But what
shall be the test? Surely the experience of the past
affords us test enough. Mr. Harrison says in effect
that the tendency to think lightly of man as he is, is
the result,—and I agree with him,—of man's "dream
of celestial glory." Well, but what has been the
moral fruit of that stoic self-estimation and magnanimity which is now again lifting up its head, as compared with the attitude of moral humiliation which
Mr. Harrison calls "pessimism"? Whence have the
great beneficent moral agencies of the world sprung?
From the optimism of self-satisfied human dignity,
or from the pessimism,—if so it is to be called,—of
the ages of humility? Surely all that is morally
great in man, from the greater works of charity to
the greater triumphs of the spirit of truth, have
sprung out of that humility which has ascribed all

its achievements to the power of God, and has found
the confidence necessary for effecting even the greatest revolutions in human society only because it believed itself to be driven on by Him.   The grand
picturesque magnanimity of the Stoic school has done
nothing for humanity, compared with the spirit of
Christian humiliation; and, tested by the past at
least, the equanimity or magnanimity which seems
to spring from unbelief will be barren indeed, compared with the self-depreciation, or even, if you please
to call it so, self-disgust, springing out of the knowledge of a diviner Presence and a mightier Will.

XXXII

AUGUSTE COMTE'S ASPIRATION

1877

SIR ERSKINE PERRY'S account, in the *Nineteenth Century* for November, of his interview with Auguste Comte in the year 1853 is not one to be easily forgotten. It brings out in full relief, as one of the most distinguished of his disciples has lately brought out in the same journal, that the daring experiment of Comte was this,—to see if, by renouncing all talk about causes, he could not so manage that men should both reject their faith and keep it, eat their cake and have it too. It has always been a grievance with ordinary men that this seems impossible. Comte boldly availed himself of this sense of grievance, and by persuading himself that if we would give up talking about causes we might cease to suffer from this grievance, really persuaded a school, comprehending some extremely able men, to make a fight for the chance of uniting all the pleasures of aristocratic scepticism with all the pleasures of a glowing faith. And Sir Erskine Perry's picture helps us to see the kind of man to whom such an experiment was possible. The "smallish, stooping man, in long tweed dressing-gown, much bloodshot

in one eye, healthy rose tint, short black hair, small
Celtic features, forehead unremarkable, agreeable
physiognomy," who believed that in 1857 he should
be preaching Positivism "from the pulpit of Nôtre
Dame" (in 1857 he died); who was so keen for
the government of an intellectual aristocracy, and
so confident that he should found a school "like
Aristotle or St. Paul" (note the disjunctive conjunc-
tion, associating the two most different types of
founders in the world), "and one that will probably
be more important than those two joined together;"
who anticipated the time when journalism should be
replaced by broadsheets affixed to the walls of great
towns, wherein those who had anything to say should
say to the people just what they wanted, and *no
more;* who had given up reading altogether, except now and then something from a favourite poet;
who spoke of the spirit of Christianity as completely egotistical and not sufficiently 'altruistic'—
i.e., unselfish—for "positive" thinkers; who weekly
visited the grave of Clotilde de Vaux, and continued
to rent the apartment he had hired in more
prosperous days chiefly because, as he mentioned
with tears in his eyes, it was the scene of his intercourse with that "holy colleague"; and who showed
with a certain solemnity to his visitor the little
ante-room in which "many important sacraments
have already been performed,—marriages, presenta-
tion of children, etc."—the man, we say, who stood
for this picture seems a perfect equivalent in the
intellectual sphere for those tenacious clingers to the
shadow of the past after the substance has been
abandoned, of whom we so often read amongst needy
nobles of blue-blood, men who go through the solemn
form of stately life, and persuade themselves that it

is as stately as ever, when all that gave it meaning
is passed away.   Yet Sir Erskine Perry's picture is
evidently both a faithful and friendly one, indeed
the picture drawn by a disciple, or something like a
disciple.   Comte evidently hoped, and Mr. Harrison
evidently hopes, to make as grand a use of the
feelings which grow out of a profound faith, in the
absence as in the presence of that faith.   And this
he called Positivism,—that is, sticking to what you
have got in human nature, without troubling yourself as to its roots.   It was Professor Huxley, we
think, who first described Positivism as Catholicism
without God.   And I am disposed to think that
that epigrammatic description was by no means dis-
pleasing to some of the best Positivists themselves.
Certainly Mr. Frederic Harrison has been doing a
good deal, in those eloquent articles of his on
"The Soul and Future Life," to justify the phrase.
He uses all the words appropriate to Catholic faith
in the new sense which excludes that faith,—speaks,
for instance, of the "Soul" as the mere "harmony
of man's various powers,"—of "Providence" as the
mysterious power by which man controls his own
destiny,—of "immortality" as "posthumous energy,"
and then boldly claims for words which he has carefully disembowelled of their old meaning, all the
charm and magic of associations which that old
meaning had alone bestowed.   Now, the picture of
the founder of this system, as painted by the kindly
and admiring hand of Sir Erskine Perry, more than
justifies this procedure.   He paints us a man of
thin fanaticism, a dreamer who lived on a few
unsubstantial ideas *plus* an excitability of brain
which made the eye bloodshot and the unreal seem
real.   Comte thought it a duty to 'personify,' after

he had given up believing in a person. He discoursed at great length to Sir Erskine Perry, in reply to that gentleman's sturdy English objections to such a procedure, and discoursed with what Sir Erskine Perry called " his brilliant flow of words," on the necessity for speaking of humanity as a *Grand Être*, " in order to concentrate ideas." Nay, he justified the use of the female form, as the most natural " type of what is excellent and loveable," for the purpose of rendering the personification more lively, and justified expressly on that ground his habit of frequently substituting the strange phrase *Déesse* for *Grand Être*. In the same way, Comte made as much or more of the Sacraments —minus their ancient meaning—as the Roman Catholics themselves who regard them as conveying a real stream of divine grace. He wanted, too, to get all the advantages exerted by a sacred caste—a priesthood—in subduing the minds of the people, without attributing to the priesthood any of those supernatural gifts on the belief in which the power of the priesthood really rests. If any one thwarted him in this attempt to combine what seemed legitimately uncombinable, his method of dealing with his critic was remarkable. For instance, Sir Erskine Perry, as I have already intimated, told him he did not think the coarse common-sense of mankind would stand being told to worship a *Grand Être* or even a *Déesse* which had no more existence than an abstract idea. Comte was equal to the occasion. " Ah ! " said he, " I fear you do not render justice to the middle-ages, and have too many prejudices still in your mind belonging to the last century. The services which the Church rendered during a very long period, though for five centuries it has been undoubtedly retrograde, are inestimable. The spiritual dominion erected as a Power, the complete union of the affections and the intellect in pursuit of a common object, yielded fruits such as the world now knows nothing of." No doubt the world has nothing like it now; and why? Because M. Comte and others have done their best to persuade the world that the affections of Christians in the middle-ages were fixed not on real objects, but on a vacuum, occupied only by the empty intellectual abstractions of the human intellect. And then he endeavoured to restore the warmth of the old affections, after he had himself done all in his power to dry up the very source of them. The attempt to love a *Grand Être*, or even a *Déesse*, in the existence of which the mind does not believe, must always be a futile one, which only men of more fancy than realism, or some lesion of the brain, will be able to accomplish. Comte would probably say that as the affections formerly fixed on what he held to be a non-existent Deity were really strong, there is no reason why they should not become strong again, even though the existence before imagined were now intellectually denied. And of course for those who hold, as I do, that the frightful blunder is made by the deniers and not by the believers, it is impossible to argue with those who would prove the possibility of strong ideal affections by showing how strong they have been when fixed on beings who (mistakenly) seem to them merely ideal, though as they hold, superstitiously supposed by the common people to be real. Still, I should think that even Positivists must be struck by the actual results to those affections they say so much of, caused by dispelling what they deem the illusion as to the reality of their object. You may in a dream fall in love with a phantom, so long as

you believe it to be real; but, once convinced
(whether rightly or wrongly) that it is a pure
phantom, the power to love it vanishes at once.
Comte, however, and his disciples will have it otherwise. They think by the mere force of their in-
sistency, and the glowing words they use, to reconcile in man the sceptical mind and the believing
heart,—to inspire in him all the contempt for the
supernatural which is fostered by modern science,
and all the fervour of humility and affection towards
a caste of spiritual teachers which can only be felt
for men regarded as the depository of supernatural
inspiration or supernatural grace. In a word, the
aspiration of Positivism is an aspiration to combine
all sorts of moral contradictions; to get the masses
of the people to obey an intellectual oligarchy, without
attributing to that oligarchy any qualities which the
masses of the people can really revere,—to get them
to love what is unreal more fervently than they love
those whom they come across in the ordinary paths
of life; to regard with awe sacraments in which
nothing is ever supposed to pass, except an electric
spark of feeling between human beings; to worship
a Providence whose decrees are half of them mistakes,
and the other half mere conclusions of common-sense;
and to dwell in imagination on a future life in which
nothing will live that has any but an historical
relation to the nature which anticipates it. Comte
deliberately contemplated, no doubt, combining all
the advantages of caste government with all the
advantages of popular liberty; all the authority of
a Church, with all the scorn for superstition
characteristic of free thought; all the meditative
ecstasy of those who wished to live in God, with the
cold conviction of the student of mere phenomena

that there was no God to live in ; (Comte read a page of the *Imitatio* every day); all the rigidity and superficial simplicity of the phenomenal philosophy, with all the devout earnestness of devotees to a supernatural *régime*.   Now one can, of course, well understand and appreciate the wish to indulge at once the habit of doubt and the habit of faith, just as one can appreciate the desire of children both to eat their cake and have it.   But in such a world as the present, it does not seem to be a wise aspiration. Thinkers, like other men, should be content to take the good and evil of their systems as they are, and not aim at combining all the good of all sorts of incompatible systems, and then expect credit for their logic as well as for their breadth.   Hegelianism is not usually thought to have much affinity with Comteism.   But even Hegel never assumed to re-concile such utterly opposite and mutually incon-sistent habits of mind as Sir Erskine Perry's dis-tinguished teacher, Auguste Comte.

XXXIII

MATERIALISM AND ITS LESSONS

1879

UNDER this title, Dr. Maudsley dilates, in the August number of the *Fortnightly Review*, on the lessons to be learned from Materialism, and on the injustice of the reproaches so often directed against it. His paper, however, will hardly strike readers accustomed to discuss the questions on which it turns, as a very strong one. In the first place, Dr. Maudsley avails himself of the fact that a few great believers in the orthodox theology have, like Milton, and, at one time, Robert Hall, been materialists, to plead that Materialism is not inconsistent with orthodox theology; while the whole implicit tenor of his paper, and the explicit tenor of its conclusion, is to depreciate prayer, and even " penitence,"—indeed all the religious exercises on which theology of any school whatever would insist,—in favour of a strict conformity to the laws of social "evolution," whatever they may be, as the only upward path for man. His earlier plea, then, that a man may be a materialist and yet retain a tolerably orthodox creed, is a plea which weakens the effect of the rest of the paper, and gives an impression that Dr. Maudsley is anxious to find a mode of escape from the conclusions which, to him at least, seem the right and logical consequences of Materialism, for such of his readers as may shrink from holding those logical consequences as he holds them.   And it always puts a writer in a false position, that he should go painfully out of his way to show weaker brethren how they may, if they please, adopt his premises, without being absolutely compelled to come to his conclusions, though it is plain enough that he thinks the latter the only proper inferences deducible from the former.   This is the first note of weakness in the paper.   The second is more serious,—namely, that while Dr. Maudsley is very strong on "the lessons of Materialism," so far as they appear to sustain the accepted morality of the day, he does not seem to have the courage to note the lessons which are of an opposite tendency, though they appear to follow as clearly from his materialistic principles as the others.   Thus, he says, "When we look sincerely at the facts, we cannot help perceiving that it [moral feeling] is just as closely dependent upon organisation as the meanest function of mind; that there is not an argument to prove the so-called Materialism of one part of mind, which does not apply with equal force to the whole mind;" and he argues therefrom that all the highest phenomena of conscience and will are just as much functions of the physical organisation, as the suspension of conscious life is the result of the pressure of a piece of bone upon the brain.   That, I understand; and I understand also the satisfaction with which Dr. Maudsley notes the interchangeability of mental disease and moral degeneracy, the emphasis with which he insists that moral degeneracy is often the first sign of a coming mental alienation; and

again, that mental deficiency in the parent will come
out sometimes in descendants, in the form of a
deficiency of moral sense.   All this is evidently part
and parcel of Dr. Maudsley's case.   But then, what
can be clearer than that it is also part and parcel of
the same case to maintain that in no intelligible
sense of the term is any man more "responsible"
for anything he is, does, or suffers, than is the
victim of a fracture of the brain for the suspension
of consciousness which that fracture of the brain
causes.   Dr. Maudsley is never weary of insisting
that all the phenomena of mind, great and small,
are just as much functions of the material organisation, as are the phenomena of brain-disease in a
man whose brain has been staved in by the kick of a
horse, or whose blood has been drugged with opium.
Well, if that be true, he is, of course, quite right in
saying, "Whether this man goes upwards or down-
wards, undergoes development or degeneration, we
have equally to do with matters of stern law."   But
what can he mean by his very next sentence ?—
"Provision has been made for both ways; it has
been left to him to find out and *determine* which way
he shall take."   Why, if Dr. Maudsley's philosophy
has any truth in it at all, this is precisely what is
not "left to him."   It may, indeed, be given to men
of acuteness, if they be adequately endowed, to *find
out* which way they are to take, but as for determination,—that is, as Dr. Maudsley himself insists,
according to his belief, a "matter of stern law."   It
has been determined for them by the long and iron
chain of natural law, or else his doctrine is vicious
from beginning to end.   If it be, in any conceivable
sense of the word, more "left" to man whether he
shall take the upward path of development or the

downward path of degeneration, than it is "left" to the particle of dust whether it shall be blown this way or that way by the wind, the whole meaning of Dr. Maudsley's essay vanishes. What would he have said, if any one had told him that it was "left" to the lad whose brain was exposed, and on the exposed part of whose brain the doctor was sometimes pressing, and sometimes ceasing to press, whether he would answer the question put to him or not. He would have laughed at the unscientific statement, and ridiculed it as pure ignorance. Yet he has himself maintained that this case is a typical case, illustrating, so far as dependence on the physical organisation is concerned, all man's reasonable and moral life. If there is any reason at all in Dr. Maudsley's assertion that "when we look sincerely at the facts, we cannot help perceiving that it [moral feeling] is just as closely dependent upon organisation as is the meanest function of mind ; that there is not an argument to prove the so-called Materialism of one part of mind, which does not apply with equal force to the whole mind," what he means is this,—that the physician who experimented on the lad's exposed brain, by asking him a question, and then pressing on it, so producing complete unconsciousness, and then, again, discontinuing the pressure, when the lad answered the question just as if it had only been that instant asked, was just as much, and just as little, able to determine for himself whether he would or would not press on that exposed brain, or act otherwise than he did act, his own physical organisation and his own antecedents being what they were, as the boy under his finger was to determine whether he would or would not answer the question put to him, without reference to the

continuance or discontinuance of the pressure.   At
least if this be not Dr. Maudsley's doctrine, the
whole paper seems to me simply without meaning.
Once admit that man, at any moment in his existence,
has a real power of choosing in which of two
alternative ways he will go,—the upward path of
development, or the downward path of degeneration,
—and Dr. Maudsley's doctrine that " there is not an
argument to prove the so-called materialism of one
part of mind which does not apply with equal force
to the whole mind," is false.   For unquestionably he
believes that the lad with an exposed brain of whom
he speaks had no choice whether he would answer or
no, so long as the physician was pressing on that
exposed part of his brain ; and unless therefore,
there is precisely as absolute a dependence between
the determination which any man takes, at every
epoch in his life, whether he will choose the upward
path of development or the downward path of
degeneration, and the organisation which induces
him to take that determination, the general doctrine
announced by Dr. Maudsley cannot be sustained.
Yet the whole essay assumes its truth, and so far as
I can grasp its meaning, has no point, unless its
truth be assumed.   The whole attack upon the
doctrine of sudden solutions of continuity, the whole
"lesson" derived from the gradual enlargement, by
minute, but constant causes, of the brain of the
savage into the brain of modern civilisation, appears
to go for nothing, if it be admitted that any man
can so far emancipate himself from the influence of
his own organisation as to change its line of development, counteract the resultant of its existing forces,
and shift it from the downward to the upward path
of evolution, or *vice versâ*.   And yet, despite this

apparent confidence of Dr. Maudsley's in the iron logic of his position, he puzzles this reading by continually insisting on what he calls the "stern feeling of responsibility" which his principles enforce, and repeating that it is left to man "to determine which way he shall take." All we can say is that if it is so left to man, in any case whatever, to determine which way he shall take, there is no real analogy between the case of the patient with the exposed brain, who had no power at all to determine whether he would answer the question put to him or not, so long as the physician's finger pressed on his brain, and ordinary human beings in the act of determining on their course; whereas, if there be no such analogy, the large materialistic generalisation of Dr. Maudsley's essay is a false generalisation, and the moral significance of his elaborate introduction is utterly unintelligible. As it seems to me, Dr. Maudsley uses the materialistic hypothesis so long as he likes it, and dispenses with it just when it suits him to dispense with it, though, of course, he is not conscious of his own inconsistency. While he wants to enforce the absolute dependence of the mind on the body for the purpose of ridiculing the hypothesis of a separate spirit, he keeps our attention constantly fixed on those phenomena which are typical of this dependence,—on the injured brain, the mental phenomena in connection with which you can produce at will by physical means as you play on a piano with your fingers,—on the moral effect of drugs which in some directions is equally sure,— on the connection finally between physical and mental disease. But the moment he wishes to expound the high "morality" of materialism, he changes his policy; he then begins to talk quite freely of our power of determining whether we will strike into the upward or downward track ; of our stern responsibility for our choice ; and so forth. While he is in this vein, we hear nothing of our moral actions being as much functions of our physical organisation, as insane illusion is a function of physical disease. We are, on the contrary, represented as having real alternatives before us, and as if no tyrannical physical organisation were dictating to us what we should be. The analogy of the trephined patient is here utterly forgotten. The higher moral feelings are appealed to as if they were the feelings of a totally different being from him who is thus made to respond to the proper stimulus, just as a nerve responds to an electric excitement,—and the great law of Dr. Maudsley's essay is forgotten. Now, I submit that this is not philosophy. Let Dr. Maudsley choose which he will have. Is the patient on whose brain you can play as certainly as on a piano, the type of all moral agents in all moral actions, or not ? If he is, let us hear nothing of the high morality which gives us a choice between the upward and downward path. If he is not, let us hear nothing of the great generalisation which deduces that " there is not an argument to prove the so-called materialism of one part of mind, which does not apply with equal force to the whole mind."

For my part, I have no hesitation in saying that Dr. Maudsley is quite right when he recognises that there are acts as to which we have an absolute choice, and quite wrong when he tries to make the wholly involuntary response of the mind to a physical stimulus, the type of all our mental actions. The structure of our language, the laws of our country, the assumptions of common-sense in every minute of our lives, all affirm this ; and yet all affirm that there are also mental functions which follow as inevitably from the application of a physical stimulus, as the striking of a clock follows the descent of the striking-weight.   But then, if there be two quite different types of the workings of our mental life,— the optional and the involuntary,—the free cause and the bound effect,—the philosophy of Dr. Maudsley falls to pieces.   Not only is his rationale of the mind incomplete, and incomplete at the most important point, but his rationale of the universe fails with his rationale of the mind.   If the mind be not a mere function of a material organisation, the whole of his dogmatic denial that there is any room for the spiritual interaction of a divine mind with the human, collapses at once, and indeed, the thesis of his paper becomes false.   Of course, Dr. Maudsley will not admit this.   He will zealously maintain that what he calls the responsible act of man in choosing between " development" and "degeneration," is quite as much an effect of material organisation as any other.   And of course, he has a perfect philo-sophic right to maintain this, only I think he should explain clearly that what he means when he speaks of the momentous responsibility of choice, is nothing at all,—nothing, at least, more than what Calvinism means when it talks of the same thing.   He should confess frankly that it is a mere illusion, not a reality, that he refers to,—that the question between development and degeneration is determined for everybody for all time, as surely as it was deter-mined for all time whether the seed which existed before animal life had ever appeared on the earth, should develop into the flower, or should rot into the elements from which it sprang.   Again, if this be, as I suppose, Dr. Maudsley's solution of the question, why, instead of *assuming* that the phenomenon of a spontaneous response to physical stimulus is the type of all mental action, did he not endeavour very carefully to prove this, and to bridge over the immense chasm between such cases as that of the lad whose mind was prevented from acting by pressure on the brain, and that of the man who stands at the meeting of the two ways between "development" and "degeneration," and to whom he himself ascribes the stern responsibility of choosing between the two?   In shirking this demonstration, Dr. Maudsley shirks the very kernel of the question he was discussing.

MOZLEY'S UNIVERSITY SERMONS

1876

It is curious, and to some extent, no doubt, a bitter disappointment to those who believe in the Christian faith, to see how very few traces we have had, of late years, of what may be called religious genius,—such genius, for instance, as shows itself in the sermons of Dr. Newman; and again, though in a very different form, in the sermons of Mr. Maurice; or again, under another totally different shape, in the sermons of Dr. Martineau. As a rule, just in proportion as a subject is capable of exciting strong feeling, it is capable of attracting originality and creative power. Science and Art get their full share of genius, and so, till lately, have fiction and politics. But for many years back, religion has hardly been able to boast of any real genius specially appropriate to its own sphere. Mr. Kingsley, for instance, was a man of genius, but the special sphere of his genius was assuredly not religious. He could throw infinitely more genius into a page or two of his description of a hunt than he put into a whole volume of sermons, excellent and earnest as some of those sermons were. Sermons are by no means the dreary things they are called.   One is always meeting with good sermons, thoughtful, earnest, even wise.   But what one now hardly ever meets with are sermons wherein it is clear that an original mind is working under the influence of that specially congenial atmosphere which breathes a new life into its powers.   For some time back, it has seemed as if original genius of a specially appropriate kind were developed by almost every kind of strong influence except religion.   And years had elapsed since I took up any new religious book showing the sort of special power to deal, after a masterly and peculiar fashion of its own, with the subject treated in it, till a few weeks ago there appeared the Oxford University sermons of Dr. J. B. Mozley.   Here, at last, I found something more than capacity and clearness of thought and earnestness and qualities of that kind.   I found, or thought I found, that special aptitude to deal with the subject which, though of course in a far higher degree, has obtained for Dr. Newman's Oxford University sermons their wide and very just celebrity.   Dr. Mozely is not so wide in his scope as Dr. Newman. There is probably far less in him of that marvellous capacity for illustrating the secrets of character, which made even the plainest of Dr. Newman's sermons so wonderful as studies of the natural history of the moral nature of man.   Dr. Mozley's genius is of a slighter kind, and runs within narrower limits.   Still, it seems to me to be true genius, and true genius of the religious kind,—the sort of genius which would *not* have been equally elicited by ethical or psychological questions of any other sort, but which is brought into play only under the definite influence of the faith of which these sermons are scattered expositions.   There is in Dr. Mozley

that reality and simplicity of style which, though it
does not necessarily imply genius, does imply that,
where there is genius, it is in its natural home, and
not merely borrowed from some other sphere.   'Take,
for instance, such a sentence as the following, about
a future life :—"No ground lays firm hold on our
minds for a continuation of existence at all, except
such a ground as makes that continuation an ascent.
The prolongation of it and the rise in the scale of it
go together, because the true belief is, in its very
nature, an aspiration, and not a mere level expectation of the mind ; and therefore, while a low eternity
obtained no credit, the Gospel doctrine inspired a
strong conviction, because it dared to introduce the
element of glory into the destiny of man."   That is
a noble saying, and one which should warn the
Spiritualists of to-day that even if they can persuade
the world of the facts they insist on, they will
substitute, *not* a faith like that of Christ for a doubt
or a guess, but a certainty which may be in great
danger of making the invisible world as dusty and
wearisome to many of us as the visible world already
is.   Or take, again, the following, as to the test of
true faith :—"Activity is not the Gospel's sole test.
It requires faith too.   It speaks of much work, and
work which we know was not mere formal and
ceremonial, but real work,—active, strong work,—
as dross ; as dead works, which had physical vivacity,
but not the breath of heaven in them.   Activity is
naturally, at first sight, our one test of faith,—what
else should it spring from ? we say ; and yet experience corrects this natural assumption, for active
men can be active almost about anything, and
amongst other things, about a religion in which they
do not believe.   They can throw themselves into

public machinery and the bustle of crowds, when, if
two were left together to make their confession of
faith to each other, they would feel awkward. But
there is something flat, after all, in the activities of
men who *accommodate* themselves to the Gospel."
Or again, take this fine description of the effect
produced by the realistic sceptic, who sees that the
belief in the future life is, in great multitudes, a
mere customary idea or picture, not founded deep in
their spiritual nature, and therefore that it can be
dispelled by the kind of questions which make the
unsubstantial character of the vision suddenly
apparent to them:—"Do you really believe in this
idea? Examine it, he says—is it not a mere idea, a
mere image that you have raised, or that has been
raised for you? Where is this heaven that you talk
about? Is it above your head? Is it beneath your
feet? Do you seriously think that if you were to
go millions of miles in any quarter of the compass,
you would find it? Is it anywhere in all space?
And if not, *what* is its *where?* Is there another
world besides the whole world? When thus
suddenly challenged then, what can such minds
do? The secret is out, and the disclosure is
made to them that the idea *in them* is only
an idea. The world to come disappears in a
moment like a phantom; the reign of the ap-
parition is over, and a dream is dispelled. It
is the unbelieving counterpart of conversion;
a man awakens in conversion to the reality of the
invisible world; here he awakens to the nonen-
tity of it."

This keen simplicity and reality in the way of
putting things is characteristic of these sermons of
Dr. Mozley's, but not less characteristic of them,—

and this is what shows that the Christian faith has
in him appealed to a certain original faculty of the
kind which we call "genius,"—is the instinctive
sympathy which he seems to have with the subtler
shades of Christ's teaching, so as to make it suddenly
seem new to us, as well as more wonderful than ever.
Take, for instance, this comment on the often quoted
passage, "Many will say to me in that day, 'Lord,
Lord, have we not prophesied in thy name, and in
thy name cast out devils, and in thy name done
many wonderful works?' And then will I profess
unto them, 'I never knew you.'" This, says Dr.
Mozley, most truly, "is a very remarkable prophecy,
for one reason, that in the very first start of
Christianity, upon the very threshold of its entrance
into the world, it looks *through* its success and
universal reception, into an ulterior result of that
victory,—a counterfeit profession of it. It sees
before the first nakedness of its birth is over, a
prosperous and flourishing religion, which it is worth
while for others to pay homage to, because it reflects
credit on its champion. Our Lord anticipates
the time when active zeal for himself will be no
guarantee. And we may observe the difference
between Christ and human founders. The latter are
too glad of any zeal in their favour, to examine very
strictly the tone and quality of it. They grasp at it
at once; not so our Lord. He does not want it even
for himself, unless it is pure in the individual." Or
as Dr. Mozley remarks, in another place, Christ is
always reversing human judgments, and impressing
us, with what we have now the means of knowing
to have been his sagacious and salutary distrust of
them, even when they seemed most favourable to his
purposes. He is sanguine beyond all reason, and

yet warns his followers that half their own sanguine judgments will have to be reversed ; 'Believe it not,' 'take heed that no man deceive you.' When their hope swells high, then they are to distrust themselves ; and when despair sets in, then they are to distrust themselves still more. The source of their confidence will mortify their hopes and will rebuke their fears ; for it is deeper than either.

Such qualities as I have dwelt upon run through Dr. Mozley's sermons. Nay, now and then they are diversified by some passage showing a power of touch which again recalls the same name I have before ventured to utter in connection with him, Dr. Newman's. In the passage, for instance, in the sermon on 'The Pharisees,' in which Dr. Mozley contrasts the conscience of the heathens, "this wild, this dreadful, but still this great visitant from another world," full of dark and troubled dreams, awakening them out of their sleep, and urging them to fly, without telling them whither they could fly, with the "pacified," "domesticated," "tame" conscience of the Pharisee, "converted into a manageable, an applauding companion, vulgarised, humiliated, and chained," Dr. Mozley touches a chord which for many a year has been little sounded. For religious genius has long been a stranger to our Churches, though there has been plenty of the best kind of religious purpose and sincerity. It seemed that for a few years the magic spell of Christianity for the heart of Englishmen had thus far been lost, that no special faculty prepared by the past, and fed with the specific food which is alone fitted to stimulate faculty of the higher order, had been germinated by the Christianity of our own day, so that as the greater religious minds of the past lost their control of one generation, none appeared in their place to teach us anew, in the dialect of our own time, the secret of the Christian life. In Dr. Mozley's Oxford University sermons, such a mind, I think, will be recognised.

PROFESSOR HUXLEY ON THE EVOLUTION OF THEOLOGY

1886

PROFESSOR HUXLEY'S article in the *Nineteenth Century* for March on "The Evolution of Theology" is not, I think, worthy of his great ability. There is little in it that properly justifies the word "evolution" at all, and it is marked by a scornful tone of contempt for those who are likely "to meet with anything they dislike" in his pages, which is hardly conceived in good taste. Still I am not amongst those who think that "in dealing with theology we ought to be guided by considerations different from those which would be thought appropriate if the problem lay in the province of chemistry or mineralogy," except, indeed, so far as the difference of province involves necessarily a difference of method. I should be eager to maintain that there is as genuine evolution in theology, as there is in any human science. If Mr. Spencer is right in holding that the development of organisation in general, means the gradual increase in the correspondence between the organ and that which environs it, it is as true of the development of theology, as of any other department of human life. But I do not hold, as some evolutionists appear to hold, that there is no real object external to man into a more complete correspondence with which the evolution of theology brings us; nor does that appear to me an opinion proper to true evolutionists at all. On the contrary, I hold that there is such an object; that that object is the great Being infinitely above us, in whom all the tentatives towards a more complete correspond-ence between us and him have originated, and from whom they go forth; and that the Bible, though it undoubtedly is what Professor Huxley calls it, a literature and not a book, has its unity in the fact that it is the literature of a race specially educated by that great invisible Being himself, to perceive that righteousness is of his essence, and that no "correspondence" between man and God is possible except on condition of a greater and greater reflection by man of that essence. Why it should be held, as it seems to be held by some of the evolutionists, that while every other regular development of man's nature issues in a more delicate and a more compre-hensive "correspondence" between man and the universe outside him, theology should be the one exception in which the development of our mind only brings upon us a liability to greater and greater illusions, I cannot conceive. The nerve which is at first only dimly sensitive to light, is supposed by the evolutionists to emerge at last in that wonderful combination of all kinds of co-operating powers, the eye of man. The nerve, which is at first but dimly sensitive to the vibrations of the atmosphere, is supposed by the evolutionists to emerge at last in that wonderful organ to which the oratorio speaks in mystic language such as the highest mind cannot adequately interpret. The feeble faculty of counting on the fingers is supposed by the evolutionists to develop into that wonderful calculus by which we compute the path of the comet, and weigh the sun itself in a balance. Can it possibly be true that the mind and the conscience are exceptions to this law of the senses and the judgment? Is the mind alone not in "correspondence" with the law of the environment, when it discerns purpose in the universe? Is the highest aspect of man's mind, his sense of duty, not in correspondence with the spirit of the environment when it discerns righteousness and purity at the heart of the universe? If so, surely man is indeed what some of the evolutionists hold,—what, indeed, Professor Huxley seems to hold,—a worshipper of magnified ghosts. But why sensitive nerves should bring us true knowledge of what is outside us, and sensitive consciences false knowledge of what is outside us, it passes my comprehension to say.

Nevertheless, those who read the article on "The Evolution of Theology" will find him, as it seems to me, extremely anxious to make the most of what may fairly be called the crude theology of the earlier parts of the Old Testament, not with a view to showing how it develops into what is greater and nobler, but with a view, on the contrary, to dwelling with a kind of triumph on its poverty. I have no objection to admit to the fullest extent the poverty of these elements. I think it quite probable that, as Professor Huxley holds, the writer of the third chapter of Genesis conceived the Lord God walking in the Garden in the cool of the day as a figure in the form of man. I believe it to be true that in the earlier books of the Bible, Jehovah—(why does Professor Huxley insist on the pedantic Jahveh?)—

was conceived only as a much mightier God than the gods of the heathen,—a mightier being of the same order. I have no objection to admit that in the earlier days of Israel it was supposed,—as Isaiah certainly shows evidence that it was supposed, or he would not so passionately denounce the impression, —that God took delight in the burnt sacrifices. In a word, nothing can be truer than that the Bible shows a steady evolution of the conception of God, from the early chapters of Genesis to the revelation of Christ. If it be true that the teraphim of the Israelites were something like the *lares* of the Romans, I am not startled by it. But what surprises me in Professor Huxley's essay is the apparent inability to see the vast gulf between the most inchoate forms of Israelite theology and the foolish superstitions of the natives of Torres Straits,—whom, by the way, he and his friend very unjustifiably did their best to confirm in the most foolish of those superstitions, simply in order that they might avail themselves of them to widen their own anthropological knowledge,—or of the natives of the Tonga Islands. Nothing can be more instructive than the comparison between these superstitions and the rudest of all the forms of Israelite theology, as showing not only that the latter had the power of firmly impressing spiritual truth from which whole nations have derived their highest elements of civilisation, but also that the earliest germs of the Jewish theology' were far beyond what they could have been, had they not been developed *ab initio* by an impulse not from within, but from above. Take what Professor Huxley calls the "freshest,"—meaning, I think, the oldest and rudest,—of the "fossiliferous strata" in the Books of Judges and Samuel,

and compare them with the superstitions which he
relates with such gusto as those in which his friend
and he confirmed the natives of the Torres Straits,
and which Mariner discovered in the Tonga Islands.
We seem to be in a totally different world. From
the beginning to the end of Jewish history we find
the deep, though ever-growing, belief in a personal
power, who from the first "killeth and maketh alive,
bringeth down to Sheôl and bringeth up;" who sets
his brand upon the murderer's forehead; who tasks
to the utmost the love of him whom he recognises as
his friend; who gives a strict moral law to a
licentious people, by which they are to be severed
from the rest of the nations; who expects his people
to recognise the invisible impress of his spirit on the
hearts of their judges and prophets, and not only to
recognise it, but to recognise also the disloyalty to it
of which those judges and prophets were often guilty;
who chooses the king most after his own heart, and
then sternly rebukes him when he breaks his law;
who inspires the noblest devotional lyrics which the
world has ever known, and the noblest prophecies
of a divine universalism, amidst the narrowest of
fierce race prejudices; and who finally reveals himself
in the one character which, after two thousand
years, even sceptics treat as raised so high above the
level of humanity, that we can only toil after it
through the ages with a growing sense of its hopeless
superiority to human aspiration.   That is what I
call "evolution," and evolution of the highest kind.
Do the superstitions of the Torres Straits, to which
Professor Huxley's friend and he himself lent their
sanction, show any sign of an evolution such as this?
Do the superstitions of the Tonga Islands develop
into a great history and divine order such as this?

They are, in fact, what Professor Huxley calls them, "ghost-worship." But, whatever he may say, there is absolutely no sign of ghost-worship in Israel, unless Saul's visit to the witch of Endor,—a visit which on the face of it was unfaithful to all the higher principles of his own life, and of the law in which his faith had resulted,—is to be so called. Never was a paper with a noble title so disappointing as that in which Professor Huxley endeavours to minimise the true significance of Jewish theology by grouping together all the poorer elements in the Israelite religion, and showing their (very slight) affinity to the savage superstitions of the present day.

Professor Huxley's second paper on "The Evolution of Theology" is even more unsatisfactory than the first. So far as he confines himself to the exposition of the superstitions of the Tonga islanders or the Samoan islanders, he does not throw any light on what he means by evolution. He shows that there was a certain similarity between the practices by which Saul, for instance, endeavoured to discover something hidden from him, and the practices of the Pacific islanders when they attempt divination of the same kind; and that there is a close analogy between David's prayer to have his offence visited exclusively on his own head, and the desire of a Tongan prince to secure the same result. I cannot say that either of these analogies seems to me at all important. The impression that you can discover by a sort of natural magic what you do not know, and desire to know, is not confined to rude peoples. It is implied in the popular usages of almost every people in the world, and I do not believe that it is half so vivid an impression among any class of minds on which revealed religion has taken a strong hold, as it is among those given up to the eager superstitions of the uneducated heart. That Jehovah was consulted by Urim and Thummim, by casting lots, and other Hebrew methods of divination, is quite true ; but the question is not whether such modes of discovering the secrets of destiny prevailed among the Hebrews, but whether they did not prevail much *less* among the Hebrews in consequence of the revelation they had received, than they prevailed amongst the Gentile nations to whom there was no such revelation, and who sent near and far to consult oracles in time of danger. Again, that David prayed that the consequence of his supposed disobedience might be visited exclusively upon himself, is no doubt as true as it is true that the Tongan chief did the same ; and, indeed, there is hardly a noble-minded ruler, or a true father or mother, in existence, who has not prayed to be allowed to bear, on behalf of those for whom the heart has been deeply moved, the penalty which might otherwise be expected to descend on those whom it is desired to shield. But I think it would be easy to show that, natural as this passionate desire to be allowed to suffer vicariously for another is, to the heart of a loyal ruler, or parent, or protector of any kind, revelation has always tempered, instead of stimulating, this unchastened eagerness, by enlightening the conscience, and showing those who have any real knowledge of God that his ways are higher than our ways, and his thoughts than our thoughts. What Professor Huxley utterly fails to do is to show that in any sense whatever the higher ideas of revelation can be traced to the gradual accretions of human superstition. For all we know, the religion of the Tongan islanders has had a longer time in which to evolve itself than the religion of the Jewish Prophets had had in the days of Isaiah. But compare the two results. The one is all magic and intellectual groping ; the other was a coherent, severe, and sublime faith.

But, as I understand Professor Huxley, the Prophets did not, in his opinion, continue the line of theological evolution. On the contrary, they did their best to purge away the adventitious sacerdotal and ceremonial elements from the Hebrew religion. They tried to bring Israel back to the worship of a " moral ideal,"—Jehovah being, in Professor Huxley's opinion, a mere moral ideal. In Professor Huxley's view, the Prophets were the reformers, the Puritans of the Hebrew people. Far from developing the dogmas and ceremonies handed down to them, " they are constantly striving to free the moral ideal from the stifling embrace of the current theology and its concomitant ritual." Yet in spite of his two papers on "The Evolution of Theology," I have arrived at no clear impression at all of what Professor Huxley understands by theology ; for a more extra-ordinary statement as to the aim of the Prophets than that they were always engaged in attempting to free their moral ideal from the stifling embrace of the current theology, I never read. As I understand the Prophets, a theological revelation is the alpha and the omega of their power. "Thus saith the Lord" is not only the formula under which they speak, but the key-note of their convictions. It is because they believe, and only because they believe, that they can announce the true will of God, that they hope to be able to elevate the true nature of man. If Professor Huxley should reply that he meant to lay a special emphasis on the adjective " current " which he attached to the word "theology," and that he regards the Prophets as endeavouring to refute the prevalent theology, and to set up a purer theology in its place, I should reply that it was not a theology at all which the Prophets tried to clear away, but a conventional and punctilious faith in religious observances, and that he cannot produce the least trace in Hebrew history of the false theology which he supposes. On the contrary, the ceremonialism and formalism which the Prophets assailed were rooted in the oblivion of theology, in the loss of that very revelation of himself by God of which from the earliest times we have a continuous series of records in the Old Testament. And why, while Professor Huxley dwells so much on ephods, and high priests' bells, and the Witch of Endor's incantation, and the casting of lots, and the offering of sin-offerings, he steadily ignores all the true theology of the Old Testament,—I mean · the declarations of God concerning his own will and purposes,—I cannot even imagine. "From one end to the other of the Books of Judges and Samuel," he says, "the only 'commandments of Jahveh' which are specially adduced refer to the prohibition of the worship of other gods, or are orders given *ad hoc*, and have nothing to do with questions of morality." Undoubtedly the Book of Judges is a story of barbarous times, in which it is often difficult to trace the predominance of any moral spirit; but equally undoubtedly the Book of Samuel begins with the announcement of the severe sentence of God on the immorality of the sons of Eli, and on the weak indulgence shown to them by their father ; and how

it is possible even for Professor Huxley to ignore
the moral revelation running through these books,
which, contain, for instance, Samuel's grand protest
against the popular unbelief which could not accept
God's guidance through the agency of uncrowned
kings, but craved the outward show of a regular
monarchy; and again, the noble Psalm in which
David anticipates the building of a temple for the
Ark, and expresses his own deep humility and infinite
trust in God; and most of all, the announcement to
him by Nathan of the judgment of God upon his
sin, in the beautiful parable of the rich man's
seizure of the poor man's pet lamb,—is to me quite
inexplicable. Nor is the record of the revelation of
the Divine nature during the time of these chronicles
confined to these books, for all those of the Psalms
which belong to this period,—and even the most
sceptical critics assign a few of them to this period,
—tell us far more of the real progress of revelation
than the terse chronicles of those violent times
themselves. As it seems to me, from the judgment
on the first murderer in Genesis to the times of the
Prophets, there is one continuous and steadily
increasing testimony to the righteousness and purity
of God, which, so far from being in any way inconsistent with the prophetic teachings, is the very
heart of them. Indeed, Professor Huxley is inconsistent with himself when, on the one hand, he is so
anxious to show that a great part of the Levitical
law dates from a far later period than that to which
it is referred; and yet, on the other hand, is so
eager to attribute to the Prophets an effort to purify
the Jewish religion from "the stifling embrace" of a
ceremonialism which, according to his view, had not
at that time been even conceived.

Where Professor Huxley gets his evidence for that worship of ancestors among the Hebrews to which he refers so large a part of all theology, is to me a profound mystery. He referred in his first article to the evidence that the Patriarchs carried about teraphim, and he enlarged greatly on the story of the Witch of Endor. But when he has made the most of these matters, he has done nothing more than show that superstitions common everywhere else were not absolutely excluded by the light of revelation from Hebrew religion. This may be granted. But to grant this is no more to assert that the belief in a righteous God, which is the main subject of the Hebrew revelation, originated in these superficial superstitions, than to grant that the Celts believe in second-sight is to assert that they regard second-sight as the root of their religion. The truth is that Professor Huxley has no consistent conception of what it is that he means by evolution. He seems to think that to trace out a few superficial analogies between the superstitions of savages and the superstitions of the Hebrew people, establishes a high probability that the noblest beliefs of that people originated exactly as the superstitions of savages have originated. I should have supposed that a very different inference was justified by these analogies. The superstitions of the Tongan and Samoan islanders are still, after we know not what period of development, crude, inconsistent, debasing. The faith of the Israelite attained, on Professor Huxley's own showing, in the time of the Prophets, to a noble and sublime type, of which the very essence was *not*, as Professor Huxley puts it, " to do justice, love mercy, and bear himself humbly before the Infinite," but " to do justice, love mercy, and walk humbly with God,"—God being to the Hebrew in every sense a real person, one in whom he had trusted and did trust, and through his trust in whom, and through that alone, he found it possible to do the justice and love the mercy which had their fountain in the Divine nature. Was this great result due to precisely the same groping of the unassisted human understanding at great problems which, in the case of savage tribes, has issued in results so confused and unmeaning? Or was it due to the direct influence of him whose mighty hand and stretched-out arm had, in the belief of the Hebrews, guided the destiny of the nation? Surely evolution in theology has a far better meaning, a meaning far more closely analogous to its meaning in science, if it be taken to express the gradually unfolding conformity of the inward creed to external realities, than it can ever have if it is only taken to express the shifting mists and vapours in which the nervous affections of man unfold themselves when they recall the ancestors who are lost to their view, and dream of other invisible agencies which may be even more formidable than those of their ancestors themselves. I believe in a real evolution of theology, —an evolution in conformity with the revealing righteousness in which alone theology originates. So far as I understand him, Professor Huxley believes only in the evolution of a dreamland of confused fears and hopes, which it is the true function of the ethical nature to repress, if not to extinguish.

XXXVI

MR. SCOTT HOLLAND'S SERMONS [1]

1882

THERE is a great difference between the power of the different sermons in this volume, but some of them are as powerful as any preached in this generation, and, indeed, full of genius, original thought, and spiritual veracity. Of the three first, it would be hard to speak in terms toò high ;—they show something of the painstaking originality, the careful searchingness, the candid courage, of Bishop Butler, though clothed in an oratory of higher force than anything which was at all in Bishop Butler's way,—an oratory, indeed, which men who choose to judge *a priori* would suppose to be inconsistent with any gifts at all resembling those displayed by Bishop Butler. Still, the fact is that Mr. Holland combines with an oratorical power which sometimes runs away with him, and diffuses itself like a flood till the mind is almost overpowered by the wealth of his accumulated illustration, very nearly as careful and precise an appreciation of the ins and outs of the

[1] *Logic and Life, with other Sermons.* By the Rev. H. Scott Holland, M.A., Senior Student of Christ Church, Oxford. London : Rivingtons.

question with which he is dealing, the qualifications
of a truth, the set-offs against an argument, the
difficulties in a true position, the plausibilities in a
false one, as the great bishop himself could have
displayed. I do not say that any of the sermons
in this volume cover anything like as wide a ground
as the great sermons on human nature, nor even that
they display a strength as remarkable as the sermons
on " Compassion," " Resentment," and "The Ignorance
of Man."   But the first three sermons in this volume,
to say the least,—and several of the others approach
them in power,—appear to me sermons that deserve
to rank high in the theological literature of England,
and that appear likely to maintain their place there
as long as sermons on the greatest subjects that
affect human nature continue to be preached and
read.

The first is on the place of reasoning in relation
to its influence over life, especially, of course, with
regard to the assertion of the Rationalists that
spiritual truths are not verified. After pointing out
that men now pay less and less attention to abstract
arguments, and appeal from all such abstract
arguments,—especially, for instance, in relation to
politics,—to the concrete lessons of experience, and
that even men of science are perfectly indifferent to
the verification of the great primary assumptions of
all science, like the law of causation, so long as they
find that they actually gain power over nature by
virtue of their scientific discoveries, Mr. Holland goes
on :—

" This modern way of regarding things does not in
reality suppose itself irrational, because it distrusts
abstract argument : rather, it is the conception of reason
itself which is changed ; reason is regarded, not in its

isolated character as an engine with which every man starts equipped, capable of doing a certain job whenever required, with a definite and certain mode of action ; but it is taken as a living and pliable process by and in which man brings himself into rational and intelligent relation with his surroundings, with his experience. As these press in upon him, and stir him, and move about and around him, he sets himself to introduce into his abounding and multitudinous impressions, something of order, and system, and settlement. He has got to act upon all this engirdling matter, and he must discover how action is most possible and most successful ; he must watch, and consider, and arrange, and find accordance between his desires and their outward realisation : so it is that he names and classifies : so it is that he learns to expect, to foretell, to anticipate, to manage, to control : so it is that he rouses his curiosity to ever new efforts, and cannot rest content until he has got clearer and surer hold on the infinite intricacies that offer themselves to hand, and eye, and ear, and taste. Continually he reshapes his anticipations, continually he corrects his judgments, continually he turns to new researches, continually he moulds and enlarges, and enriches, and fortifies, and advances, and improves the conceptions which he finds most cardinal and most effective. Undisturbed in his primary confidence that he has a rational hold upon the reality of the things which he feels and sees, he acts on the essential assumption that, in advancing the active effectiveness of his ideas, he is arriving at a more real apprehension of that world which he finds to move in increasing harmony with his own inner expectations. This effective and growing apprehension is what he calls his reason ; and its final test lies in the actual harmony, which is found to result from its better endeavours, between the life at work within and the life at work without. Reason is the slowly formed power of harmonising the world of facts ; and its justification lies, not in its deductive certainty so much as in its capacity of *advance.* It proves its trust-worthiness by its power to grow. It could not have come so far, if it were not on the right road ; it must be right, because ever, in front of it, it discovers the road continuing. Reason moves towards its place, its fulfilment, so far as it settles itself into responsive agreement with the facts covered by its activity, so far as its expectations encounter no jar or surprise, so far as its survey is baffled by no blank and unpenetrated barrier. Every step that tends to complete and achieve this successful response tends, in that same degree, to enforce its confident security in itself and in its method. . . . It is on our inner and actual life, then, that the action of our reasoning depends. Deep down in the long record of our past, far away in the ancient homes and habits of the soul,—back, far back, in all that age-long experience which has nursed, and tended, and moulded the making of my manhood,—lies the secret of that efficacy which reason exerts in me to-day. That efficacy has, through long pressure, become an imbedded habit, which if I turn round upon it and suddenly inspect it, will appear to me inexplicable. Why this gigantic conclusion ? Why this emphatic pronouncement ? Why this array of dogmatic assumptions ? I may take those assumptions up in my hands, and look them all over, and poke and probe them, and find no answer in them for their mysterious audacity. No, for they have no answer within themselves : their answer, their verification, their evidence, their very significance, can only be got by turning to and introducing all that vast sum of ever-gathering facts which the generations before me, under the weight of the moving centuries, pressed into these formulæ, ordered under these categories, wielded by the efficacy of these instruments, harmonised, mastered, controlled in obedience to the judgments,—judgments which justified their reality and their power by the constant and unwavering welcome with which the advance of life unfailingly greeted their anticipations, and fulfilled their trust. I am, of necessity, blind to their force as long as I have no corresponding experience,—so long as that body of fact which they make explicable remains to me unverified and unexplored. What to me, for instance, can be the potency of the conception of Soul, if I have no soul-facts that require explication? I feel the need and necessity of a name only when there are certain phenomena before me which no other name suits or sorts. What need or necessity, then, can I see for the word Spirit, unless I have, within my experience, those spiritual activities which were to my forefathers so marked, so distinct, so unmistakable, so constant, that it became to them a mental impossibility to retain · them under a material name, and a practical impossibility to carry on an intelligible common life without distinguishing those activities from the motions of their flesh? What sense or reason can I discover for the assumption of a God, unless I can repeat and re-enact in the abysses of my own hidden being those profound impressions, those ineradicable experiences, those awful and sublime ventures of faith to which the existence of God has been the sole clue, the sole necessity, the one and only interpretation, the irresistible response, the obvious evidence, the unceasing justification?"

Thus far the first sermon takes us. In the next one, "The Venture of Faith," Mr. Holland paints a most powerful picture of the manner in which man is impelled by the imperious nature within him to assume that the outside world is really akin in its laws and principles to the world within him; that even though nature is wholly independent of our feelings, yet it is not by discharging all feeling, but rather by the free use of our feelings, as well as of our reason, that we can best learn to control nature; that even our passions become intelligent, and help to feed the force of our intellectual power; that without passions and emotions and affections which

have so often been called irrational, we could never
have, or make manifest to others, that fundamental
basis of personal character on which alone men can
rely for the purposes even of intellectual life ;—in
short, that what seems most alien in us to the causes
at work in the external universe, is really essential
to the progress which we make in investigating the
nature of that universe, and building up the habits
and rules by which we learn to make the most use
of it.   I have rarely read a passage of more pregnant
and impressive force than the following, for instance,
describing how the passions essentially contribute to
the growth of that natural order with which, as it is
so often supposed, they are at variance :—

" We each individually reveal a character built up out
of feelings which, at first sight, we class with the instincts
of the animal, or attribute to the blind influences of
fleshly impressions.   And yet, after all, it is out of these
that our *rational* character emerges ; it is out of these
feelings that we elaborate a history which is perpetually
advancing its problems, its needs, its solutions, its satis-
factions ; it is in these very feelings that we make
manifest to all who have eyes to see, or ears to listen, the
tokens of an enduring self, whose actions men can count
upon and calculate, whose movements they can classify
and connect, whose growth they can confidently anticipate.
And still deeper down in our self-study, we discover
strange effects in those impulses which at first we called
animal.   They are not content to lie back behind the
narrow barriers within which the simple passions of that
dim animal world run their unchanging round.   They
break through that ancient monotony ; they take to
themselves larger powers ; they feel their way towards
new possibilities ; they increase the force and extend the
range of their desires.   The passions, in becoming human,
are no longer animal.   It is not that they are differently

managed and treated ; it is that they themselves are changed ; they themselves desire what no animal desires ; they themselves exceed, as no animal exceeds ; they themselves disclose in their very excess a secret instinct of self-discipline, in which lies the seed of the new law, the law of Purity and Holiness. The appetite that is capable of self-assertion is driven by its own inner necessities to the task of self-control. Morality, as we look at it closely and carefully, is no system imposed on passion from without ; it is itself the very heart of all desire, the very principle of all human impulse, the very inspiration of all passion. Out of the growth and increase of these vaster passions, righteousness springs like a flower to perfect, like a revelation to interpret, all that without its manifestation is left unfulfilled and unexplained. And if so, then these passions, these impulses, cannot be altogether blind and unpurposing. They have it in them to produce a rational order ; they hold, hidden within their extravagance, the mystery of control ; they inevitably tend towards temperance and chastity. They are, then, already rational ; they are, from the very start, already moral."

And yet, as Mr. Holland shows, this essential individuality of the reason in every man, which makes that reason blend with his passions and affections, so that you can hardly say whether his impulses be rational, or his reason impulsive, is so far from making men really solitary,—so far from separating them into units, that, on the contrary, it is always found that the literatures and languages which most powerfully represent the turns and distinctions of individual feeling and thought, also appeal most powerfully to the reason and imagination of the whole race. In short, the intensely individual character of reason in each man is not only not inconsistent with the power to awaken response in the race, but is essential to it :—

"Do men find that there follows, on the use of their reason, a sense of bitter loneliness, of horrible isolation? Do they, the more they think, hold ever more aloof from their fellows? Do they find themselves thrown back, shocked, jostled, when they utter their minds? Are they, when they try to argue or discuss, ever running their heads against hard walls? Or is it not exactly the contrary? Is it not in ignorance of each other's minds that men meet with rude rejections, and batter vainly against blind barriers? Is not the exercise of thought one long and delightful discovery of the identity that knits us up into the main body of mankind? If ever we do succeed in putting our thoughts into words that others understand, is it not a sure road to their hearts? Do they not run to greet us with open arms? Our sympathies, our hopes, our desires, do we not, when once we can find a language to express what they are to us, rediscover them all in the soul of our fellows? Is not all language one enduring and irresistible witness to the reality and depth of the communion which our thought arrives at, as soon as man touches man? And each new tongue or dialect brings with it new and delicious proof."

So that even in relation to society, the growth of the reason is not only identified with the growth of the passions and affections, but inseparable from it; and you cannot wield a great power over others, without digging down deep into that part of your nature which seems most purely individual. Not only does the love of righteousness, the love of holiness, the love of all things most potent for the government of society, grow out of the grafting of what seemed purely individual emotion and desire on the reason, but we learn that the very constitution of the universe is at bottom based upon this blending of reason with desire and affection against which we are often warned, as if it prejudiced our minds against the light of truth :—

"Does reason itself refuse to exist, except to those who venture with⁻no faint heart to follow the fascination of hope? Is it impossible to be rational without passing beyond the bounds of reason, without surrendering reason itself to the compulsion of a prophetic inspiration? Does all thinking hang on an act of faith? Can it be true that we can never attain to intellectual apprehension unless the entire man in us throws his spirit forward, with a willing confidence, with an unfaltering trust, into an adventurous movement; unless the entire man can bring himself to respond to a summons from without, which appeals to him by some instinctive touch of strange and unknown kinship to rely on its attraction, to risk all on the assumption of its reality? A touch of kinship! Yes, kinship alone could so stir faith; and the call, therefore, to which it responds must issue from a Will as living, as personal, as itself. Ah! surely, then, 'God is in this place, and I knew it not.' From the first dawn of our earliest intelligent activity we move under the mighty breath of One higher and lordlier than we wot of; we walk in the high places, we are carried we know not whither. Not for one instant may we remain within the narrow security of our private domain; not for one moment may we claim to be self-possessed, self-contained, self-centred, self-controlled. Every action carries us outside ourselves; every thought that we can think is a revelation of powers that draw us forward, of influences that lift us out of the safety of self-control. To reason is to have abandoned the quiet haven of self-possession; for already in its first acts we feel the big waters move under us, and the great winds blow."

The third sermon is on M. Renan's assertion that "A man who would write the history of a faith must believe it no longer, but must have believed it once," a maxim on which Mr. Holland comments with curious power :—

"How, then, are we to prepare ourselves for historical and critical treatment of religion ? How can we be sure of securing the fit conditions ? Can we believe experimentally merely for the purposes of discovery ? Can we be certain of being able to cease from our belief at the moment at which we propose to begin our critical examination ? Or must all then be left to happy chance ? Must the historical study of religions be confined to those who have happened by good luck to fall outside the faiths which once they held ? It is an awkward test to have to apply to candidates for the study. And, again, are we to consider them fortunate or unfortunate to find themselves so qualified ? Which is the healthier condition of mind,—the earlier, or the later ? If the later is the more natural and the more perfect, how can the earlier be at all sound or entire ? And, if not sound, how can it be the essential groundwork of the critical temper ? It can hardly be that the later temper is a product of the earlier,—that the natural evolution of uncritical faith is into critical doubt. For what happens in the loss of the temper of faith is, that we abandon the attempt to develop our faith."

And he goes on to observe that we accept implicitly the ordinary assumptions as to the freedom from preconception in which all history ought to be written, until we discover that the very forces of history are passions, that unless we can enter into these passions, we cannot write history at all, and that the spirit of indifference has no balance by which " it can test the fury of warring opposites." "Without some living interest in the issue, history looks to us as the wild melody of madmen, whose rage, and anxieties, and dangers, fill us with a painful distress at their reckless exaggeration, and their ungentle obstinacy." If, then, a strong sympathy with one kind of issue is far from a disqualification for entering into history, it is hardly possible that the possession of a belief is a positive disqualification for the study of ecclesiastical history or theological controversy. Mr. Holland, in the most powerful pages of his book, recalls to us what it is that faith really means,—over how many of the various chords of human life it has the mastery, —and how impossible it is even for the believer to recall fully all the influence which from time to time his faith has exerted over the spirit and practice of his life. Yet if it be difficult for the believer to recall that of which he has still the moral traces left in him and the full possibility of experiencing again, how much less possible must it be for one who has left behind him what he thinks illegitimate spiritual emotions, so to recover and revive them, as to present to the rest of the world an adequate insight into their essence and significance. He reminds us how widely the *historical* criticism of a religion depends for its results on the critic's apprehension of the forces actually at work in the world, on his "experimental insight into the Presences and Powers whose efforts he is measuring, and whose significance he professes to declare." It is, he says justly enough, at once rational and inevitable, that one who does not believe any longer in special supernatural influences, should distrust the statements of all who profess to record facts assuming such influences ; and that he should consequently look at the assertions of fact which imply such occurrences, in a wholly incredulous spirit. Mr. Holland concludes, then, that if to have believed *once* is necessary for a true historian of religion, it is impossible that he should ever enter into the history truly when he has ceased to believe and has declared to himself that all the cardinal facts with which he has to deal are founded on illusion ; but he adds the following fine remark, on the true drift of M. Renan's warning :—

"Has belief, then, by its own faithlessness, incurred this taunt against its honesty, its uprightness, its courage ? Has it, indeed, feared to face its own problems with the reality and the singleness of heart which unbelief can bring to their unravelling ?   Has its sincerity, then, fallen so low that it cannot be trusted to use an equal scale ?   Has it had to appeal to those who have not enjoyed its good chances, nor possess its excellent tools, to assist it in the task for which it alone is adequately equipped ?   These are solemn questions for us.   They cannot be dismissed by a brave word of frank denial ; they arouse in us shameful and humiliating doubts.   We ought to have seen for ourselves long ago much that now we are shown by others' guidance.   We ought to have learned to correct our blundering misapprehensions, without having had to undergo such late and painful schooling."

I have tried to show something of the power of these sermons.   They are, I think, the finest, in a volume of which the majority are really fine ; but they are not so much finer than many others, that, even had these been wanting, we should have failed to discern the great powers of this preacher, and the promise of this volume for the Christian Church of our day.

XXXVII

SIR JAMES PAGET ON SCIENCE AND THEOLOGY

1881

THE Address delivered by Sir James Paget to the
students preparing for ordination at the clergy school
of Leeds, which has just been published by Messrs.
Rivington, might very well supply the basis of a very
original and very striking book on the divergences
and the points of approach between Theology and
Science. It is marked not only by the rare moral
thoughtfulness and candour of the most accomplished
of the great surgeons of his day, but by that keen
insight into the limitations of science which only the
habitual study of science and the mastery of its
principles can give. Sir James Paget points out, in
a passage of much beauty, that though, as amongst
the various branches of Science, the specialisation
which has become so extreme of late years has tended
to estrange the master of one from the master of the
other, and to render the very language of the students
of the different departments unknown tongues
to each other, yet that, nevertheless, this extreme
division of labour ends in bringing all the different
departments of science to converge, in ways hitherto

quite unsuspected, in the great central truth of that
unity of method which implies unity of authorship
and unity of purpose :—

"It may even seem likely that, in the future, as
knowledge widens and divides its fields, and men's
studies become more specialised and distinct, the opposition will become more intense, the deviations wider, the
difficulty of reconciliation greater ; for each group will
become less and less able to appreciate the works of the
others. A learned professor of Tübingen speaking, not
long ago, of the progress of knowledge, said that he
feared that the temple of science would fail of being
finished for the same reason as did the Tower of Babel,
because the workmen did not know each other's
language. And there is, indeed, great truth in the
symbol. There are very few men living who can, I will
not say study, but even understand the language of the
whole of any recent volume of the *Philosophical Trans-
actions of the Royal Society*. But on this point the
history of science is opposed to what we might expect.
As the field of science has been more divided, and studies
have been more special, and men have worked on
narrower fields, so has the unity of nature become more
evident ; they have dug deeper and come nearer to a
centre. Here is a point which seems to me most worthy
of your regard. Let me illustrate it by some instances.
In my early studies it was held by many that life, or the
vital principle, that which was deemed the active power
in all living things, was not only different from the
principles at work in dead matter, but absolutely and
essentially opposed to them all. It was thought in
some measure profane and irreligious to hold that life,
regarded not as a condition but as a thing, could be in
any kind of relation or alliance with anything acting in
dead matter, as with chemical affinity, caloric, magnetism,
or anything of the kind. But, while men have been
more and more separating themselves into groups of

physiologists, and physicists, and chemists, and each of these again into lesser groups, the intimate relation of all the forces of matter, whether living or dead, their correlations and mutual convertibility, have become more and more evident. Similarly, it was believed, hardly more than half a century ago, that the chemical compositions of organic and of inorganic matter were essentially unlike, and that the organic could not be attained except through operations of a vital power. Now, chemistry makes hundreds of compounds not distinguishable from those formed in living bodies ; and the late researches of M. Friedel, showing that carbon, the most characteristic element of organic compounds, can be replaced in some of them by silicon, one of the most characteristic elements of the inorganic, seem to show that all attempts to indicate a clear line of distinction between the chemistry of the living and that of the dead will fail. Again, the likeness of things that were deemed diverse is illustrated by Darwin's observations on the carnivorous plants. One used to think that if there were a sure mark of distinction between plants and animals, it was that these had, and those had not, stomachs with which they could digest, change, and appropriate alien nutritive substances. He has shown as true digestion in plants—especially by the leaves of the Drosera, the little Sun-dew which you may gather on the moors—as can take place in any of our own stomachs ; a digestion true, complete, and similar to our own. Yet further, Darwin's last book, on the *Movements of Plants*, makes it more than ever clear that we must think very cautiously in assigning the existence of a nervous system as a really characteristic distinction between plants and animals. So, in respect of diseases, I have lately tried to show that between ours and theirs there is no difference of kind, however much theirs may be, in comparison, free from the complications of nervous system, moving blood and mind in which we have to study our own. Nay, even beyond plants ; I have ventured to suggest that a truly

elemental pathology must be studied in crystals, after
mechanical injuries or other disturbing forces. I might
cite many instances more, but these may suffice for
illustration of the general fact, that in the progress of
knowledge, while scientific men have seemed to be
working more and more widely apart, they have found
more and more near relations among all the objects of
their study. As the rays of knowledge have extended
and diverged, so has their relation to one common centre
become more evident, and the unity of nature has become
more significant of the unity of God.

And what Sir James Paget insists upon as the result
of pursuing the teaching of facts in different departments of science, however widely they appear to
diverge from each other, he believes to be equally
applicable to the opposite divergences between the
drift of theology and the drift of science as a
whole. In point of fact, of course, theology first
taught us that unity of cause and drift which science
is slowly verifying, though it insisted boldly on a
mental origin for that unity which the modern
scientific school strives in vain to dispense with.
And not only did theology anticipate science in
teaching us the unity of creation, before that unity
had been verified by study, but as Sir James Paget
hints, it also anticipated science in warning us that
we must not trust our reasoning powers too confidently, when they appear to us to deduce positively
from one truth what seems inconsistent with another
truth. Theology teaches us, for instance, the fore-
knowledge of God, and as positively the responsibility
and free-will of man ; and yet to very many men's
minds, these truths appear wholly incompatible, just as
the evidence of our senses appeared to teach us that
the sun moves round the earth, while the evidence of a

much more important body of fact taught, on the contrary, that the earth moved round the sun. Alike by revelation and by science we have been warned not to believe too easily in the incompatibility of truths independently established on firm grounds, simply because we fancy that we can demonstrate to ourselves their inconsistency :—

"And yet more, let me venture to say, each side should avoid the habit of thinking that they can safely impute inferences as necessary consequences of the beliefs held by the other ; that they can easily show what must come of carrying-out a belief to what they call its logical consequences. It is from this that much of the bitterest part of controversy is derived. It is declared that if this or that probably harmless opinion be allowed, some grievous error or some utter folly must come next. 'It stands to reason,' they say. 'Stands to reason.' One is tempted to ask, first, whose reason ? Is it the reason of a really reasonable man ? and of one well instructed in the subject of inquiry ? But in any case, it should be remembered how many things that did stand to reason have fallen at the test of fact. I am sure it is true in science—I suspect it is true in theology—that all the beliefs which we now know to have been erroneous, and all the denials of what we now know to have been true, did once 'stand to reason.' They did so stand, with all seeming strength and security, in the minds of those who maintained them and were ready to defend them as certain truths. It stood to reason that the sun moved round the earth, and that people could be bewitched, and that the moon had much to do with lunatics ; it stood to reason, even with the rare power of reasoning of Bishop Berkeley, that tar-water would cure and prevent many serious diseases. And I suppose that in every heresy the error has stood to reason in the minds of many who held to it. There are few expressions which, in serious matters, we should more carefully avoid than this, or any which imply that we can of our own mental power infer certainties, or settle the boundaries of probabilities, or the consequences of beliefs, in subjects which we have not thoroughly studied."

And most aptly does Sir James Paget quote from the late Canon Mozley the weighty sentence—"It were to be wished that the active penetration and close and acute attention which mankind have applied to so many subjects of knowledge, and so successfully, had been applied in a somewhat greater proportion than it has been to the due apprehension of that very important article of knowledge,—their own ignorance."

On the theological side, however, Sir James Paget's fine address certainly needs some expansion and illustration.   Much that he says goes to prove not only that the supposed divergency of drift between the different sciences is more or less imaginary, but that "our future knowledge will not be merely heaped on the surface of that we now possess," but that "it will penetrate the mass and fill its gaps and interspaces, and make many things one, which as yet seem multiple and alien."   What he does not do quite so successfully, and what is yet quite within the scope of his address, is to show that this filling-in of the blank "interstitial spaces" between science and science, will be accompanied by a similar filling-in of the blank interstitial spaces between science and revelation.   If it be so, there should already be instances in which science has verified, from a totally new side, truths anticipated by revelation, though not anticipated in the manner or form in which science brings its truths to light.   I have already referred to one case of this kind suggested in Sir

James Paget's address, namely, to the anticipation
by revelation of the unity of Nature.   But there is,
of course, a possible interpretation of this anticipation which would deny that it was, properly speaking,
an anticipation of an important truth at all.   I turn,
therefore, to what I hold to be the most striking
of all the anticipations by revelation of a doctrine
only now being slowly verified by science, and one
filling up "the interspace" between two very different
regions of human investigation.   Sir James Paget
refers to Mr. Darwin's teaching as to "the survival
of the fittest " thus :—" Man has reached his present
state in civilised races through an incessant struggle
not only for food and life, but for intellectual
mastery ; for virtue, as against those vices that are
only brutality surviving ; for truth, as against error.
The influences of Christianity and of civilisation
have made the struggle more gentle ; the better
sort of men do not destroy one another ; but the
law of conflict is not abrogated.   The struggle which,
from age to age, has ensured the survival of the
fittest, has been under a law which includes intellectual conflicts, and has constantly helped to the
attainment of the truth."   Sir James Paget here
uses the phrase "survival of the fittest" in a sense
different from Mr. Darwin's, but one of which it is
most important to notice the true applicability to
moral types.   Mr. Darwin's "survival" depends on
the organic transmission to descendants of all the
habits and variations of physical organisation favourable ·to the preservation or multiplication of a race,
and on the tendency which those habits and physical
variations have to shelter the individuals possessing
them from destruction, and to give them special
advantages in the conflict with other races for food

and mastery.   But Sir James Paget uses the phrase
in a very different sense.   The only sense in which
controversy and collision amongst human minds
tend to the "survival of the fittest creed," is by
sifting belief, and bringing to the side of the more
reasonable or more potent and inspiring thought,
those who were previously on the side of the less
reasonable or less potent and inspiring thought,—in
other words, by persuading men who were not
adherents of a particular conviction to adopt and act
upon that conviction.   It is the ultimate power of
gaining adherents which in this sense secures the
survival of beliefs; and if those be the "fittest"
beliefs which seem most to strengthen and vivify the
minds of the most dominant races of men, just as
those are the fittest races for the earth which gain the
securest and most dominant position in it, then, no
doubt, revelation has anticipated in a most astounding
way the survival, and therefore, the fitness of certain
beliefs which had nothing in the world to suggest
them as fit beliefs for men at all, unless we can
ascribe that suggestion to the inspiration of a superhuman mind.   For revelation anticipated that that
belief should most "survive" which should range on
its side the most profound indifference to its own
adherents' survival; that the survival of the belief
should be secured by the suffering and death of the
believer; that it should triumph through his defeat;
become strong by virtue of his weakness, and
conquer in his humiliation.   In the Jewish revelation,
the promise is to the righteous servant who shall
go like a lamb to the slaughter, and who, as the
sheep before the shearers is dumb, openeth not his
mouth, and who is even to be "numbered with the
transgressors."   But in the Christian revelation the

principle of a survival ensured by death is carried to its utmost extent. It is made in some sense a condition of the triumph of Christianity that with no weapons of the flesh shall it resist evil,—that it is to yield before injustice and indignities, as the air yields before a blow;—that unless it can face death as the ear of wheat does when it is sown, it shall not "bring forth much fruit"; that without shame it cannot be glorified; that without taking the lowest place, it can never reach the highest. Now I venture to say that the power which could steadily predict, as the most fitting of human beliefs to survive all other beliefs, and to inspire those in whom it does survive to great achievements, such readiness, not to say ardour, to lose, to suffer, to die, in its name, was a power which Science itself ought to admit,—now that history has verified the prediction,—to the rank of superhuman. What could seem less likely to improve the position of life on this earth, than the teaching that earthly life itself was utterly insignificant, compared with a particular state of heart towards a world which nobody could see? What could promise less of dominance, less of achievement, less of distinction, than this constant exhortation to covet lowliness, to be patient of injustice, to welcome dishonour? Imagine the world from the Agnostic point of view, and you can hardly conceive a doctrine more likely to secure its own speedy extinction, than the doctrine that the world is to be won only by despising the world, and true life gained only by encountering death. Yet this is precisely the paradox which Judaism first taught, and Christ accepted as the very key-note of his revelation, but of which it has taken centuries to verify the power. Ought not Science to admit that not even the first predicted and verified eclipse of the sun, tested the principles of science more effectually than this century-old anticipation of a type of belief as the fittest to survive all other human beliefs and to dominate the mind of man, which no one without superhuman help could have conceived as appropriate to earthly life at all?

XXXVIII

MR. WILFRID WARD'S WISH TO BELIEVE

1882

MR. WILFRID WARD, in an extremely thoughtful and able dialogue on "The Wish to Believe," which appears in the new number of the *Nineteenth Century*, maintains that it is very far from true that in the case of any serious belief, the wish is father to the thought. On the contrary, he holds,—or at least the chief interlocutor in the dialogue, whom I take to be the spokesman of the author, holds,—that the more we wish to believe in anything which it is of the first importance to us to find true, the less importance do we attach to our own wishes as affecting the truth, nay, the more jealously do we guard ourselves against being misled by these wishes. When, on the other hand, it is not of any critical importance to us to know the truth, when it is of much more importance to us to be able to indulge comfortably a dream of our own as if it were the truth, than to know what is truth, and what is not, then Mr. Wilfrid Ward holds that the wish is often father to the thought. For example,—the example, is mine, not his, I will give his own example directly,—a man finds that his hereditary religious

creed is an obstacle in his way in some important
concern of life.   It hinders his chance of marrying
the wife on whom his heart is set, or it hinders his
chance of moving in the social circles in which it is
his ambition to move.   If this be his only reason
for being well inclined to reconsider his faith, and
see the error of his ways, and, indeed, to adopt, if
he can, the creed which will aid his suit, or help him
in his social aspirations, it is very likely that the
wish will be father to the thought of a change of
belief.   What he really desires is not to know the
actual truth, but to be able to take up a certain
attitude of mind without conscious insincerity,—that
is, to have sufficient to say for it to render this
attitude of mind tolerably consistent with self-respect.
And in that case, the wish not so much to *believe*, as
to entertain a view that may do duty for belief, will
probably render it very easy to entertain that view,
and will hoodwink the mind to the fact that this
view is not in any strict sense a belief at all, but is
only such an equivalent for it as the mental and
moral proprieties require.   But if, on the contrary,
the man's one desire is to be sure that what he
believes corresponds to reality,—that by believing it
he will not be living in a fool's paradise of hope, but
will know the truth about the highest end of life,
and about the great hereafter,—then the desire to
believe this or that, will not in the least help him to
the belief, unless he can find evidence that is to his
mind demonstrative that the belief is true.   So far
from being able to hoodwink himself by any juggle
between his wish and the reality, he will find it all
the more difficult to believe as really true what he
wishes to find true ; his strong wish will make him
all the more unable to be credulous in the matter.

The very strength of his wish will render him
nervously sensitive to the weakness of the evidence
for what he wishes to believe, where it is weak, and
to the strength of the opposite case, where it is
strong; he will be in the condition of mind of the
father or mother who is listening to a consultation
of physicians on the crisis through which a beloved
child is passing. He will hear what can be said on
the side of hope with hungry avidity, but he will
hear what can be said on the side of despair with at
least an equal passion of appreciation of its significance and terror. He will be almost overwhelmingly
afraid to hope; he will dwell even more intensely
than he ought on the ground for fear; and he will
be in the end much slower than the physician himself
to anticipate recovery. Such I understand to be
Mr. Wilfrid Ward's view of the relation of the wish
to believe, to actual and genuine belief. And now
I will give his own illustration of the connection
between the two :—

"'Then,' said Darlington, slowly, 'as I understand
you, you hold that where there is a real anxiety and wish
about the *thing*—an honest desire for the truth of the
thing, and not merely for the pleasure of the *thought*—
that desire makes you *less* ready rather than more ready
to believe.' 'Precisely,' said Walton; 'a shallow, self-
deceitful thought, called only by a misnomer "belief,"
may well enough be the result of wishing to believe;
but true conviction never. I remember well a lady of
my acquaintance who used to think her nephew a perfect
paragon of perfection, and far the cleverest man at his
college at Oxford. She sucked in eagerly all the civil
things that people said in his favour, and systematically
disbelieved less flattering reports. Here was one sort of
belief. It arose from her wish—but her wish for what?

That her nephew should *really* be the cleverest and most successful man?' 'I suppose so,' said Ashley, unguardedly. 'Not entirely so, I think,' said Walton; 'but mainly from her wish for the *satisfaction of thinking* that he was so. The actual fact was of secondary importance to her; but it is of primary importance to him who wants a real and deep conviction. I remember, too, in that very case that the truth of this was evidenced in a most amusing manner when this brilliant nephew was trying for a fellowship which was of some consequence to him. She paid far more attention to and was rendered far more anxious by arguments against the probability of his success, and seemed very doubtful as to the result——quite prepared for his failure; and why? Because *here* it was the *fact* of his success which was of moment, and not the pleasure of her own subjective impression.'"

And again, Mr. Wilfrid Ward illustrates the same conception of the relation between the wish to have a decent excuse for believing, on the one hand, and the earnest wish to believe, if it be possible to believe truly, on the other, by a second hypothesis which may seem to some to cast an even stronger light on the discussion :—

"'Well,' said Walton, 'I have been trying while you were talking to see the essential distinction between the cases that have been cited on both sides. I think I can point it out by an example which has occurred to me, which I think you will admit to be true to nature. There are two very different states of mind—anxiety that something should be really true, and the wish to have the pleasure of believing something. Here are two pictures. First take some lazy, comfort-loving, and selfish man. He is walking with a companion on a sea-beach. No one is visible near him. Suddenly he hears what he takes to be the shriek of a drowning man,

beyond some rocks at the end of the beach. His companion thinks it is only children at play. The rocks are
hard to climb, and at some distance off. The man is
readily persuaded that it *is* only children at play, and
that there is no call on him to climb the rocks, or assist
anybody. There is one attitude of mind—one picture.
Now for another. An affectionate mother is placed in
exactly the same circumstances as my lazy man. She
thinks she recognises in the shriek her son's voice. Her
companion says it is only children at play ; but this *does
not satisfy her.* She entreats him to help her to climb
the rocks, and they arrive just in time to rescue her son
—for it is her son—from drowning. Now, surely you
won't deny that the mother would be far more desirous
to be convinced that her son was not drowning than the
lazy man in the parallel case ; yet her wish, far from
making her believe it, only makes her take all the more
pains to satisfy herself as to the true state of the case.
Genuine conviction that the fact is really as she hoped is
what she wants ; and wishing for it does not help her a
bit to get it. Our other friend, on the contrary, was not
really and truly anxious to ascertain the *fact*. He wished
to banish an unpleasant idea from his mind. I do not
think he was truly or deeply convinced that there was no
call on him to climb the rocks. He was not anxious to
be *convinced* that there was no call ; he only cared to
think that there was none. He did not care *to adjust his
mind to the fact* at all ; he only wished to have a comfort-
able *idea*, and to banish an uncomfortable suspicion. He
was not anxious that the *fact* should be as he wished ; if
he had been, he would have used every means to ascertain whether it were so or not.' "

I hold that Mr. Wilfrid Ward is substantially
right in the very important distinction here drawn.
In other words, I am quite willing to admit that the
earnest desire to believe in a particular state of facts

of vast importance to the person entertaining that
desire, does not usually tend to make *men in general*
more credulous of that belief.   It has that effect on
what are called sanguine or optimistic men,—that
is, on men of a special temperament, who are in the
habit of confounding their eager wishes with their
confident expectations.   On the other hand, it has
the opposite effect on men of the pessimistic turn of
mind, who are in the habit of thinking that what
they very earnestly hope for is hardly possible.   But
on mankind in general, on men whose temperament is neither specially sanguine, nor specially the
reverse, I agree with Mr. Wilfrid Ward that the
keener the desire, the less disposed we are, as a rule,
to mistake the mere desire for evidence of the thing
desired.

But this conclusion, valuable and important as it
is, does not by any means exhaust the question as to
what the total influence of a desire to believe, on
the actual state of human belief, is.   And some
further light on this subject may, I think, be arrived
at, by asking what the causes are by virtue of which
optimists are made credulous of the things they hope,
and pessimists are made credulous of the things they
fear.   I believe that, in the main, optimists become
optimists through the habit of fixing their attention
much more vividly and steadily on those tendencies
which indicate the result they desire to believe in,
than they fix them on the causes which tend to
bring about the disappointment of their hopes ; and
that pessimists become pessimists by the habit of
vividly dwelling on the causes which tend to produce
the events which they fear, and passing over, com-
paratively speaking, those which are of better omen.
And the same thing happens, though from other

causes, in the case of persons of average temperament
Wherever a man who is neither optimist nor pessim
ist in ordinary affairs knows very much more of the
modus operandi of the set of causes leading to one
result, than he does of those leading to an opposite
result, he is almost sure to exaggerate the chances of
the result with the approaches to which he is so
much more familiar than he is with the approaches
to the opposite result.   Take the case of two
tolerably equal players at chess, neither of them
particularly inclined to expect what they wish for,
or to anticipate what they fear.   Each of them,
however, knows his own plans and his own strategy
much better than he can possibly know those of his
antagonist; and the result is that, however strongly
experience may asseverate that till the game is really
won his antagonist has just as good a chance as he,
you will, on interrogating them, almost always find
that each player believes himself to have the
advantage, long before he really has gained any
advantage worth the name.   It is an illusion due to
having preoccupied your imagination with all the
modes by which you may gain the victory, and
having failed to appreciate equally,—because you
had no equal insight into your adversary's plans,—
the modes by which you may be crushed.   Of
course, even in such a case as this, temperament
tells.   A sanguine player will be much more completely occupied with his own plans for victory than
a timid player,—and consequently, he will be even
more sure that he has got a definite advantage, when
he has got nothing of the kind, than a timid player.
But even the timid player will often be found to
have over-calculated his chances of success, not from
any predisposition so to do (for his predisposition is

the other way), but because his mind is much more occupied with the avenues which would lead to success, than it is with the avenues that would lead to failure. Indeed, I am strongly disposed to believe that what is called a cheerful or sanguine temperament does not really affect at all the esti-. mates formed of *particular evidence ;* but that what it does affect is the choice of the evidence to which special attention is paid, and the choice of the evidence which is allowed to fall into the shade. A sanguine man will see the weakness of a weak case as well as another, but his mind dwells more constantly and vividly on the strong evidence which favours the belief he wishes to entertain, and less constantly and vividly on the strong evidence against that belief, while in the mind of a timid and fearful man just the reverse takes place, and so it comes to pass that the mind of each is disproportionately influenced by the kind of evidence on which it has most anxiously dwelt. Even with people who are neither sanguine nor fearful, the same kind of thing happens, wherever there are other circumstances helping them to master one side of a case, and to keep the other hidden from them. And on the whole, I should say that any man who has *forced* his mind to weigh carefully all that is advanced against a belief that he wishes to entertain, and is still satisfied that that belief is true, need not fear that the wish is, in his case, father to the belief. With a certain kind of mind, the wish to believe is just as likely to be father to a *dis*belief; and in any case, the way in which the wish biases towards belief is, I take it, not a direct way, but depends on securing an amount of attention to one side of the case disproportionate to that which is given to the other side of the case. The cynic who habitually dwells on the deceitfulness of human nature has often a painfully strong desire to believe in the goodness of *a* particular character, and yet cannot succeed in doing so simply and solely because he is so accustomed to interpret apparent goodness as hypocrisy, that he has lost the power of regarding a frank and cordial air as anything but assumed for a selfish purpose.

THE METAPHYSICS OF CONVERSION

1875

I never felt any doubt at all that the process known
in the terminology of Evangelical Churches as 'conversion' is in very many cases indeed a real one,
though it is a very mischievous sort of thing for
Revivalists or any one else to teach that there can be
no true religion without some sudden spiritual crisis,
such as John Wesley, for instance, dated in his own
case as having happened precisely at a quarter before
nine on the 24th May 1738. No doubt there are
many persons and some social classes for whom there
is far more chance of 'conversion,' in Messrs. Moody's
and Sankey's sense, than of any gradual change;
and unquestionably this would be true of all persons
like the famous Colonel Gardiner, for instance (the
officer whose life and marvellous conversion was
recounted by his friend, Dr. Doddridge)—persons, I
mean, embarked in a life of conscious evil,—a life
which, unless arrested in mid-career, is pretty sure to
waste the available forces of character, and before
long to leave too little strength of purpose of any
kind for an effectual change. But the curious thing
is that the high doctrine of 'conversion,' though it
may have won its greatest number of apparent
triumphs over persons, whether poor or rich, of

Colonel Gardiner's type—*i.e.*, persons who had never been earnest either in morality or religion till the moment of their conversion,—has derived all its authority from men of a very different type indeed, men like St. Paul and John Wesley, whose whole life has been in some sense profoundly religious, and in whom the convulsive change called 'conversion' has represented *not* a change from a life of reckless pleasure or license to a life of faith, but only a change from one type of faith to another type of faith,—the distinction between the two being frequently by no means apparent to the external world. In St. Paul, no doubt, the change was intelligible enough,. because it marked the moment when he surrendered his character to a new personal influence, an influence in many respects in vivid contrast to that exerted by the Judaic hopes and traditions in which he had been brought up.   But in a great many famous cases of 'conversion,' there is no passage over an external boundary of this kind to mark the change.   John Wesley, for instance, had been engaged in voluntary spiritual and religious duties of precisely the same kind as those of his later life, for nearly ten years before he admitted his own conversion.   Eight years before its date he had cut himself off from the Academic world around him, had visited the prisons of Oxford till all his friends thought him mad, and had sailed with some Moravians to Georgia to help in the work of the Gospel there ;—and yet it was not till after his return to England that, under the teaching of Peter Böhler, he became suddenly convinced that he had at last obtained the saving faith of which he was in search.   He had persuaded himself that faith must be all or nothing, that it hardly admitted of degrees, and that for eight years and more before he obtained it he had had as little of what he held to be saving faith as in the days of his school-boy unconcern. Yet so fine was the change, even to his own consciousness, that though Wesley could date the minute of his conversion, he was compelled to note that at first it brought him no joy, even if it brought him comparative peace, and that it was consistent with much doubt and fear; and he was fain to apologise for his state to the teachers of a yet higher doctrine, who held that any one who could feel doubt or fear, could not be said to have even a weak faith, but must be declared to have no faith at all, by quoting St. Paul's language to the Corinthians, whom he declared to be "not able to bear strong meat," and to be even "carnal," "Ye are God's building, ye are the temple of God," which, argued Wesley, could not have been said of them if they had had no saving faith at all, but must have referred to persons who *had* saving faith, but who had it in a weak form. Thus we see that this great preacher of conversion had already been compelled to distinguish sharply between three very fine shades of his own religious belief,—the shade of mere belief, which left him still beyond the pale of salvation owing to want of faith, though he was earnestly and persistently seeking it,—the shade which amounted to saving faith, but only in a weak measure, like that of the Corinthians who were still 'carnal,'—and the shade which was not only adequate for salvation, but adequate also for producing peace and perfect freedom from doubt.

Now what is the mental rationale of this curious religious tendency to insist not merely on 'conversion' in the sense of a great change from one kind of aim, and purpose, and drift in life to a totally different one, but on conversion within conversion,—on a conversion which affects not so much the attitude

and direction of the mind's movement, as the refine-
ments of its own conscious manipulation of its inward
condition? St. Paul, though his own change was
much more tangible, since it marked his acknowledg-
ment of a new master, yet set the example of this
anxious manipulation of the intricate inward drama
of the heart, in his careful discrimination of the
"law" by which he was condemned as dead in tres-
passes and sins, from the new personal life in which
he was restored to peace and freedom. It would
seem, indeed, that there is a large class of religious
minds in whom the real change from worldly to
spiritual life is so far from sudden that nothing could
well be· more gradual, and yet in whom there is,
nevertheless, some imperious subjective necessity
compelling them to draw an invisible equator between
the opposite hemispheres of condemnation and salvation. Is there not something strange in the fact
that the metaphysics of Conversion, as one may call
them, do not really arise out of the cases of sudden
change from a life of crime or profligacy to a life of
self-devotion, but rather out of the cases of the most
gradual change—change which has been as steady
and uniform as the growth of the dawn into the day?
   I believe that the explanation of this curious fact
is to be discovered in the craving, which marks all
religious as distinct from merely moral life, for finding a completely new spiritual departure from a base
that can be contrasted in the broadest way with the
structure of the character itself standing in need of
regeneration. The most fundamental phenomenon
of the religious life in all Churches and Creeds is
weariness, not to say sickness, of self, and a passionate desire to find some new centre of life—a "not-
ourselves," as Mr. Arnold would say—which can re-
novate the springs and purify the aims of the soiled

and exhausted nature. Now this craving, so far from being confined to those who have led a life of vice or self-indulgence, is perhaps even more powerfully exhibited in men of strong self-control and highly-disciplined nature, provided their spiritual affections be also deep and warm. In men like John Wesley, for instance, the weariness of self probably arises in large measure from the very constant use of the will in small manipulations of the inner life. Nothing is more touching in John Wesley's journal than the constant recurrence of lamentations that he cannot permanently feel the new wave of emotion which swept over his mind about the period which he calls his "conversion," that he "cannot find in himself the love of God and of Christ," that he is conscious of "deadness" and of "wanderings" in prayer, and so forth. What he is craving is not at all a new habit of the will, but a refreshing spring of external influence of which he may always be conscious. It is in great part *against* the accurate and formal goodness of old habit that his heart really protests. He wants to feel himself borne up on a tide that sweeps him away with it, not pacing carefully on a dusty road of small duties. The passionate need for a release from themselves is certainly felt even more by the patient and painstaking souls that have always been carefully disciplined, than by those who, like Colonel Gardiner, make a vast change in their outward lives at the moment when they acknowledge the inward change. And there is a natural enough reason for this. In the case of the conversions which cause a great change of outward life and habit, a good deal is apt to be referred to new divine influence, which is really nothing but the reassertion of itself by a temporarily suppressed element of character or inherited disposition. Colonel Gardiner, when he saw the light shine about him, and believed that Christ upon the cross was reproaching him with his share in the sufferings of Calvary, was probably totally unaware of the strong protest which the moral nature inherited from his mother, and carefully cultivated in childhood by both Mother and Aunt, had long been making in him against the course of profligacy in which he was engaged. He referred to this super-natural event in his life, as he at least deemed it, almost the whole stock of new emotions which now overwhelmed him; and yet it is quite certain, I take it, on the evidence he himself furnishes, that the sense of the misery of his vices had been long grow-ing on him, and the lessons of his childhood long reasserting themselves,—and reasserting themselves almost in direct proportion to the weights he had been piling over that compressed spring of inherited piety and childish integrity. When he came to him-self, and with the military courage which was so conspicuous a characteristic in him, broke off at once and finally with his pleasant vices, he hardly recog-nised in his new mind the suppressed and neglected currents of his old mind; rather he referred the whole change to the supernatural revelation which he had, as he did not doubt, received. Nevertheless, no one with any judgment can question at all, after reading Dr. Doddridge's account of his own state-ments, that the new self was, in a considerable measure, a reassertion of the nature partly inherited from and partly cultivated in him by his mother; and the same may be said of St. Augustine's character after his conversion, and of that of a great many other converts manifested in the same manner. No small part of the elasticity and joy which 'conver-sion' causes in those whose external life it really revolutionises is, I do not doubt, due to the satisfaction the change gives to an overpowered element in the men themselves, which, like a compressed spring, has been steadily pushing against the life led in the past. The proof of this I take to be that it is far rarer to find that wonderful exhilaration and joy which there showed themselves, for instance, in the life of Colonel Gardiner and of St. Augustine, in the so-called 'conversions' of men who have never given the rein to their lower nature ; and again, that it is still rarer to find it in the case of the criminal classes, whose lives are reformed, if at all, slowly, and not *per saltum*. After all, the theory of inherited modifications of character,—the theory which is now so much connected with the name of Darwin, though this part of it at least was preached long before Mr. Darwin's speculations were known, and is closely connected with the theory of inherited automatic habits,—accounts for a good deal of the passionate joy with which misdirected characters spring back into the deeper groove of feeling impressed on their parents, or themselves, or both, long before the superficial aberrations began.

And yet, as I have said, the best explanation of Conversion is to be traced to quite another source,—to the supreme weariness of self which is apt to be felt even more intensely by strongly-controlled natures, capable of deep spiritual affections, than even by those who have gone far astray. It was St. Paul who had lived "in all good conscience before God" up to the very day of his conversion, who first expounded the metaphysics of conversion ;—he who was ever yearning to say, when asked as to the source of his own highest feelings and actions,—"Not I, but Christ that dwelleth in me." It is not those who can speak of their conversion as bringing with it directly, as Colonel Gardiner did, seven years of something like transport, who are apt to expound the metaphysics of conversion at all ;—for such happiness as that, there must be a concurrence between the belief in divine help and the release of a long suppressed, but deeply ingrained natural bias. The "conversions" of men like Wesley are dim and twilight affairs of extremely gradual and ambiguous character, as compared with such conversions as Colonel Gardiner's. And yet it is the profound recoil from self in men whose own habitual goodness has shown them how superficial even the best habitual goodness is, that has led to all the dogmatising about the character of conversion, about the complete repudiation of human good works, and the absolute reliance on the merits of another as the only source of true life. Indeed nothing seems more instructive than to observe that the specific religious yearning for a complete escape from self is strongest in those who have the best self from which to escape rather than the worst; and this is so, simply because it is in them that the contrast between the new and old self seems the least complete and satisfactory,— because a good deal of the minute and painstaking scrupulousness of which they are so weary, necessarily accompanies them even into the region of the new emotion for which they long, but in which too often they only faintly participate.

END OF VOL. I

Printed by R. & R. CLARK, *Edinburgh.*

The Eversley Series.

Globe 8vo. Cloth. 5s. per volume.

The Works of Matthew Arnold.
ESSAYS IN CRITICISM. First Series.
ESSAYS IN CRITICISM. Second Series.
EARLY AND NARRATIVE POEMS.
LYRIC AND ELEGIAC POEMS.
DRAMATIC AND LATER POEMS.
AMERICAN DISCOURSES.

The Holy Bible. Arranged in paragraphs, with an Introduction by J. W. MACKAIL, M.A. In 8 volumes. Vol. 1. GENESIS—NUMBERS. Vol. 2. DEUTERONOMY—2 SAMUEL. Vol. 3. 1 KINGS—ESTHER. Vol. 4. JOB—SONG OF SOLOMON. Vol. 5. ISAIAH—LAMENTATIONS. Vol. 6. EZEKIEL—MALACHI. Vol. 7. MATTHEW—JOHN. Vol. 8. ACTS—REVELATION.

Essays by George Brimley. Third Edition.

Chaucer's Canterbury Tales. Edited by A. W. POLLARD. 2 Vols.

Dean Church's Miscellaneous Writings. Collected Edition. 9 Vols.
MISCELLANEOUS ESSAYS.
DANTE : and other Essays.
ST. ANSELM. | SPENSER. | BACON.
THE OXFORD MOVEMENT. Twelve Years, 1833-1845.
THE BEGINNING OF THE MIDDLE AGES. (Included in this Series by permission of Messrs. LONGMANS and Co.)
OCCASIONAL PAPERS. Selected from *The Guardian, The Times*, and *The Saturday Review*, 1846-1890. 2 Vols

Life and Letters of Dean Church. Edited by his Daughter, MARY C. CHURCH.

Emerson's Collected Works. 6 Vols. With Introduction by JOHN MORLEY.
MISCELLANIES. | ESSAYS. | POEMS.
ENGLISH TRAITS AND REPRESENTATIVE MEN.
THE CONDUCT OF LIFE, AND SOCIETY AND SOLITUDE.
LETTERS AND SOCIAL AIMS.

Letters of Edward FitzGerald. Edited by W. A. WRIGHT. 2 Vols.

Letters of Edward FitzGerald to Fanny Kemble, 1871-1883. Edited by W. A. WRIGHT.

More Letters of Edward FitzGerald.
[*In the Press.*

Pausanias and other Greek Sketches. By J. G. FRAZER, M.A.

Goethe's Prose Maxims. Translated, with Introductions, by T. BAILEY SAUNDERS.
*** *The Scientific and Artistic Maxims were selected by Professor Huxley and Lord Leighton respectively.*

Thomas Gray's Collected Works in Prose and Verse. Edited by EDMUND GOSSE. Vol. 1. Poems, Journals, and Essays. Vols. 2 and 3. Letters. Vol. 4. Notes on Aristophanes and Plato.

Works by John Richard Green.
STRAY STUDIES FROM ENGLAND AND ITALY.
HISTORY OF THE ENGLISH PEOPLE. 8 Vols.
THE MAKING OF ENGLAND. With Maps. In 2 Vols.
THE CONQUEST OF ENGLAND. With Maps. In 2 Vols.

Guesses at Truth. By TWO BROTHERS.

The Choice of Books, and other Literary Pieces. By FREDERIC HARRISON.

Poems of Thomas Hood. Edited, with Prefatory Memoir, by ALFRED AINGER. In 2 Vols. Vol. 1. SERIOUS POEMS. Vol. 2. POEMS OF WIT AND HUMOUR. With Vignettes and Portraits.

R. H. Hutton's Collected Essays.
LITERARY ESSAYS.
ESSAYS ON SOME OF THE MODERN GUIDES OF ENGLISH THOUGHT IN MATTERS OF FAITH.
THEOLOGICAL ESSAYS.
CRITICISMS ON CONTEMPORARY THOUGHT AND THINKERS. 2 Vols.
ASPECTS OF RELIGIOUS AND SCIENTIFIC THOUGHT. Selected from the *Spectator*, and Edited by his Niece, ELIZABETH M. ROSCOE. With Portrait.

Thomas Henry Huxley's Collected Works. 9 Vols.
Vol. 1. METHOD AND RESULTS.
Vol. 2. DARWINIANA.
Vol. 3. SCIENCE AND EDUCATION.
Vol. 4. SCIENCE AND HEBREW TRADITION.
Vol. 5. SCIENCE AND CHRISTIAN TRADITION.
Vol. 6. HUME. With Helps to the Study of Berkeley.
Vol. 7. MAN'S PLACE IN NATURE : and other Anthropological Essays.
Vol. 8. DISCOURSES, BIOLOGICAL AND GEOLOGICAL.
Vol. 9. EVOLUTION AND ETHICS, AND OTHER ESSAYS.

MACMILLAN AND CO., LTD., LONDON.

The Eversley Series.—*Continued.*

Globe 8vo. Cloth. 5s. per volume.

French Poets and Novelists. By HENRY JAMES.

Partial Portraits. By HENRY JAMES.

Letters of John Keats to his Family and Friends. Edited by SIDNEY COLVIN.

Charles Kingsley's Novels and Poems.

WESTWARD HO! 2 Vols.
HYPATIA. 2 Vols.
YEAST. 1 Vol.
ALTON LOCKE. 2 Vols.
TWO YEARS AGO. 2 Vols.
HEREWARD THE WAKE. 2 Vols.
POEMS. 2 Vols.

Charles Lamb's Collected Works. Edited, with Introduction and Notes, by Canon AINGER. 6 Vols.

THE ESSAYS OF ELIA.
POEMS, PLAYS, AND MISCELLANEOUS ESSAYS.
MRS. LEICESTER'S SCHOOL, and other Writings.
TALES FROM SHAKESPEARE. By CHARLES and MARY LAMB.
THE LETTERS OF CHARLES LAMB. 2 Vols.

Life of Charles Lamb. By Canon AINGER.

Historical Essays. By J. B. LIGHTFOOT, D.D.

The Poetical Works of John Milton. Edited, with Memoir, Introduction, and Notes, by DAVID MASSON, M.A. 3 Vols.

Vol. 1. THE MINOR POEMS.
Vol. 2. PARADISE LOST.
Vol. 3. PARADISE REGAINED, AND SAMSON AGONISTES.

John Morley's Collected Works. In 11 Vols.

VOLTAIRE. 1 Vol.
ROUSSEAU. 2 Vols.
DIDEROT AND THE ENCYCLOPÆDISTS. 2 Vols.
ON COMPROMISE. 1 Vol.
MISCELLANIES. 3 Vols.
BURKE. 1 Vol.
STUDIES IN LITERATURE. 1 Vol.

Science and a Future Life, and other Essays. By F. W. H. MYERS, M.A.

Classical Essays. By F. W. H. MYERS.

Modern Essays. By F. W. H. MYERS.

Records of Tennyson, Ruskin, and Browning. By ANNE THACKERAY RITCHIE.

Works by Sir John R. Seeley, K.C.M.G., Litt.D.

THE EXPANSION OF ENGLAND. Two Courses of Lectures.
LECTURES AND ESSAYS.
ECCE HOMO. A Survey of the Life and Work of Jesus Christ.
NATURAL RELIGION.
LECTURES ON POLITICAL SCIENCE.

The Works of Shakespeare. With short Introductions and Footnotes by Professor C. H. HERFORD. In 10 Vols.

Works by James Smetham.

LETTERS. With an Introductory Memoir. Edited by SARAH SMETHAM and WILLIAM DAVIES. With a Portrait.
LITERARY WORKS. Edited by WILLIAM DAVIES.

Life of Swift. By Sir HENRY CRAIK, K.C.B. 2 Vols. New Edition.

Selections from the Writings of Thoreau. Edited by H. S. SALT.

Essays in the History of Religious Thought in the West. By B. F. WESTCOTT, D.D., D.C.L., Lord Bishop of Durham.

The Works of William Wordsworth. Edited by Professor KNIGHT.

POETICAL WORKS. 8 Vols.
PROSE WORKS. 2 Vols.

The Journals of Dorothy Wordsworth. 2 Vols.

MACMILLAN AND CO., LTD, LONDON.

CL. 10.5.00.

www.ingramcontent.com/pod-product-compliance
Lightning Source LLC
Chambersburg PA
CBHW021535110726
47902CB00004B/890